Adolescent Rorschach Responses

Developmental Trends from
Ten to Sixteen Years

Also from the Gesell Institute of Child Development

Child Rorschach Responses

Rorschach Responses in Old Age

Adolescent Rorschach Responses

Developmental Trends from Ten to Sixteen Years

LOUISE BATES AMES, Ph.D.
Director of Research, Gesell Institute of Child Development; Member of the Society
for Projective Techniques and the Rorschach Institute, Inc.

RUTH W. MÉTRAUX, M.A.
Rorschach Consultant

RICHARD N. WALKER, Ph.D.
Research Associate

Paul B. Hoeber, Inc.
Medical Book Department of Harper & Brothers

ADOLESCENT RORSCHACH RESPONSES
Developmental Trends from Ten to Sixteen Years

Copyright © 1959, by Paul B. Hoeber, Inc.
Medical Book Department of Harper & Brothers

Printed in the United States of America

H-K

REPRINTED 1961

Library of Congress catalog card number: 59-6148

Contents

Contents

List of Tables

Preface

This book is a sequel to our earlier volume *Child Rorschach Responses* in which we traced developments in many aspects of Rorschach performance between 2 and 10 years of age. The present volume continues this survey for the years from 10 to 16. We believe that it should be of practical usefulness to clinical psychologists, because it presents descriptions of characteristic findings at successive ages for a large group of bright, normal adolescents. Viewed against this descriptive background, an individual Rorschach record gains in interpretive significance and diagnostic value. Our findings may also be of interest to developmental psychologists, for the Rorschach test variables offer evidence for certain principles of growth in this period. Any adolescent's Rorschach protocol seems most profitably considered as a single point in an ongoing developmental process.

At the time we began the investigation reported in our earlier book, many psychologists questioned the usefulness of the Rorschach test at the younger ages. This was because the records of many children, even obviously healthy children, contained responses that would have pathological significance in the adult. However, our findings suggested that some types of response having malignant significance when appearing in adult records are given with such frequency by children at particular levels of development that they must be recognized as characteristic of those levels. It is in fact their regressive character that makes these behaviors indicative of disturbance in adulthood.

The present, as well as the earlier study, indicates that a child's Rorschach response, when viewed against a background of responses characteristic of his age, provides information (or, better, hypotheses) concerning both his developmental status and his individual personality features. This and further studies yet to be published also indicate that any single Rorschach record must be considered as representative of a subject's response only at a specific time. While a strong thread of individuality runs through a single individual's successive records, substantial changes from year to year are the rule for many children.

Our earlier study raised many questions in our minds about the teen ages and suggested some possible answers to them, answers confirmed by the present study. We anticipated that characteristic changes would still be discerned from year to year during the adolescent period but that the rate of change would slow down, while sex differences would increase in size. We further expected that some responses considered traditionally to represent disturbance might actually be found with some frequency in a group of normally functioning children and adolescents. The present study has confirmed these possibilities—the Rorschach response does continue to change in a patterned and somewhat predictable way in the years from 10 to 16.

The present study suggests that, though in the years from 10 to 16 the Rorschach response changes gradually toward one which increasingly approximates the normal adult response, ages at which the response is full and expansive tend to alternate with ages at which it is definitely restrictive. The suggestion is that the so-called introversive phase of adolescence may be not a single limited span of a certain number of months or years, but may occur more than once and may alternate with ages of full and expansive behavior.

We were here interested in testing the general assumption, which we question, that the Rorschach response of the adolescent and young adult remains essentially constant over a long period of time, in the absence of external events of traumatic force. An earlier study, *Rorschach Responses in Old Age,* has shown that the response continues to change in the years after 70, though in this period of life the change is often in the direction opposite to earlier changes. That is, after 70, records tend to become more restricted, less accurate, less varied as to content. Individual differences in rate of change stand out especially in this later period. Subsequent studies will investigate changes and constancies in response from age to age of subjects in their twenties and thirties.

Meanwhile, the present study is offered as a demonstration of age changes in the Rorschach records of pre-adolescent and adolescent boys and girls. It indicates that these changes occur, for the group of normal young people whom we have studied, in a patterned, somewhat predictable manner. The findings of this Rorschach study are compared with those reported in *Youth: The Years from Ten to*

Sixteen (Gesell, Ilg, and Ames) which were derived from observations of, and interviews with, adolescents and their parents. The age trends revealed in the two studies show general correspondence in their broad outlines; in their details each supplements and enriches the significance of the other.

L. B. A.
R. W. M.
R. N. W.

Acknowledgments

Foremost acknowledgment must be made to the many teen-age boys and girls who patiently, year after year, coöperated with us in this investigation.

Special acknowledgment must also be made to the faculty members of the several schools which allowed us to test their students. Outstanding among these are Mrs. Martinson and Mr. Stephen K. Lovett of the public schools of Norwalk, Mrs. Pauline Olson of the New Canaan Country Day School, Mr. Edward Summerton, formerly of the Hurlbutt School in Weston, and the staff of the Hamden Country Day School in New Haven.

Among the several staff members of the Gesell Institute who helped in the gathering and analysis of data were Dr. Janet Rodell, Mrs. Janice Goldstein, Miss Elizabeth Binz and Mrs. Barbara Tice. We wish also to acknowledge the editorial help of Mrs. Marjean Kremer, our Research Assistant.

Thanks are especially due to Dr. Frances L. Ilg, Director of the Gesell Institute, not only for practical help in the giving of many of the tests to individual children, but also for much of the theoretical formulation of our developmental concepts of the specific behavior characteristics of the several ages considered.

Part One

CHAPTER ONE

Introduction

Two earlier studies, *Child Rorschach Responses* (1) and *Youth: The Years from Ten to Sixteen* (11), have led directly to the present investigation. The first of these examined the development of the Rorschach response between 2 and 10 years. This study revealed first that an orderly sequence of change appears in children's Rorschach responses during that period, and second that the full significance of an individual child's Rorschach can be determined only in the light of knowledge of the normal course of development.

The design of this first study involved comparison of the Rorschach records of samples of children at successive half-yearly, then yearly age levels. Descriptive statistics for many Rorschach variables were presented for each age. In an effort to obtain a more integrated picture of the successive levels, a qualitative, composite description of the Rorschach behaviors most characteristic of each age was drawn up.

The Rorschach, unlike many other techniques, provides us with a test stimulus that remains essentially constant throughout the entire age span, and is thus of particular value for comparative studies. Several findings of our study of 2- to 10-year-olds seemed interesting in their general developmental implications. First of all, the sheer amount of change that occurs over the age range studied is impressive. When one reads the qualitative description of the 2-year-olds' Rorschach response and then that of the 10-year-olds, one is struck by the profound changes in organization that have occurred.

Next, a reading of the descriptions intervening between those for 2 and 10 years suggests that the course of this growth is not in a straight line. It tends to be curved, with the greatest changes taking place during the early years. Age 6 lies midway between age 2 and age 10; but the Rorschach response of our typical 6-year-old resembles that of the 10-year-old much more closely than it does that of the 2-year-old.

And finally, on this hypothetical curve of development from 2 to 10 years, the successive ages do not simply represent successively closer

3

approximations to the "typical" 10-year-old picture. The over-all trend is clearly in that direction. But different age levels bring forth different forms of patterning of the total Rorschach response. Growth occurs through a constant reorganization of levels.

Thus, in our presentation of "age sketches" for regular, chronological intervals, we found ourselves describing many apparently irregular, sudden changes, newly emerging behaviors, even apparent reversals of the over-all course. Certain ages appeared especially significant as marking changes in direction of development. Seven years, for example, was perhaps the most outstanding of these (a finding of some interest in relation to developmental observations by Freud and by Piaget). But for each age grouping, however arbitrary in relation to the length or timing of steps in the underlying developmental process, a description could be composed that sets it apart from adjacent ages. These Rorschach findings implied differences in the fullness and richness of response, in the relative stability or equilibrium of behavior, in emphasis on inwardizing of experience, or thrusting outward to meet the world.

The clinical usefulness of such developmental information is twofold. It enables one to evaluate the stage of maturity that a given child's Rorschach response has reached. And it throws into sharper relief the individual characteristics of the child's Rorschach response by contrast with characteristics of others at his level.

The finding of such striking developmental changes in the Rorschach response during the first 10 years of life led us to inquire whether similarly distinctive changes might not occur during succeeding age periods, particularly in the years of preadolescence and early adolescence. Reinforcing our interest from the Rorschach study was the completion of a second study, a survey of general behavior characteristics during this period, *Youth: The Years From Ten to Sixteen* (11). This latter study, by means of standard tests and interviews with adolescents, their parents, and their teachers, depicted developmental sequences in a wide variety of behavior areas in the 10- to 16-year period, again through the device of comparison of successive yearly groupings of subjects. As in our earlier growth studies and in our earlier study of the Rorschach, this behavior survey revealed a process of growth through successive reorganization of energies, abilities, and interests, with some levels tending to emphasize expansiveness of affect and behavior, others to emphasize inwardizing, even withdrawing tendencies.

Our present investigation, therefore, was initiated in an attempt to answer questions raised by these two previous studies. The first, a study of the development of Rorschach responses in the first 10 years, raised the question of whether or not comparable distinctive age changes appeared in the next 6 years. The second, which studied adolescent development chiefly by observational and interview methods, raised the question of whether developmental changes in the Rorschach would to any extent correspond with behavior changes observed by other methods.

Several further related problems suggested themselves when we considered undertaking an investigation of the Rorschach response in the preadolescent and early adolescent years.

As the human organism matures from conception to birth and then from birth throughout infancy and childhood, both structural and behavioral changes tend to occur ever more slowly. The negative acceleration of development on the Rorschach in the 2- to 10-year segment of growth has already been mentioned. One of our interests in the present investigation has been to determine the extent to which the rate of change in Rorschach response continues to slow down in the years after 10.

Any survey of child or adolescent Rorschachs is naturally concerned to discover the extent to which responses approximate the patterns that we have come to expect from the normal adult. Our earlier analysis of responses in the years 2 to 10 indicated a decided over-all trend in the direction of normal adult expectancies, but still a substantial gap from them even as late as year 10. We could anticipate that Sixteen should be closer to the typical adult response than is Ten, but were very curious to see just how close this would be, since Sixteen is in many ways near adulthood, yet in a complex society still far away.

Related to the difference between child and adult Rorschachs is the problem of evaluating children's records according to adult standards on certain particular points, namely the so-called "danger signals" or "neurotic signs." Our survey of the first 10 years showed clearly that, as clinical experience had suggested, the young child commonly gives many responses that would be considered suspicious if not malignant if they occurred in an adult record. (In fact, it is precisely because they reflect a perceptual approach characteristic of the young child that many of these responses are considered "malignant" in the adult years.) We expected, therefore, that a number of specific response qualities, presumably of a more subtle sort, which might in fact suggest disturbance in an adult, could occur with some frequency in the records of normal adolescents.

A further important area of exploration is that of sex differences in this period. Though the behavior of boys and girls has been observed to differ in many respects during the earliest years (10), so far as the Rorschach is concerned sex differences in the first 10 years are small in comparison to age differences. We anticipated that sex differences would increase and stabilize during the years from 10 to 16, perhaps equaling age differences as a source of variation in the Rorschach response.

In our previous study (1), we ventured the hypothesis that in the earliest years the Rorschach may reveal more about the developmental status of the subject than about his individual personality (to the extent that these two factors can be separated). That is, we suggested that in the early years the Rorschach differences that appear among individuals at the same level are less striking than the differences that appear within the same individual at different levels. Then increasingly as the child matures, the Rorschach reveals a more individual personality structure. At some later age (adolescence? the twenties?) individual personality factors substantially overshadow developmental factors on the Rorschach. And then again, at some much later age, possibly in the seventies or eighties (the time of reaching this level would differ for different individuals), maturity factors may once again play the dominant role in determining Rorschach response qualities (see our *Rorschach Response in Old Age,* 2). The present investigation should provide some estimate of the relative strength of these two factors in the years from 10 to 16.

CHAPTER TWO

Review of the Literature

The use of the Rorschach test with preadolescents and adolescents has had a rather different history from that of its use with young children. Early experience convinced some clinicians that the test was not applicable at the lower age levels, mainly because of the "psychotic-like" appearance of young children's responses when judged by adult standards. However, as clinicians developed standards for evaluating children's records, the test's value was demonstrated, and gradually a considerable body of literature on its use at this younger level grew up (see Ames *et al.,* 1; Klopfer *et al.,* 40). The Rorschach responses of adolescents and preadolescents, on the other hand, do not differ dramatically from those of adults. Adolescents' records were found to be useful early in the test's history and required no period of discovery before being recognized. It is apparently for this reason that the body of literature on adolescent records has been later in developing than that on child records.

While less specialized knowledge of the age period is required for interpretation of adolescent records, it is becoming recognized that for greatest usefulness in individual diagnosis some sort of normative background is valuable. This chapter surveys the English-language literature on the use of the Rorschach test with subjects aged 10 to 16 years, with a view to defining what approaches have been taken, what variables have been considered worth studying, and what normative material is available. Studies are grouped under four general headings: methodology, normative and developmental studies, validation studies using the method of contrasted groups, and validation studies using correlation techniques. Single-case reports have not been considered here.

METHODOLOGY

Notable both as first and as most productive in the study of the Rorschach in adolescence is Dr. Marguerite Hertz. Much of her work has been concerned with the careful definition of the Rorschach scoring system, with special attention to development of criteria for scoring the "relative"

7

variables: D, F+, P, and O (23, 24, 25, 26, 29, 30). Her original papers list the statistically determined normal details, the popular forms, and the good-form responses for a group of 300 junior high school students. This material was assembled in her useful *Frequency Tables for Scoring Responses to the Rorschach Inkblot Test* (30), new editions of which have appeared as new groups of subjects have contributed records. The present, third edition lists all responses appearing in 1,350 records of children aged 11 to 16 years, scored for location, form accuracy, and popularity-originality. With slight emendations to fit our own group, these norms have been used for scoring the protocols of the present study.

NORMATIVE AND DEVELOPMENTAL STUDIES

Much of the existing normative information on adolescent Rorschachs has likewise been contributed by Hertz. For many years her 1935 norms (22) were the only ones available for American adolescents. Her subjects, the same 300 boys and girls on whom her scoring criteria were first developed, range from 12 to 16 years of age, most of them being 13- and 14-year-olds. Mean scores for 12 scoring variables, for all ages and both sexes together, are presented in this paper.

A second set of papers, written with Baker, (31, 32, 33, 34), compares in detail the movement and color responses of 76 of Hertz's subjects who took the test at both 12 and 15 years of age. This longitudinal study points up the substantial amount of change that occurs in individual children's responses from 12 to 15. The characteristic change within this period is a swing introversively or a "contraction of the whole personality." The 15-year-olds are less impersonal and objective in their approach to reality, more influenced by emotional factors. (To anticipate our own findings, we might remark that they parallel Hertz's very closely but that this introversial swing is not a steady trend from 12 to 15. Rather, the 15-year-old introversivity or constriction contrasts as sharply with 14- as with 12-year-old personality.)

An important group of publications on adolescent Rorschach responses has come from the Institute of Child Welfare at the University of California at Berkeley. A number of authors have been associated with this research, the records for which were collected as part of an 18-year longitudinal study under Jean Walker MacFarlane. Subjects were tested in alternate years, with over 100 children tested at 11, 13, and 15, smaller numbers at 12, 14, and 16, and all subjects tested at 18 years. Though the material was collected longitudinally, it is presented cross-sectionally. The first of these studies, by McFate and Orr (43), is a statistical presentation of age norms, giving means and standard deviations, medians, first and third quartiles, and percentage-using scores for many of the usual Rorschach scoring variables. (Many of the more important ratios are not given, however. One misses especially some presentation of W%, D%, F%, and F+%.) For the variables considered, a fairly full picture is given of the score distribution for boys and girls at each age.

Additional studies in this series analyze the Rorschach records in further detail. Ranzoni, Grant, and Ives (49) examine the stimulus properties of the individual cards, comparing the location, determinant, and content scores most commonly elicited by each card at ages 11, 13, 15, and 18 years. The authors point out the way in which knowledge of normative trends must affect some of the more usual types of interpretive statements. In another paper, Ives, Grant, and Ranzoni (37) present the incidence of "neurotic signs" and "adjustment signs" in the Rorschachs of this group at each age. Many of the "neurotic signs," derived from studies by Miale and Harrower-Erickson, show very high incidence in this group of normal adolescents, some of them apparently increasing with age, some decreasing. The 17 "adjustment signs," as proposed by Davidson, likewise vary considerably in incidence and show consistent sex differences, in all cases favoring girls. The characteristics of both "neurotic" and "adjustment" signs in this group "make questionable their validity and usefulness as a diagnostic technique with adolescents."

A pair of articles by Beck and his associates (Rabin and Beck, 48; Thetford, Molish, and Beck, 57) present data on a sample of children partly overlapping in age with the 10-to-16 range of interest here. Both articles present norms for 62 10- to 13-year-olds; the latter article also gives data for 24 14- to 17-year-olds. For these combined groups, the sexes together, mean scores and some actual frequency distributions are presented for most of the usual Rorschach variables (excepting Klopfer's FM and m). In addition, the articles present means for Beck's Z score and his lambda index (essentially F%, including FM+m), as well as mean R for each blot, distribution of sequence types (methodical-irregular-confused) and of experience-balance types (M : ΣC balance). As compared with the preceding articles, the norms presented in these papers show the greatest differences from our own norms. This is most marked in the location of variables, where it seems evident that Beck's students score W far more critically than we do (their mean W% for ages 10 to 13 is 15 per cent; ours is 48 per cent).

Some normative data are presented in Hertzman and Margulies' comparison (35) of Rorschach responses at the college and the junior high school levels. For 60 boys, averaging 13 years 9 months, mean scores are presented for most of the usual Rorschach variables, as well as distributions on M : ΣC and W : M ratios. The incidence of nine of Miale and Harrower-Erickson's "neurotic signs" is also presented. Findings for this group of boys are compared with those for an equated group of college students.

For a group of 15 boys and 15 girls, all juniors in high school and averaging 16½ years of age, Hershenson (20) presents means, standard deviations, and ranges for a dozen of the usual Rorschach scoring variables. Her main point of concern, however, was with their preference ranking of the ten Rorschach blots. After obtaining mean rankings of the cards for each sex, she ran rank-order correlations between each individual's preference sorting and the total group's, to give "individual conformity" indexes. Though these did not appear to relate to the more usual Rorschach scores, they offer an interesting method for calculating one dimension of divergence from statistical normality and may, as the author suggests, have some value in differentiating clinical groups.

A study that overlaps partly with the age range of interest here is Paulsen's (44) study of the same 30 school children at ages 6, 8, 10, and 12. Although the longitudinal, predictive aspects of this study are of greatest interest, she does present cross-sectional norms for the usual Rorschach variables in terms of means, quartiles, and percentage-using scores. Comparisons of extent of individual changes in paired ages are of particular interest. A large proportion of the children showed extreme shifts in experience balance during this period; only one child showed a consistent experience balance throughout. Paulsen points out that personality development shows certain general trends but that it does not proceed regularly or uniformly in the individual child; "rather, spurts, plateaus, and occasionally regressive movements are characteristic," perhaps appearing in rather rhythmic fluctuation.

Also longitudinal in design is a study by Suares (56) in which she obtained Rorschachs on 21 boys, aged 15 to 17, tested five years earlier by Loosli-Usteri, and on 21 girls, aged 12 to 14, tested two years earlier by Shapiro. (She also presents material on 21 boys aged 14 to 18 in college preparatory courses and 21 boys of the same age who were miscellaneous clinic referrals.) Like Hertz and Baker, she reports that the boys first tested at 10 to 12, then again at 15 to 17, show considerable variability in the type of $M : \Sigma C$ change, but that the general trend is clearly in the direction of increased introversivity. The girls, on the other hand, in developing from 10-12 to 12-14 years, tended to show increases in extratensiveness. With her findings we are in accord, but her conclusions seem to strain the data. She appears to believe that the increase on the M side of the *Erlebnistyp,* as shown by the boys, indicates presence of the puberty crisis, while increase on the C side, as shown by the girls, indicates passing of the puberty crisis. That the 12-year-old girls would thus be considerably in advance of the 15-year-old boys in development she considers reasonable, "since it is known that girls develop faster than boys after the age of 12 or thereabouts."

Differing from the preceding studies in using physiological status rather than age as a developmental criterion is Steiner's report on Rorschach findings from the Caroline Zachry Institute's study of adolescent girls (55). This study compares group Rorschach responses of 100 prepuberal girls, aged 10 to 14, with those of 100 puberal girls, aged 10 to 15 (as well as with those of 100 adolescent girls, all 17 years or older). The median prepuberal girl is aged 12 years, the median puberal girl is aged 13 years 3 months, so that age as well as physiological maturity is a factor in the differences. While the group administration makes the absolute levels of the scores of little value for comparison with studies that use individual administration, the comparison of the two groups is of some interest. From group averages, the puberal group appears as more constricted than the prepuberal group, showing lower mean scores in R, M, and FM, all color scores, and shading scores; higher use only of W% and m. The authors state that, in general, "many of the traits which characterize the growing girl—many of the defensive mechanisms, healthy or neurotic—have their numerical peak at puberty" (53, p. 58).

VALIDATION STUDIES: CONTRASTED GROUPS

School Achievers and Nonachievers

Margulies (42) reports a study in which successful and unsuccessful students, mean age 13, equated in I.Q. and social status, were compared on a number of Rorschach variables, particularly the W : M ratio and signs of "shock." The unsuccessful children tended to show more signs of color and shading shock, while the successful children showed more Fc, FC, and m, lower A%, and more of Davidson's "signs of adjustment." In a study of 25 high school failures compared with 25 honor students, Beckham (5) found the unsuccessful students to give many more refusals, fewer responses, poorer F%, fewer M.

Delinquents

By far the greatest number of studies of particular groups of adolescents deal with delinquency. While the diagnosis "delinquent" has no sharper age limits than behavioral limits (Pescor's study, 45, for example, includes some 77-year-old delinquents), most of the subjects so designated fall in the adolescent age range. Schmidl (53) has surveyed the status of the Rorschach in juvenile delinquency research as of 1947, reviewing the European as well as the American literature. He points out a number of general shortcomings, primarily noting that many authors apparently regard delinquents as a homogeneous group in personality make-up. No satisfactory typology of delinquency has been established and, since it is evident that any single institution samples the delinquent population unevenly, Schmidl recommends pooling of samples, as well as more careful definition of samples. Much of the research on delinquency since then retains many of the faults he pointed out.

While most authors contrast their findings on delinquent groups with some sort of normal controls, a number of authors simply present the findings for single groups. Weber (58), for example, gives a nonstatistical description of the Rorschach records of 15 juvenile auto thieves, age 15 and 16 years, and Bowlus and Shotwell (6) describe the Rorschachs of 12 girls aged 15 to 27, nine of them under 21, diagnosed as psychopathic delinquents. Endacott (9) presents means, standard deviations, and ranges for Rorschach scores of 100 male delinquents, aged 9 to 17 years, comparing them with the published norms of Hertz and several European investigators.

In a study of the efficacy of a number of tests for distinguishing between 47 16- and 17-year-old girls in a state reform school and 50 girls randomly selected from public high schools, Boynton and Wadsworth (7) include the Rorschach test, scoring it only for Do, FC, CF, C, and O. Their finding that nondelinquent girls score significantly higher in C and O is difficult to interpret in the light of the many differences between their samples apart from delinquent status.

Gorlow, Zimet, and Fine (17) contrast the Rorschachs of 13 "adolescent" delinquents (mean age 12.3 years) with 13 nondelinquent children of the same age and I.Q. levels, in order to validate a method of scoring content for anxiety and hostility indexes. Significant differences appear between the groups, with delinquents obtaining higher scores for both anxiety and hostility, thus lending some confidence to the indexes.

One of the earlier studies using delinquent subjects, that of Helene Hertz (21), makes an intra-institutional comparison between nine well-adjusting and nine poorly adjusting girls, matched for I.Q. (ages not given). The groups are contrasted on several single Rorschach variables, and detailed interpretations of two sample cases are presented.

Jacobs and Graham (38) compare the Rorschachs of juvenile auto thieves and juvenile burglars, hypothesizing that "joy riders" would show personality differences from the burglars. No statistical data are presented, but the authors state that the groups show differences significant at the 5 per cent confidence level "in the areas of fantasy and anxiety," with auto thieves showing more autistic fantasy and greater anxiety.

Kogan (41) likewise uses no nondelinquent controls, but instead compares the paired Rorschach records of six boys, tested just before and again some weeks after their appearing before a parole committee. These boys, aged 14 to 17 years, were grouped regardless of outcome of the committee's decision, on the grounds that a decision either way would be a relief from the tension existing at the time of the first test. Results are presented descriptively, the main trends reported being an improvement in the M : FM balance and an increase in F% at the time of the second test.

By far the most impressive study of the Rorschach used in delinquency is that by Schachtel (12, 52) in Glueck and Glueck's large-scale study of 500 delinquents and 500 matched controls. While this study has been criticized for its general design, it stands head and shoulders above other Rorschach studies in this field. The two groups of subjects, mean age 14½, were matched for age, intelligence, ethnic origin, and neighborhood of residence. Schachtel was not informed as to which boys were delinquent and which were not until completing his evaluations of the records. In his discussions comparing the two groups, he is clearly wary of statistical presentations. Nevertheless, he does present mean scores for a number of variables as well as a few total frequency distributions of scores and percentatge distribution of subjects on certain ratios. He finds that nondelinquents give higher R and higher Dd%, more nondelinquents use S, and nondelinquents give higher mean M and Mt (FM+m) scores. The color score distributions are presented in some detail; more delinquents had CF+C scores exceeding FC scores than did nondelinquents. And more delinquents had introversive or ambiequal M : ΣC ratios while more nondelinquents had constricted or extratensive ratios.

More important to Schachtel than mean scores, however, was his use of a checklist of 54 psychological traits (e.g., self-assertion, hostility, vivacity, etc.) to be rated +, —, or ? on the basis of the total Rorschach impression. This set of ratings was made for each record and a diagnosis arrived at, which included a judgment as to whether the subject was delinquent or not. Of the 991 blind judgments made, 67 per cent were correct and only 7 per cent were incorrect (delinquents called nondelinquent or vice versa), while in 26 per cent of the cases the Rorschach failed to provide adequate material for judgment. Schachtel (52) discusses some considerations entering into his judgments and presents two sample cases in some detail.

Neurotics

Goldfarb (13) offers a comparison of 20 adolescent subjects having obsessional Rorschachs with 20 unselected subjects who had been referred for educational guidance. All subjects were foster children, and mean ages of both groups fell near 14½ years, but the mean I.Q. of the obsessionals was 120, that of the controls 97. Individual scores for the two groups are compared, with many marked differences, and qualitative reactions are described for the obsessional group (e.g., need for reassurance, qualified response, etc.). The differences between the groups are convincingly presented, but since the author had selected the obsessional group precisely on the basis of these differences, he is evidently only saying, "This syndrome exists," and the "control" group appears to serve no important purpose.

Cox (8) contrasts the Rorschach scores of 60 boys attending a child guidance clinic with 60 boys from public schools, in an effort to define a "neuroticism" dimension on the Rorschach. Subjects range in age from 8 to 12 years and the two groups are close in mean I.Q. scores. Of the clinic group, about half seem to be characterized by the descriptions "aggressive," "destructive," "temper tantrums," while half are "withdrawn," "submissive," "faddy," etc. Statistical tests show the clinic group to have fewer D, F, F+, and P, as well as more C and more refusals. A content category including art, blood, emblem, ghosts, mud, and statues, is also higher for the clinic group. Twenty-six of the variables were then intercorrelated, a factor analysis was done, and finally a discriminant function study using factored scores was made for differentiation of the groups. This resulted in a multiple regression equation having a correlation of .59 with the dichotomous criterion. This is remarkable separation, considering the nature of the task: to differentiate a group containing an assortment of overly aggressive and overly withdrawn children from a group containing children having unknown behavior traits. It seems doubtful, however, that the differentiating power would stand up well under cross validation.

A pair of studies by Goldfarb (14) and Goldfarb and Klopfer (15) present Rorschach characteristics of adolescents who had been reared in institutions during infancy. Eight institution-reared boys and seven girls, aged 10 to 14 years when tested, are compared with a matched group reared in foster homes. Mean values of single Rorschach scores are compared, as well as percentage incidence of various "signs," revealing a number of significant differences. Goldfarb concludes that the institution children, compared with the foster home children, tend to be: "(1) less mature, less controlled, less differentiated, more impoverished; and (2) more passive and apathetic, less ambitious, and less capable of adjustment related to conscious intention or goal."

Racial Groups

Stainbrook and Siegel (54) compared 40 white and 40 Negro tenth grade students in Southern schools (as well as white and Negro college students) on single Rorschach variables. No figures are reported, but the authors state that significant differences appeared in mean scores, with R, D, S, m, K, and CF lower in high school Negros, FC higher. Since the groups differed in I.Q. scores and in schools attended as well as in race, one does not know to which source to attribute these differences.

VALIDATION STUDIES: CORRELATION TECHNIQUES

In Paulsen's longitudinal study (44) of public school children, she was able to secure follow-up ratings of the social adjustment of 21 children at age 16. These were made on a three-point scale by a social worker, on the basis of parent interviews, subject interviews, and school file data. Independently of these ratings, Paulsen made a similar evaluation (poor-moderate-good) of the children's Rorschach records at ages 6 and 12 years. Correlations with the 16-year-old social adjustment ratings ran to .66 for the 12-year-old Rorschach evaluations and .50 for the 6-year-old Rorschach evaluations (our computations from Paulsen's tables). Considering the time lapse and the probable real changes in adjustment status, the effectiveness of Paulsen's evaluations is impressive.

Less encouraging are the results of validation studies by the California Guidance Study group. In their efforts to find Rorschach predictors of self and social adjustment levels, they have used both sign-list approaches and global ratings by experts. Adjustment ratings were made by social workers following interview with each child. An article by Ives, Grant, and Ranzoni (37) correlates these interview ratings with a number of Davidson's "adjustment signs" in the records at ages 11, 13, 15, and 18, finding that the correlations in general vary nonsignificantly around zero. In a second study, Grant, Ives, and Ranzoni (18) had three experienced Rorschach users rate the 146 protocols for the subjects at age 18 on a four-point scale of over-all adjustment. Correlations between these judges' ratings and the social workers' ratings of adjustment were mostly low positive, too low for clinical usefulness. Rorschach workers may take some comfort in the belief that "adjustment" is too broad to evaluate from the Rorschach protocol and that such evaluations must consider the individual's life situation, the stress to which he is subjected as well as his potentiality for successful response, and so cannot be made blind. But this carefully done study must give pause to any thoughtful user of the test. It is interesting to see that Rorschach judges placed from 60 to 70 per cent of these normal subjects at the "maladjusted" end of the scale. It seems evident that much less is known about normality on the Rorschach test than about abnormality.

CHAPTER THREE

Subjects and Methods

Subjects

This study is based upon 700 Rorschach records, those of 50 boys and 50 girls at each yearly age level from 10 to 16. These 700 records were contributed by 398 different children, since some children contributed records at more than one age. Single records were given by 271 children; the remaining 429 records were given by just 127 different children. The extent of overlapping of subjects at each pairing of ages is shown in Table 1. As this table indicates, between one third and one half of subjects seen

TABLE 1. OVERLAPPING OF SUBJECTS
(Number of subjects seen at each pair of ages)

Age	Number seen at age	Seen also at age					
		11	12	13	14	15	16
10	100	33	29	29	15	8	5
11	100		36	33	22	12	12
12	100			50	43	29	23
13	100				45	30	23
14	100					47	34
15	100						41
16	100						

at any given age were also seen at adjacent ages. With increasing distance between ages, the amount of overlap decreases.

The semilongitudinal nature of the sample was not utilized in analysis of the age groups (except in Chapter 17). The inclusion of repeat cases in the year-to-year comparisons serves to make the age differences smaller than they would be if entirely different subjects were compared. Thus, the results of the statistical tests of age differences are on the conservative side.

The subjects we have tested are not a representative sample of adolescents. Just about half the records were contributed by subjects whose fathers were professional workers, over three fourths by subjects whose fathers had professional, semiprofessional, or managerial occupations. Table

2 presents the percentage distribution of paternal occupations on the Minnesota Scale (36) for the 515 records having this information.

TABLE 2. Socioeconomic Distribution of Subjects: Percentage of All Records at Each Level of Minnesota Scale of Paternal Occupations

(N=515 records having this information)

Level	Percentage
I. Professional	52.0
II. Semiprofessional, managerial	26.8
III. Clerical, skilled trades, retail business	11.7
IV. Farmers	.0
V. Semiskilled, minor clerical, minor business	5.8
VI. Slightly skilled	3.7
VII. Day laborers	.0
Total	100.0

Correspondingly, the group shows an above-average intelligence distribution. I.Q. scores of some sort were available for 78 per cent of records. Most of these are individual Wechsler-Bellevue scores, but a number of school-administered group test scores are also included in our calculations, since we consider them adequate for our purpose of obtaining a rough picture of intelligence status. As Table 3 shows, the over-all mean I.Q. for

TABLE 3. I.Q. Distribution of Subjects: Test Means and Standard Deviations at Each Age

		I.Q.	
Age	N	Mean	SD
10	65	118.1	14.3
11	72	117.4	13.4
12	86	115.9	13.2
13	88	115.1	13.5
14	92	116.9	14.6
15	89	113.0	10.3
16	55	115.8	11.2
All	547	115.9	13.1

our sample is 116, with a standard deviation of 13. Figures for the individual ages all approximate this over-all figure. Thus, the group as a whole centers in the high average or bright normal range, with a mean about one standard deviation higher than the national average and a dispersal about this mean somewhat smaller than that expected in a more representative sample.

Administration

Approximately one third of the Rorschach records were obtained, and recorded stenographically, in the course of developmental examinations of longitudinal research subjects at the Gesell Institute of Child Development. An additional group of records, somewhat over a third, were also obtained at the Gesell Institute, but as part of a briefer battery of tests, recorded by the administering examiner. The remaining records were obtained in school settings, and were administered individually and recorded by one of the authors.

Presentation of the test was kept as simple as possible. The following instructions were approximated:

There are no right or wrong answers to this. The main thing is, what does it look like to you? Different people see different things. Now, what does this first one look like to you?

Essentially these same instructions were repeated for all subjects, including those who had taken the Rorschach test one or more times previously.

Inquiry was conducted in two stages, as was done in our earlier study of young children (1). Most of the inquiry questions were asked immediately following the subject's indication that he had finished with a given card. In particular, questions of location and nonleading questions regarding determinants were asked at that time. Where necessary for clarification of scoring, certain questions that might otherwise influence subsequent responses to the blots were asked following completion of the entire series of Rorschach cards. These were particularly questions dealing with the enlivened determinants: movement, shading, and color.

Following the subject's completing spontaneous response and inquiry, he was asked to indicate the card he liked best and the one he liked least of the series.

Scoring

Our scoring procedure has been described in previous publications (1, 2). It derives from that of Loosli-Usteri, which, in the Swiss tradition, closely resembles that of Rorschach. Among American scoring methods it is probably closest to that of Hertz. In general, where it departs from American methods is in the direction of greater simplicity.

LOCATION As is noted in Chapter 5, we tend to score W somewhat more liberally than do some American authors, notably Beck. We attempt to consider the subject's general intention and do not score D when the subject includes nearly all the blot but fails to specify inclusion of some particular area. Among details, we distinguish D from Dd by Hertz's *Frequency Tables* (30), which list the D for each blot statistically determined from responses of a junior high school sample. White space responses are scored S; combinations of white space with global interpretations are scored WS. We do not score DS, but score either D or S according to which location appears to have the greater significance.

DETERMINANTS   Scoring of form (F), movement (M, FM, m), and color (FC, CF, C) is the same as that described by Klopfer (39). In addition, F responses are scored F+, F±, or F—. Scoring of F+ is determined primarily by Hertz's *Tables* (30). The score F± is assigned when the concept given is inherently vague in shape (e.g., design, rocks) or where the fit of concept and blot is only mediocre but not so poor as to warrant an F— score. F+% then equals (F+ + ½F±) divided by total F.

The one point at which we differ from most American scorings is the point at which American scorings differ from each other: shading. We use a single score to cover nearly all varieties of shading: F(C). The only use of shading not covered by this symbol is that which Loosli-Usteri terms Clob, and which Piotrowski terms c'. This is a response based on a diffuse impression of the blot, stemming from its darkness, producing concepts having unpleasant, dysphoric content. This category is not further elaborated here, since it has a mean occurrence of less than 0.1 per child. While the many remaining varieties of shading are covered by a single score, F(C), these are analyzed into subclasses in Chapter 6, and the reader can label them with whatever shading scores he is most familiar with.

CONTENT   The content categories used are listed in Chapter 7. These arose in part from the Rorschach material itself, but the listing used resembles those used by most authors.

POPULARITY   Our list of forms scored popular is presented in Table 4. This is based on the list in Hertz's *Tables* (30), which was slightly emended according to our findings with our own subjects. This change involved the dropping of six forms considered popular by Hertz but not occurring with such frequency in our own group. All these appear on the last three cards: three of them on Card IX, for which we consider no

TABLE 4.   POPULAR FORMS

Card	Response
I.	Bird, bat, butterfly (W)
	Face—human, animal, mask (WS)
II.	Two people (W)
	Two animals—bears, dogs, elephants (W)
III.	Two persons (W)
	Butterfly, moth (center D)
	Bow, tie (center D)
IV.	Skin, fur, rug, pelt (W)
	Boot, shoe (lower side D)
	Person, giant (W)
V.	Bat, butterfly, bird (W)
VI.	Skin, fur, rug, pelt (W)
VII.	Two persons or one person mirrored (tiers 1+2 or W)
	Two animals (tiers 1+2 or W)
VIII.	Animal (side figure)
X.	Spider, crab, octopus (side blue D)
	Rabbit's head (lower green D)

response popular, two on Card VIII ("tree" and "ribs"), and one, a borderline popular, on Card X (the "green worms"). We have also added three forms to the remaining list: "bow" or "tie" on III, "person" or "giant" on IV, "two animals" on VII. All these are also popular in the 4- to 10-year-old age range.

A response is scored P when the popular form was given either by itself or as part of a larger concept. Thus, "sea scene" on Card X, as a W response, would be scored P if the side blue forms were enumerated as crabs. But only a single P would be given to a single response: "man with boots on" for IV or "two men fighting about a bow tie" on III.

CHAPTER FOUR

Analysis of Results

Statistical analysis of the Rorschach scores of our subjects serves two related but essentially separate purposes: (1) to determine *trends* associated with age and sex differences, and (2) to provide rough normative data on the *levels* of performance for different age and sex groups. The first function relates most closely to the over-all purpose of this book. It is concerned with comparing age and sex groups to define *changes in direction,* rather than with assessing specific average scores. (What we are doing, essentially, is using cross-sectional data to estimate longitudinal trends.) For making such global evaluations as our descriptions of the "distilled essence" of Rorschach performance at each age level, information on the comparison of ages is of far more value than knowledge of means for any single age. Here we are asking such questions as: Do boys give as many, more, or fewer M at age 13, when compared with 12 or 14?

The second purpose is the presentation of statistical norms for the evaluation of the scores of a single individual in relation to the scores of a particular age-sex group. Here the question asked is: Should this 13-year-old boy's score of 3 M be considered average, high, or very high, in relation to scores for 13-year-olds in general? Since it is an open question how well our sample represents 13-year-olds in general, such a comparison can serve only as a rule of thumb. Perhaps not much more precision is necessary for this purpose, however, since external comparisons of individual scores serve primarily to allow the clinician to get his general bearings. Further comparisons must be internal, among the different scores and actual responses of the individual record. At any rate, the 14 sets of scores—for girls and boys at seven ages—represent response characteristics of children from relatively similar backgrounds, who were given the test under similar conditions, and whose responses were scored by the same criteria. They can serve at least to provide a starting point for the beginning clinician and to supplement the rule-of-thumb norms built up by the experienced Rorschach worker.

Methods Used

In summarizing a collection of scores, descriptive statistics should tell as much as possible as succinctly as possible. The information of greatest interest usually concerns the central tendency of the scores and the spread of individual scores around this central value. When the scores are normally distributed, the mean and standard deviation convey this information with elegant precision and brevity. Such is not the case with Rorschach scores.*

In order to summarize adequately the wide variety of Rorschach scores, several different statistical approaches are generally necessary. In this study, four different types of statistics have been used: (1) percentage-using scores, (2) raw frequency of occurrence, (3) means and standard deviations, (4) percentile scores (medians, quartiles, 1st and 9th deciles).

The first statistic is, in some ways, the basic one. It poses the question: How many individuals use this particular variable at all? A few Rorschach scores occur so nearly universally that for them the answer to this question provides very little information for comparing groups. This is the case with W, F, A, and P. For nearly all other scores, however, the information is important, especially because without it an average value can be misleading. (For example, if mean F(C) is .5, it is important to know whether 50 per cent of the subjects gave single F(C) responses or whether 10 per cent gave five responses apiece.) Table 5 presents percentage-using scores for the major Rorschach variables.

A second type of statistic, here used mainly for describing variables that are not the usual Rorschach scores, is simple raw frequency of occurrence. Such figures are reported only where general trends, not particular individual values, are of interest. This is the case with the adjective count, for example, where it is of interest that 15-year-olds as a group use the most dysphoric adjectives, but where we are not trying to propose a "dysphoric adjective ratio" as a new individual score.

Third are the means and standard deviations. Values of these statistics are presented for the major Rorschach variables in Table 6. With a few exceptions, means have been reported to the nearest tenth, in order to avoid the temptation of finding "trends" in the second decimal place.

Finally, percentile values for the major Rorschach variables are presented in Table 7. Three main percentile statistics are presented: the median (the score of the middle person) and the first and third quartiles

---

* Whereas most psychometric tests are in their initial construction manipulated until particular statistical properties appear in their scores, the Rorschach test did not undergo such a treatment. Its creator apparently saw the scores as shorthand notations for the complex processes observable in subjects' responses. In his many comparative tables of different scores, he simply struck "rough averages" (reported as ranges) for the different groups as they appeared to him (51, p. 23).

TABLE 5. PERCENTAGE OF SUBJECTS USING MAJOR RORSCHACH VARIABLES*

	10 Years		11 Years		12 Years		13 Years		14 Years		15 Years		16 Years	
	Boys	*Girls*	*Boys*	*Girls*	*Boys*	*Girls*	*Boys*	*Girls*	*Boys*	*Girls*	*Boys*	*Girls*	*Boys*	*Girls*
D	96%	98%	92%	100%	96%	98%	98%	98%	96%	98%	96%	90%	94%	96%
Dd+Do+S	54	48	52	52	54	56	42	60	54	64	26	62	54	50
M	78	78	78	76	84	84	72	88	84	92	66	88	84	92
FM	78	78	78	72	84	76	82	66	80	82	66	82	88	82
m	48	48	42	36	54	58	52	48	44	56	32	34	50	44
FC	20	24	22	28	20	28	24	30	26	30	14	24	34	46
CF	54	54	50	50	50	44	36	48	44	48	36	62	46	54
C	14	14	8	6	12	16	14	10	10	24	12	10	10	10
Any color	64	66	64	66	68	64	52	52	60	68	46	70	66	82
F(C)	38	44	40	34	36	48	52	62	46	58	46	66	50	66
A	100	96	100	96	98	100	100	100	100	100	100	100	98	100
H	90	94	90	100	98	98	90	100	94	98	82	94	92	98

* At all ages, 100 per cent of both boys and girls use the following: R, W, F, P

TABLE 6. MEANS AND STANDARD DEVIATIONS FOR THE MAJOR RORSCHACH VARIABLES (N=50 in each sex group)

		10 Years			11 Years			12 Years			13 Years			14 Years			15 Years			16 Years		
		Boys	Girls	Total	Boys	Girls	Total	Boys	Girls	Total	Boys	Girls	Total	Boys	Girls	Total	Boys	Girls	Total	Boys	Girls	Total
R	mean	18.2	20.1	19.2	19.5	19.5	19.5	20.5	23.4	22.0	18.2	22.1	20.1	20.0	26.9	23.4	15.5	21.1	18.3	20.2	24.8	22.5
	SD	9.2	12.5	11.0	9.5	13.4	11.5	9.6	16.4	13.5	9.8	12.2	11.2	11.3	15.2	13.7	7.9	10.3	9.5	12.0	17.2	14.8
W%	mean	52.4%	50.3%	51.4%	52.4%	43.8%	48.1%	48.0%	45.8%	46.9%	55.6%	36.8%	46.2%	49.4%	35.8%	42.6%	53.4%	47.6%	50.5%	48.6%	50.4%	49.5%
	SD	19.0	22.4	21.8	22.8	25.4	24.5	22.1	25.4	23.8	22.0	26.2	25.6	24.2	27.0	26.3	24.1	26.8	25.4	21.1	22.3	21.5
D%	mean	40.2%	42.4%	41.3%	39.9%	47.8%	43.9%	44.6%	45.0%	44.8%	39.4%	52.4%	45.9%	42.6%	52.0%	47.3%	42.8%	44.2%	43.5%	44.4%	42.4%	43.4%
	SD	18.0	17.8	17.9	20.2	20.5	20.4	17.7	19.9	18.8	18.7	18.9	18.8	20.2	20.0	20.4	21.9	22.4	22.0	20.6	22.1	21.2
Dd%	mean	7.4%	7.3%	7.3%	7.6%	8.4%	8.0%	7.4%	9.2%	8.3%	5.0%	10.8%	7.9%	8.0%	12.2%	10.1%	3.8%	8.2%	6.0%	7.0%	7.2%	7.1%
	SD	10.3	12.7	11.6	9.3	10.2	9.7	11.0	12.4	11.7	8.1	11.5	10.2	11.5	14.3	13.0	8.0	10.2	9.4	10.0	9.4	9.7
F%	mean	59.6%	64.5%	62.1%	60.5%	63.1%	61.8%	63.0%	59.7%	61.3%	59.9%	65.4%	62.7%	62.7%	63.4%	63.1%	65.3%	60.0%	62.7%	60.5%	51.3%	55.9%
	SD	19.9	19.4	19.7	17.3	21.0	19.2	15.7	18.9	17.4	18.5	21.6	20.2	18.5	17.1	17.6	23.4	17.0	20.3	23.2	20.5	22.2
F+%	mean	90.1%	91.6%	90.9%	89.2%	91.4%	90.3%	92.4%	92.3%	92.4%	91.8%	93.7%	92.8%	92.0%	93.4%	92.7%	91.2%	93.0%	92.1%	92.6%	92.9%	92.7%
	SD	7.0	10.7	9.0	11.5	10.2	10.9	6.7	6.6	6.7	7.9	6.2	7.1	7.6	5.5	6.6	8.6	6.1	7.2	6.7	7.2	6.9
M	mean	1.9	2.1	2.0	2.2	2.2	2.2	2.1	3.0	2.6	1.9	2.3	2.1	1.9	2.9	2.4	1.3	2.4	1.8	2.0	2.7	2.3
	SD	1.8	1.8	1.8	1.8	2.0	1.9	1.7	2.4	2.1	2.1	2.1	2.2	1.5	2.8	2.3	1.4	1.7	1.8	1.7	2.1	2.0
FM	mean	2.3	2.4	2.4	2.5	2.4	2.5	2.4	2.0	2.2	2.3	1.6	2.0	2.4	2.1	2.3	1.3	1.9	1.6	1.9	2.9	2.4
	SD	2.4	2.5	2.5	2.2	2.2	2.2	2.1	1.8	2.0	2.1	1.5	1.9	1.8	2.0	1.9	1.4	2.4	1.5	1.6	3.1	2.5
m	mean	.7	.6	.6	.7	.5	.6	.9	1.0	1.0	1.1	.8	1.0	.6	.9	.8	.4	.5	.5	.9	1.0	1.0
	SD	1.0	.8	.9	1.3	.8	1.1	1.0	1.4	1.2	1.1	1.2	1.1	.9	1.0	1.0	.9	.8	.8	1.3	2.0	1.7
FC	mean	.3	.4	.3	.3	.3	.3	.2	.5	.3	.3	.3	.3	.3	.4	.3	.2	.3	.3	.4	.7	.5
	SD	.6	.6	.6	.6	.6	.6	.4	.9	.7	.5	.6	.6	.5	.6	.5	.6	.7	.6	.6	1.0	.8
CF	mean	.8	.9	.9	.7	.8	.7	.8	.8	.8	.7	.8	.7	.6	.9	.8	.6	.9	.7	.8	1.7	1.2
	SD	.9	1.1	1.0	.8	1.0	.9	1.0	1.2	1.1	.8	1.1	.9	.8	1.5	1.2	1.1	.9	1.0	1.0	2.3	1.7

		10 Years			11 Years			12 Years			13 Years			14 Years			15 Years			16 Years		
		Boys	*Girls*	*Total*	*Boys*	*Girls*	*Total*	*Boys*	*Girls*	*Total*	*Boys*	*Girls*	*Total*	*Boys*	*Girls*	*Total*	*Boys*	*Girls*	*Total*	*Boys*	*Girls*	*Total*
C	mean	.2	.2	.2	.1	.1	.1	.2	.2	.2	.1	.1	.1	.1	.3	.2	.1	.1	.1	.1	.1	.1
	SD	.5	.4	.5	.3	.1	.2	.6	.4	.5	.4	.4	.4	.3	.5	.4	.2	.3	.3	.4	.3	.3
ΣC	mean	1.2	1.3	1.3	1.0	1.1	1.0	1.1	1.3	1.2	1.0	1.1	1.1	1.0	1.5	1.2	.8	1.2	1.0	1.2	2.2	1.7
	SD	1.3	1.3	1.3	1.0	.9	.9	1.3	1.5	1.4	1.5	1.7	1.6	1.2	1.8	1.5	1.3	1.2	1.3	1.3	2.5	1.9
F(C)	mean	.6	.8	.7	.7	.6	.6	.7	1.1	.9	1.0	1.1	1.1	.8	1.5	1.2	1.0	1.7	1.3	1.2	2.0	1.6
	SD	.8	1.3	1.1	.9	1.3	1.1	1.5	2.0	1.8	1.3	1.5	1.4	1.4	1.9	1.7	1.4	1.8	1.6	2.2	2.7	2.5
A%	mean	46.5%	51.0%	48.8%	47.4%	53.4%	50.4%	50.9%	47.3%	49.1%	45.3%	48.3%	46.8%	47.9%	44.5%	46.2%	49.1%	45.3%	47.2%	49.6%	42.3%	46.0%
	SD	15.6	19.8	18.0	17.7	16.6	17.5	18.0	11.8	15.2	12.2	13.3	12.7	12.6	13.4	13.0	15.9	16.8	16.3	15.9	14.7	15.6
H%	mean	19.5%	18.2%	18.9%	18.4%	19.6%	19.0%	18.0%	20.2%	19.1%	15.8%	20.9%	17.8%	16.7%	21.7%	19.2%	13.9%	21.9%	17.9%	16.1%	20.1%	18.1%
	SD	16.5	12.4	14.7	12.2	14.2	13.2	15.9	10.7	13.5	11.3	13.6	12.7	10.2	11.2	10.9	10.6	9.5	10.7	10.9	12.3	11.7
P	mean	5.9	6.8	6.4	6.8	6.6	6.7	6.7	6.7	6.7	6.4	6.7	6.6	6.6	6.6	6.6	5.5	6.2	5.8	6.0	6.1	6.1
	SD	2.0	1.9	2.0	2.4	1.9	2.2	2.0	1.9	1.9	1.8	1.6	1.7	1.8	1.9	1.9	1.9	1.5	1.7	1.8	1.6	1.7

TABLE 7. Percentiles for Major Rorschach Variables: Whole-Number Percentiles for Boys and Girls at Each Age and for Total 10–16 Range
(Medians in Italic)

Percentile	10 Years B	G	T	11 Years B	G	T	12 Years B	G	T	13 Years B	G	T	14 Years B	G	T	15 Years B	G	T	16 Years B	G	T	10–16 Years B	G	T	Age diff. B	G	Sex diff. B-G
R																											
90	29	35	34	33	32	33	34	40	36	30	38	35	35	46	40	26	39	34	40	36	36	33	37	35	*		†
75	23	25	24	27	21	25	25	28	25	22	26	23	24	34	29	17	26	22	22	30	26	22	27	24			
50	*15*	*18*	*16*	*17*	*16*	*16*	*18*	*20*	*19*	*16*	*18*	*17*	*17*	*25*	*20*	*14*	*20*	*16*	*16*	*22*	*19*	*16*	*19*	*17*			
25	11	13	13	13	13	13	14	12	13	12	15	13	13	16	15	11	12	12	13	14	13	12	14	13			
10	10	11	10	10	10	10	13	10	10	10	10	10	10	11	11	9	10	10	11	12	11	10	11	10			
W %																											
90	79	82	81	83	78	80	74	87	81	85	75	83	88	78	83	90	95	90	78	85	81	82	82	82		—	†
75	70	71	70	66	58	62	68	66	67	74	46	68	62	56	60	66	66	66	67	66	67	69	66	68			
50	*56*	*47*	*52*	*50*	*41*	*46*	*44*	*39*	*42*	*56*	*31*	*42*	*46*	*29*	*39*	*56*	*46*	*51*	*46*	*54*	*50*	*52*	*41*	*49*			
25	35	30	34	36	26	33	33	29	30	39	21	28	30	17	23	32	25	29	30	20	28	34	24	29			
10	23	19	20	21	13	19	19	16	18	28	15	18	20	11	17	20	15	17	19	16	17	20	14	16			
D %																											
90	63	64	63	63	67	65	66	68	66	63	70	67	68	75	72	72	73	72	70	70	70	67	70	69			*
75	56	57	56	56	60	58	60	59	59	52	65	61	58	67	62	62	62	62	56	60	58	56	59	58			
50	*42*	*49*	*45*	*44*	*49*	*47*	*48*	*49*	*48*	*38*	*57*	*49*	*45*	*57*	*50*	*39*	*45*	*43*	*45*	*43*	*44*	*44*	*50*	*47*			
25	27	28	27	26	37	31	33	35	33	25	44	30	27	40	33	31	34	33	33	27	30	28	34	30			
10	17	13	16	10	18	13	18	13	18	15	20	16	11	25	15	10	13	10	16	16	16	16	16	16			
Dd %																											
90	18	24	21	24	22	23	28	29	29	13	26	23	20	23	22	19	25	23	18	23	20	20	25	23	*	*	†
75	13	10	12	15	15	15	11	14	11	9	17	13	12	16	13	13	11	9	11	11	11	11	14	13			
50	*4*	*0*	*3*	*4*	*4*	*4*	*4*	*4*	*4*	*0*	*9*	*3*	*6*	*9*	*8*	*0*	*7*	*0*	*4*	*3*	*4*	*8*	*6*	*4*			
25	0	0	0	0	4	0	0	4	0	0	0	0	0	0	0	0	0	0	0	0	0	0	0	0			
F %																											
90	83	88	85	84	93	86	83	83	83	88	91	90	84	84	84	90	80	88	90	83	88	86	86	86		*	—
75	76	74	75	74	79	75	74	75	74	73	81	78	76	77	76	82	73	76	74	66	71	77	75	76			
50	*63*	*66*	*65*	*63*	*62*	*63*	*67*	*60*	*63*	*60*	*69*	*66*	*63*	*63*	*63*	*68*	*60*	*64*	*67*	*49*	*59*	*64*	*63*	*63*			
25	45	49	40	45	48	48	51	45	50	50	47	47	50	54	52	54	46	49	48	38	40	50	47	48			
10	38	43	40	38	38	38	43	33	38	35	35	35	38	40	39	43	38	39	25	23	23	36	36	36			
F+ %																											
75	97	96	96	100	98	98	100	98	98	100	100	100	100	98	98	100	100	100	100	100	100	100	100	100	—		*
50	*91*	*98*	*98*	*93*	*94*	*93*	*93*	*93*	*93*	*93*	*95*	*94*	*93*	*93*	*93*	*93*	*94*	*94*	*93*	*94*	*93*	*93*	*94*	*93*			
25	85	88	86	80	88	86	88	87	88	86	89	88	84	89	89	85	87	86	89	88	88	87	89	88			
10	79	84	83	73	81	75	83	83	83	81	85	83	84	86	85	78	85	83	85	81	82	80	84	83			

	%	1	2	3	4	5	6	7	8	9	10	11	12	13	14	15	16	17	18	19	20	21	22	23	24
		*																*		*			*		†
																*									†
		*		*																					—
M	90	5	5	4	5	5	5	4	4	3	5			5	5	5	5	6	4	5	5	4	4	4	5
	75	3	4	3	3	4	3	3	3	2	3	4	3	3	3	3	4	5	3	4	5	3	3	3	3
	60	2	2	2	2	2	2	1	2	1	2	2	2	2	2	1	2	2	2	2	4	2	2	2	2
	25	1	1	1	1	1	1	1	1	0	1	1	1	1	1	0	1	1	1	1	2	1	1	1	1
	10	0	0	0	0	0	0	0	0	0	0	0	0	0	0	0	0	0	0	0	1	0	0	0	0
FM	90	5	5	5	6	7	4	4	4	4	5	4	6	5	4	6	5	5	6	5	5	6	5	5	6
	75	3	3	3	3	4	3	3	3	2	3	3	4	3	3	3	4	4	4	3	4	4	3	3	3
	60	2	2	2	2	2	1	1	2	1	2	2	2	2	3	2	2	2	2	2	2	2	2	2	2
	25	1	1	1	1	1	1	0	1	0	1	1	1	1	0	1	2	1	1	1	0	1	1	1	1
	10	0	0	0	0	0	0	0	0	0	0	0	0	0	0	0	0	0	0	0	0	0	0	0	0
m	90	2	2	2	3	3	3	1	2	1	2	2	2	3	3	3	2	4	2	2	2	1	2	2	2
	75	1	1	1	1	2	1	1	1	1	1	1	1	2	1	2	1	1	1	1	1	1	1	1	1
	60	0	0	0	0	0	1	0	0	0	1	1	0	1	0	1	1	1	1	0	0	0	0	1	0
	25	0	0	0	0	0	0	0	0	0	0	0	0	0	0	0	0	0	0	0	0	0	0	0	0
FC	90	1	1	1	1	2	1	1	1	1	1	1	1	1	1	1	1	2	1	1	2	1	1	2	1
	75	1	1	0	1	1	1	0	0	0	1	1	1	0	0	0	1	1	0	1	1	1	1	1	1
	60	0	0	0	1	0	0	0	0	0	0	0	0	0	0	0	0	0	0	0	0	0	0	0	0
	25																								
CF	90	2	1	2	4	5	2	2	2	2	2	3	2	2	2	2	3	3	3	2	2	2	2	3	3
	75	1	1	1	2	3	1	1	2	1	1	1	1	1	1	1	1	1	1	1	1	1	1	2	1
	60	0	1	0	1	1	0	0	1	0	0	0	0	0	0	0	1	1	1	1	1	1	1	1	1
	25	0	0	0	1	0	0	0	0	0	0	0	0	0	0	0	0	0	0	0	0	0	0	0	0
C	90	1	1	1	1	1	1	0	1	0	1	1	1	1	1	1	1	1	1	0	0	1	0	1	1
	75	0	0	0	0	0	0	0	0	0	0	0	0	0	0	0	0	0	0	0	0	0	0	0	0
ΣC	90	3	3	3	4	5½	3½	3	3	3	3½	3½	3½	3½	3½	3½	3½	3½	3	2½	2½	2½	3	3½	3
	75	2	2	1½	2½	3½	2	2	2	1	2	2½	1	1½	1½	1½	1½	2	1½	1½	1½	1½	2	2	2
	60	1	1	1	1	1½	1	1	1	0	1	1	½	½	½	½	1	1	1	1	1	1	1	1	1
	25	0	0	0	0	½	0	0	0	0	0	0	0	0	0	0	0	0	0	0	0	0	0	0	0
F(C)	90	3	4	2	4	5	4	4	5	3	4	5	2	3	3	3	3	3	2	2	2	2	2	3	2
	75	1	2	1	2	3	1	2	3	2	2	2	1	2	2	2	1	2	1	1	1	1	1	1	1
	60	0	1	0	1	1	1	1	1	0	1	1	0	1	1	1	0	0	0	0	0	0	0	0	0
	25	0	0	0	0	0	0	0	0	0	0	0	0	0	0	0	0	0	0	0	0	0	0	0	0

See footnotes at end of table, page 28.

TABLE 7. Percentiles for Major Rorschach Variables (*Continued*)

Percentile	10 Years B	G	T	11 Years B	G	T	12 Years B	G	T	13 Years B	G	T	14 Years B	G	T	15 Years B	G	T	16 Years B	G	T	10–16 Years B	G	T	Age diff. B	G	Sex diff. B-G
A%																											
90	68	78	76	70	69	69	72	67	70	62	67	64	67	64	65	72	67	69	71	65	68	71	68	69			
75	57	67	59	58	64	61	67	55	61	55	57	56	56	55	55	57	56	56	58	51	56	57	58	57			
50	46	50	47	47	56	53	49	45	48	46	46	47	49	44	46	48	41	44	49	41	45	47	46	46		—	*
25	35	40	38	34	44	38	41	39	39	38	41	39	39	35	36	37	32	35	40	31	35	39	34	37			
10	29	33	30	25	34	29	30	34	33	28	33	31	30	28	29	33	25	28	33	24	28	31	29	30			
H%																											
90	38	32	35	38	36	36	33	38	34	34	39	36	33	38	34	28	39	35	33	35	34	34	36	35			
75	29	25	26	27	30	28	25	27	26	23	26	25	22	29	28	22	30	26	22	25	24	25	27	26			
50	18	16	17	16	19	18	18	19	18	14	19	16	14	19	17	13	20	16	14	19	16	15	19	18	—	—	†
25	11	10	10	10	13	11	14	13	13	8	11	9	10	14	11	6	11	9	8	11	9	10	11	11			
10	3	6	4	3	8	6	9	8	9	2	7	4	8	9	9	0	8	0	3	7	4	4	6	5			
P																											
90	9	10	10	10	9	9	9	9	9	9	9	9	9	9	9	8	8	8	8	8	8	9	9	9			
75	7	8	8	9	8	9	9	8	8	8	9	8	8	8	8	8	7	7	8	7	7	8	8	8			
50	6	7	6	7	6	7	7	7	7	6	7	7	7	6	7	6	6	6	6	6	6	6	6	6		*	—
25	4	5	5	5	5	5	5	5	5	6	6	6	5	5	5	4	5	5	5	5	5	5	5	5			
10	3	5	4	4	5	5	4	4	4	3	4	4	4	4	4	3	4	3	4	4	4	4	4	4			

* Differences significant at .05 level by median test.
† Differences significant at .01 level by median test.

(points that delimit the middle 50 per cent of subjects). In addition, the 10th and 90th percentile points (those that separate off the top and bottom 10 per cent of subjects) are given for a number of variables.

The median and quartiles are particularly valuable for a test like the Rorschach, which sets no top limit for most scores, because these statistics are not affected by the occurrence of a few extreme scores. (To compute percentile points, one *counts individuals* rather than *adds scores*. Since each person counts equally, an extreme score affects the median no more than a moderate score does. The top score could, in fact, be doubled without changing the median.) The quartile points have special clinical usefulness because they define a *central range* of values, and can answer the question: How high is high? If we know, for example, that the median R is 16, and subject X gives 24 responses, is that high? The answer is yes if $Q_3 = 20$, no if $Q_3 = 30$, because evaluation depends on how much the scores tend to spread out.

An additional word should be said about means and medians, since the descriptive statistic of greatest interest to most users of the test is some form of average. Both median and mean values can be found here for all major variables. In our verbal descriptions of trends we have tended to emphasize median values, because they give a better indication of the central value and because they are apparently more stable scores (i.e., insensitive to the occasional deviant scores that can so inflate the mean). However, when a minority of subjects uses a particular variable, the median cannot be used to compare different groups, since all medians will equal zero. In that case mean scores are reported.

A point to be noted is that medians can be reported in two forms, both of which are used here. The first form is the actual score of the middle person in the group. The second form, used only when a majority of subjects is distributed over a small number of scores (as in the case of all determinants except F), is a weighted or interpolated median. Interpolation allows presentation of the median as a decimal fraction, so that two groups can be differentiated when their whole-number medians are the same. For clinical use the whole-number median is more practical, but for portraying trends the interpolated median is more valuable. Whole-number medians have been presented in Table 7, where scores are collected for ease of clinical reference. In the separate sections on the different determinants, where age trends are of greater interest, interpolated medians are presented.

Evaluation of the Data

Because this study is developmentally oriented, we have been alert to the appearance of trends, as indicated by group-to-group differences in summary statistics. And, naturally, abundant differences among the statistics appeared. Age differences were not, however, the sole sources of these score differences. Twelve-year-olds might differ from 13-year-olds in mean R, say, but so too would a new sample of 13-year-olds. Thus we had the problem of distinguishing differences related to real age changes from differences related only to sampling of different individuals.

At first thought, the answer to the problem might appear to lie in the relative size of the difference between average scores for the different groups. That is, the difference between 10.0 and 10.2 does not look like much to base a trend on, still less the difference between .02 and .08, but the difference between 10.0 and 12.0 looks as if it might represent a real change. Though difference in size is one important consideration for such evaluations, several other approaches allow more dependable conclusions.

By far the most satisfactory method of distinguishing age differences and sampling differences would be to eliminate the sampling differences— that is, to compare the same subjects at the different ages. A longitudinal approach could not be made in this study,* since only about 35 per cent of the subjects overlap from one age to the next (see Chapter 3). Instead, the groups were treated as cross-sectional samples and the median test was used to test differences among the major Rorschach variables. This test evaluates differences between the sexes or differences among all the ages taken together.†

Rorschach protocols, however, provide many more variables of interest than the 18 we have tested, and our discussions probably touch on several hundred of them. Many of these, though potentially countable, are handled here in qualitative form. In judging the importance and probable dependability of group differences in these variables, we have used (explicitly and implicitly) at least four criteria. The first of these is *external consistency,* which accords greater importance to a small group-to-group difference that fits in with a larger trend than to one of equal size that appears capricious. The second is *internal consistency,* which accords relative importance to a small difference that fits into a total coherent picture of a particular group, as indicated by significant values of associated variables. The third criterion, *frequency,* is sometimes only roughly quantified, as when we make such statements as "compared with surrounding ages, many 13-year-olds appear to. . . . " Finally, *size* of a difference between groups was, naturally, a determiner of the importance accorded to it.

How these criteria were differentially weighted in our decisions con-

---

* Collection of data for a fully longitudinal study is now nearing completion. This information on age *changes,* rather than simple age *differences,* will provide the ultimate test of the findings proposed in this book.

† Essentially the median test involves striking a grand total median for all groups combined, then counting the numbers of individuals within the separate groups whose scores fall above and below this point. Because of nonindependence, owing to the longitudinal cases, the results of this test are decidedly conservative.

cerning the importance of any age or sex group difference (i.e., in our "clinical judgments") we do not know. Still less can we say how often our admitted search for consistent developmental trends actually manufactured or distorted trends. The objective evidence provided by statistical tests indicates some substantial differences between groups in their basic Rorschach framework. In our adding of flesh to this skeleton, we have at least been conscious of the possibilities of overpadding. We have also had to revise a sufficient number of our expectations, as the data contradicted them, to have developed a strong subjective feeling of our own objectivity. For the reader, however, this may not be a study that can be fully evaluated on the basis of internal evidence alone. Besides the testimony of statistical tests, external trends, and internal consistency, the reader's private verdict may also consider a factor of personal recognition—the feeling that "I've seen that 15-year-old before."

CHAPTER FIVE

Area

The areas that an individual chooses for interpretation provide some measure for evaluating his perceptive processes. His choices give us some insight into his method of attacking a situation; the succession of his responses gives some estimate of his ability or his process in organizing his thinking. The relative emphasis of areas chosen for response may tell us whether his emotional and intellectual tone is expansive or restricted, painstaking or slapdash. We derive some idea of whether his thinking tends to be generalized, abstract, perhaps at times superficial; whether he tends to be more practical, critical, and realistic; whether his ability to generalize appears to be in balance with his capacity to judge a situation realistically. In his perception of small details, we have one means of judging his ability and proclivity to refine his thinking. If there is emphasis on the white areas, we may have some insight concerning aggressivity, resistance, or negativism, and even perhaps about the kinds of difficulties or situations that provoke these characteristics. Some area responses give us clues concerning the possibility of repression, excessive control, timidity of expression.

These, then, are some of the possibilities that analysis of area affords us in individual protocols. Of course, the analysis of area cannot be taken out of context, but must be evaluated in relation to the total constellation presented by the protocol.

Age Changes

WHOLE (W) RESPONSES   For the normal adult, most investigators have indicated a W% expectancy of between 20 and 30 per cent. In our earlier study (1) of the years from 2 to 10, W% greatly exceeded this. In these younger subjects, mean W% ranged from 42 to 60 per cent with the low point at 9 years, high point at 3½ years. The average W% for the total age range that we studied from 2 through 10 years was 53 per cent.

In the present study of the years from 10 through 16, W% is somewhat less than in the earlier age range, though it does not approach the ex-

TABLE 8. AREA RESPONSES: MEAN AND MEDIAN SCORES FOR BOYS AND GIRLS AT EACH AGE

	10 Years			11 Years			12 Years			13 Years			14 Years			15 Years			16 Years		
	B	G	T	B	G	T	B	G	T	B	G	T	B	G	T	B	G	T	B	G	T
Mean Scores																					
W+W	5.7	6.0		5.9	5.1		6.1	6.3		6.7	5.3		5.9	6.0		5.9	6.3		6.8	7.4	
DW	1.1	2.3		1.9	1.8		1.9	1.7		1.6	1.2		1.4	1.2		1.2	1.3		1.1	1.7	
WS	.8	1.2		.9	.7		1.0	.7		.9	.7		.8	.5		.5	.5		.8	.7	
All W	7.5	9.6	8.5	8.6	7.6	8.1	9.0	8.7	8.9	9.2	7.1	8.2	8.1	7.7	7.9	7.6	8.0	7.8	8.7	9.8	9.2
D	8.8	8.5	8.7	9.1	9.5	9.3	9.2	11.0	10.1	7.9	12.0	10.0	9.5	14.4	12.0	7.2	11.0	9.1	9.4	12.2	10.8
Dd	1.4	1.4		1.1	1.4		1.1	2.5		.5	1.9		1.5	3.3		.4	1.5		1.4	2.2	
Do	.1	.2		.4	.4		.3	.3		.1	.4		.3	.4		.2	.3		.3	.1	
S	.3	.4		.4	.5		.8	.8		.5	.6		.7	1.1		.2	.4		.4	.5	
All Dd	1.8	2.0	1.9	1.8	2.3	2.1	2.3	3.7*	3.0	1.1	2.9	2.0	2.5	4.8	3.6	.7	2.2	1.4	2.1	2.8	2.5
Median Scores																					
All W	8	9		8	7		8	8		8	6		8	7		7	8		8	9	
D	7	8		7	8		8	10		6	11		8	15		6	11		8	11	
All Dd	1	0		1	1		1	1		0	2		1	3		0	1		1	1	

* 50 Dd's from one child; without her record, mean (N=49) is 2.7.

pected mean of the adult. Means in our present group range from 51 per cent at 10 years, the high point, down to 43 per cent at 14 years, the low point. If we consider medians instead of means, the range is much the same, from 52 per cent (10 years) to 39 per cent (14 years). Mean W% for the whole period is 48 per cent; median, 49 per cent.

Most of these W responses, as Table 8 shows, are simple, total, global responses. The average child at each age gives one to two DW responses. (Note that our DW score includes mostly successive wholes—wholes built up from separate details—rather than confabulatory wholes, which this symbol would indicate in most American scoring systems.) WS responses occur with an average of just under one per child at most ages.

It is important, in comparing results of this study with those of others, to recognize that our criterion for scoring W is not as rigid as that held by many authors, particularly Beck (4) and Piotrowski (47). We group cut-off wholes with the general W scoring category and attempt to score area according to the child's general intention, rather than try to push inquiry too far concerning inclusion or rejection of certain portions of the blot. It is our belief that too searching an inquiry distorts the child's original intent and introduces a spurious precision into location choice. This procedure results, of course, in a W category having different significance from that of the fore-named authors.

DETAIL (D) RESPONSES   D% in the normal adult record is expected to fall between 50 and 70 per cent. In the years from 2 to 10 in the group we studied, the mean D% ranged from 33 per cent at 4½ and 5½ years, the low points, to a high of 48 per cent at 9 years. Mean D% for the total age range from 2 to 10 years was 38 per cent.

D% in the years from 10 to 16, like the W response, falls a little closer to the expected adult average, though it by no means ever approximates it. Mean D% for our present subjects ranges from a low of 41 per cent at 10 years to a high of 47 per cent at 14 years. Medians are slightly higher, ranging from 43 per cent at 15 years to 50 per cent at 14 years. Mean D%, 10 to 16 years, is 44; median, 47%D.

The most conspicuous age change is the steady increase in D%, both median and mean, from 10 through 14 years, with its high at 14 years, and then a sharp drop in D at 15 and 16 years.

W:D RATIO   As in our study of the earlier ages, the present group from 10 to 16 years does not closely approach the W:D ratio expectancy of the normal adult. Some European and American investigators have indicated that children in their studies do approach the adult expectancy of 1:3 in W:D relationship.

As Table 8 shows, the median W:D ratio at each age is often closer to 1:1 or 1:1.5, with the D response taking a slight ascendancy over the W response at every age.* Only at 14 years does the comparison reach the ratio of 1:2. However, it does appear that the ratio is progressing in the expected direction, even though in our group and for the age range studied it does not reach what is considered the adult expectancy.

RARE DETAIL (Dd) RESPONSES   In the normal adult record an average of about 10 per cent Dd is expected. This figure is frequently reached or approximated in the first ten years of life, the average for the total age range being 9 per cent according to our previous study (1).

Dd% in the present age range, from 10 to 16 years, is slightly lower, the means ranging between 6 per cent at 15 years, the low point in our group, and 10% at 14 years, the high point. Medians are lower, but show the same age changes with the high point of 8% at 14 years, low point of zero per cent at 15 years. Mean Dd%, 10 to 16 years, is 8 per cent, median 4 per cent.

Do response is presented in Table 8. Here we see that its occurrence is limited, not exceeding a mean of .4 for any age-sex group. S responses are slightly more frequent and the range for different ages is wider: from .2 responses per child (boys at 15 years) to 1.1 responses (girls at 14 years).

SUCCESSION   At no age was it possible to indicate any well-defined characteristics of succession for a majority of subjects. Table 9 shows the

TABLE 9.   SUCCESSION: NUMBER OF RECORDS OF EACH CLASSIFICATION FOR BOYS AND GIRLS AT EACH AGE

	10		11		12		13		14		15		16		Total	
	B	G	B	G	B	G	B	G	B	G	B	G	B	G	B	G
Rigid	0	0	0	0	0	0	0	0	0	0	0	0	0	0	0	0
Orderly	6	8	5	5	5	9	1	3	2	5	1	8	3	5	23	43
Loose	7	6	4	7	4	11	3	8	5	15	2	3	3	5	28	55
Confused	3	0	0	3	0	0	0	0	0	0	0	0	0	0	3	3
Reversed	0	0	0	0	1	0	0	0	0	0	0	0	0	0	1	0
None	34	36	41	35	40	30	46	39	43	30	47	39	44	40	295	249

category of "no succession" or "none" as most frequent at each age. This was largely because the total number of responses for each individual seldom allowed a clear-cut succession to be determined. With the over-all median of just 17 responses per record, the occurrence of more than two responses per card was restricted. In addition, those who tended to approach the cards with a W response inclined to the same type of response

---

* The apparent contradiction between mean D exceeding mean W, while mean W% exceeds mean D%, is due to the correlation between R and D. Short records tend to be largely composed of W's, and a short record counts as heavily as a long record in computing mean W% or D%. Long records tend to be composed largely of D's and Dd's, and long records count more heavily in computing mean W and D.

throughout. If their perception seemed more oriented toward details, then D tended to be the predominant response. Whenever a different perception was introduced, it was likely to be the only response on a card.

For some 156 protocols it was possible to determine succession. It is interesting that in none of the records of these adolescents could succession be considered "rigid," as it is usually defined. The most frequent categories were "loose" and "orderly." The totals indicate that the girls far outnumber the boys in the use of both these categories, but it must be remembered that girls give more responses than do boys, so that a succession is more often established.

Succession, where it can be ascertained, may be used as an aid in evaluating individual protocols, but offers little as a tool for obtaining information regarding groups in the age ranges we have studied.

Sex Differences

In the years, from 2 to 10, according to our previous study, sex differences in area perception are small. Means for the total range are:

Girls: 52%W, 38%D, 10%Dd
Boys: 54%W, 38%D, 8%Dd

Thus, in these early years, boys gave slightly more W responses than did girls, girls more Dd responses than did boys.

From 10 to 16 years, the differences appear more marked. Means for the total range are:

Girls: 44%W, 47%D, 9%Dd
Boys: 51%W, 42%D, 7%Dd

Medians for the entire range, 10 to 16 years, highlight the differences in an even more clear-cut manner:

Girls: 41%W, 50%D, 6%Dd
Boys: 52%W, 44%D, 2%Dd

Thus we see that boys, in the group from 10 to 16 years, clearly exceed the girls in W response, while the girls exceed in D and Dd response.

Table 8, giving the mean and median number of DW responses per child by age and sex, shows that the boys exceed the girls in the number of DW responses at four ages, 11 through 14 years, and the margin is usually slight. Boys exceed in WS responses at all ages except 10 years. In D response, girls exceed at every age but 10 years where the difference is only slight. Girls give more Dd responses than do boys at every age. Girls also exceed boys in the average number of Do responses at every age except 12 and 16 years, and in the average S response at every age. At

14 years, the girls appear to be particularly oppositional with an average of 1.1S responses.

Thus, girls give a rather consistent picture of being more interested in details of the blot, both the large, "practical" details and the smaller details, with special emphasis of this tendency at 13 and 14 years, and somewhat less so at 15 years. Boys consistently respond more than do girls to the total blot, with W scores predominant for them. These differences are least at 10 years and again at 16 years of age.

Summary

Area response, in the group from 10 to 16 years which we have studied, though progressing in the direction of what we presume is the normal adult expectancy in these scores, has not by any means approximated the adult expectancy.

Means in area response for the entire group, 10 to 16 years, are 48%W, 44%D, 8%Dd. Medians are 49%W, 47%D, 4%Dd. W:D ratio as compared from medians is about 1:1 or 1:1.5 rather than the 1:3 ratio often expected.

Boys are much more inclined to give W responses, girls exceed in D and Dd responses, both rather consistently throughout.

Thus we see that area response, considered as an index to the developmental status of the individual between the ages of 10 and 16 years in the group that we have studied, suggests that although there is inclination toward greater maturity and the expected adult response, this is still a stage of change and instability. Age changes as suggested by the area response indicate that the developing adolescent becomes gradually more realistic and practical, with increased ability to refine his thinking, until by the age of 14 years he seems more mature in his perceptions than at any previous age. However, this is not a stable change and the following ages again testify to the fluctuating quality of the period. By 16 years, the developing individual in our group, in light of the area responses alone, does not have the maturity expected of the adult, but appears to be making progress in that direction.

CHAPTER SIX

Determinants

FORM

Form responses—those not determined by movement, color, or shading but by the shape of the blot alone—are generally considered to reflect the degree of a subject's intellectual control. They give an indication of his intellectual and critical ability and of his reasoning powers.

F% A desirable F% in an adult record is generally considered to be 50 per cent or below. According to Klopfer,

The control of any subject of more than average intelligence, whose record contains more than 50 per cent F can be called constrictive. . . . Among presumably normal adult subjects, any F% between 50 and 80 invariably corresponds to signs of inflexibility, or, in clinical terms, constriction with compulsive elements (39, pp. 233–234).

In our study of the Rorschach responses of children between the ages of 2 and 10 years, the mean F% ranged from 90 per cent at 2 years of age to 52 per cent at 7 years. It exceeded 60 per cent at all ages except 7 and 8, when it fell to 52 and 58 per cent respectively. In the present study of 10- to 16-year-olds, both mean and median F% remain definitely above the presumed ideal limit of 50 per cent.

As Table 6 indicates, the mean F%, both sexes considered together, falls very close to 62%F at every age except 16 years, when it drops to 56%F. The medians, which may present a more accurate picture of age changes, differ little from the means. Though age variations are very small, it is interesting that the F% is slightly higher, presumably indicating greater restrictive tendencies, at 10, 13, and 15 years.

Sex differences are initially small and variable, but tend to increase. Girls appear as the more restricted at 10 and 13 years, less so at 12, 15, and 16 years. Since the ultimate expectation for adult records is toward lower F%, the response of the girls seems to approach maturity more rapidly than does that of the boys. Highest F% for girls occurs at 13 years, while for the boys it is highest at 15 years. By 16 years more than half the girls achieve the adult expectancy by obtaining scores falling below 50 per cent.

F+% Form-determined responses differ in the accuracy and sharpness with which the concept given matches the blot. According to Rorschach, F+% is "an indication of the clarity of the associative processes and at the same time of the length of the span of attention and the capacity for concentration" (51).

In our earlier study (1) an effort was made to compare the responses of our young subjects with those of their contemporaries rather than with those of an adult population. Even so, in the first 10 years of life we found a steady increase in mean F+% from 54 per cent at 2 years of age to 89 per cent at 10 years. In fact, by 5½ years the mean F+% reached 84 per cent and thereafter it never fell below 80 per cent.

In the present study, form accuracy was scored according to the standards provided by Hertz's *Frequency Tables* (30), established from the responses of a junior high school sample. For both sexes together, our mean F+% ranges from 90 to 93 per cent with little variability from age to age (see Table 6). Median F+% is slightly higher, ranging between 92 and 94 per cent throughout the entire age range.

A small but intriguing sex difference shows up here. The mean F+% for the girls is higher than for the boys at every age except 12 and 16 years, when the sexes are about equal. The difference is consistent, though very small, with an over-all mean F+% of 91 per cent for boys, 93 per cent for girls.

Discussion

According to the results of our research, a score of over 50%F may not have for the individual up to 16 years of age any greatly adverse significance. That an F% below 50 per cent is "desirable" for the normal adult record is quite possible but, in the population we have studied, even the median or mean F% seldom falls below 60 per cent. It is true that at 16 years of age the F% takes its sharpest dip since 7 years. We may presume that the maturing individual is striving toward a satisfactory productive balance between his intellectual and emotional drives, and may anticipate that the F% will continue to decrease. This is an area where further research is desirable.

But up to 16 years of age, we cannot necessarily assume that a subject is highly restricted in his emotional expression if he responds with an F% higher than 50 per cent. We know by comparison with the earlier records of children from 2 to 10 years that individuals from 10 to 16 years have stabilized their reactions in this area a great deal, which seems a progressive step toward maturity.

We can select better bench marks for judging the significance of F%

by considering the percentile distributions. For the middle 50 per cent of all our subjects, F% falls between (approximately) 50 and 75 per cent. Scores falling below 50 per cent are as unusual statistically as those falling above 75 per cent. The latter subjects may be considered to have allowed little play of the more enlivened determinants. Responses of the former group, with scores falling below 50 per cent, can only be judged as successfully enriched or as inadequately controlled according to the over-all balance of the records.

As to the F+%, it is in this area that we have evidence of early stabilization of results. In the child from 2 to 10 years there is a steady progression toward greater precision of responses. From 5½ years on, F+% (scored by child standards) never falls below 80 per cent. In the 10- to 16-year range, the F+% has so stabilized that the median remains above 90 per cent and the first quartile above 85 per cent throughout. It may be to the F+% that we can look first for possible adverse clinical indications, since expectancies here seem so consistent and stable that deviation in this area is of primary importance.

MOVEMENT

M Human movement responses (M) are generally considered to be a key to the richness of the inner life of the individual, an indication of inner creativity. M by its nature supposedly indicates how actively the person responds, or wishes to respond—self-assertiveness being suggested by extensor movements, compliance by flexor movements, indecisiveness by blocked movements.

The number of M found in the adult record may normally range from 0 to 15, depending on the intelligence of the subject and the degree of emotional freedom. Two or three M responses are expected in adult subjects of average intelligence, five or more in those of superior intelligence.

The average number of movement responses in child Rorschach records is low but has been found (1) to increase in an almost steady progression from 2 to 10 years. In a group of subjects in this age range studied by us, the number increased from an average of .1 to 1.7 per child.

In our present pre-teen and teen-age subjects, aged 10 to 16, we find less of a consistent trend, and more specific change in direction from year to year. That is, after age 10, M does not continue to increase regularly with age, as it did earlier. Rather it fluctuates from one year to the next, with the most conspicuous changes at 13 and 15 years.

Specifically, the mean M for ages 10 to 16 is as follows: 2.0, 2.2, 2.6, 2.1, 2.4, 1.8, 2.3. An initial increase in mean M, followed by drops at both 13 and 15 years, appears in both boys' and girls' means. Median scores, presented in Table 10, parallel the means at a slightly lower level.

Eighty-two per cent of our total age range give at least one M re-

TABLE 10. MEDIANS FOR ENLIVENED DETERMINANTS:* MEDIAN INTERPOLATED VALUES FOR EACH SEX AT EACH AGE

	10 Years			11 Years			12 Years			13 Years			14 Years			15 Years			16 Years		
	B	G	T	B	G	T	B	G	T	B	G	T	B	G	T	B	G	T	B	G	T
M	1.6	1.8	1.7	2.3	1.9	2.0	1.9	2.9	2.3	1.3	1.8	1.5	1.8	2.1	1.9	1.0	2.4	1.4	1.6	2.3	1.9
FM	1.5	2.0	1.9	2.0	1.9	2.0	1.9	1.5	1.7	1.9	1.7	1.8	2.0	1.8	1.9	1.0	1.8	1.4	1.5	1.8	1.8
m	.4	.4	.4	.4	.3	.3	.6	.7	.6	.5	.5	.5	.4	.6	.5	.3	.3	.3	.5	.4	.5
CF	.6	.7	.6	.5	.5	.5	.5	.4	.5	.3	.4	.4	.4	.5	.4	.3	.9	.6	.5	.8	.7
ΣC	1.0	1.1	1.1	.9	.9	.9	.9	.8	.9	.4	.5	.5	.7	1.1	.9	.4	1.0	.6	.9	1.4	1.2
F(C)	.4	.4	.4	.4	.3	.4	.4	.5	.4	.5	.9	.7	.5	.9	.7	.5	1.1	.8	.5	1.2	.9

* The occurrence of FC and C too small to allow calculation of medians.

sponse. The largest percentage of cases (88 per cent) giving M occurs at 14 and 16 years; the smallest percentage at 11 and 15 years (77 per cent).

QUALITATIVE   We have tabulated all the more common movement responses by age and sex, grouping them as static, extensor, and flexor-passive. The extensor movements are further divided as moderate extensor

TABLE 11.   PRINCIPAL TYPES OF HUMAN MOVEMENT

	10 Years			11 Years			12 Years		
	B	G	T	B	G	T	B	G	T
Static									
Just "two people" (Card III)	8	8	16	8	7	15	5	16	21
Static postures: head up, wearing, etc.	7	8	15	0	6	6	4	3	7
Sitting, resting, lying, leaning	10	11	21	8	5	13	9	17	26
Standing	2	1	3	8	2	10	2	5	7
Looking, staring, admiring	4	2	6	3	4	7	1	6	7
Talking, explaining, planning	3	0	3	4	6	10	1	5	6
Other oral: opening mouth, singing, blowing, etc.	0	4	4	2	0	2	3	2	5
Smiling, laughing	1	4	5	1	2	3	1	1	2
Frowning, crying	2	1	3	0	1	1	0	0	0
Miscellaneous	4	2	6	4	0	4	1	0	1
Total Static	41	41	82	38	33	71	27	55	82
Moderate Extensor									
Individual arm gestures: waving, arms out, etc.	3	8	11	5	6	11	4	10	14
Interpersonal arm gestures: holding hands, etc.	6	2	8	3	4	7	4	4	8
Walking, coming, going	3	3	6	1	5	6	4	7	11
Riding on, flying on	0	1	1	1	2	3	1	1	2
Eating, drinking	1	0	1	4	1	5	0	2	2
Playing	1	1	2	1	2	3	1	1	2
Moderate work: "working," cooking, knitting, etc.	0	3	3	0	3	3	0	4	4
Miscellaneous	1	1	2	2	4	6	2	6	8
Total Moderate Extensor	15	19	34	17	27	44	16	35	51
Vigorous Extensor									
Dancing, swinging around	11	13	24	15	15	30	17	25	42
Fighting, quarreling, arguing, battling	5	6	11	10	7	17	8	9	17
Running, jumping, chasing	2	2	4	0	5	5	2	2	4
Sports: swimming, acrobatics, bowling, football	2	5	7	1	2	3	2	5	7
Miscellaneous	2	2	4	0	1	1	3	0	3
Total Vigorous Extensor	22	28	50	26	30	56	32	41	73
Flexor-Passive									
Flexing: bending down, leaning, squatting, etc.	1	3	4	5	6	11	6	5	11
Acted upon: hanging, falling, pushed, tied, etc.	4	3	7	5	5	10	4	4	8
Total Flexor-Passive	5	6	11	10	11	21	10	9	19
Mixed or Conflicted									
Lifting, holding, carrying	9	9	18	12	7	19	8	9	17
Pulling, grabbing, tug-of-war	5	3	8	5	2	7	11	2	13
Balancing, bracing	0	0	0	3	0	3	0	0	0
Total Mixed or Conflicted	14	12	26	20	9	29	19	11	30
Over-all Total	97	106	203	111	110	221	104	151	255
Percentage of total: Static	42%	39%	40%	34%	30%	32%	26%	36%	32%
Moderate Extensor	15	18	17	15	25	20	15	23	20
Vigorous Extensor	23	26	25	23	27	25	31	27	29
Flexor-Passive	5	6	5	9	10	10	10	6	8
Mixed or Conflicted	14	11	13	18	8	13	18	7	12

and vigorous extensor, and we have added the category "mixed or conflicted" to include lifting, holding, and carrying; pulling and grabbing; and balancing or bracing (see Table 11).

For the total age range, extensor movements are the most common, comprising 44 per cent of all movement responses. When separated as

RESPONSES: NUMBER OF M PRODUCED BY EACH AGE-SEX GROUP

13 Years			14 Years			15 Years			16 Years			Over-all Total			Over-all Percentage		
B	G	T	B	G	T	B	G	T	B	G	T	B	G	T	B	G	T
0	4	4	5	11	16	6	8	14	3	4	7	35	58	93	5%	7%	6%
7	11	18	7	10	17	5	15	20	7	11	18	37	64	101	6	7	7
6	6	12	4	12	16	4	8	12	7	21	28	48	80	128	7	9	8
3	3	6	4	6	10	4	3	7	3	6	9	26	26	52	4	2	3
3	2	5	2	7	9	1	3	4	3	4	7	17	28	45	3	3	3
1	1	2	4	3	7	1	5	6	4	3	7	18	23	41	3	3	3
2	3	5	2	2	4	1	2	3	1	4	5	11	17	28	2	2	2
0	0	0	0	0	0	1	0	1	0	0	0	4	7	11	1	1	1
0	0	0	0	1	1	0	0	0	0	0	0	2	3	5	—	—	
0	0	0	0	0	0	1	0	1	0	0	0	10	2	12	2	—	1
22	30	52	28	52	80	24	44	68	28	53	81	208	308	516	32	35	33
3	4	7	7	10	17	2	4	6	4	4	8	28	46	74	4	5	5
1	7	8	3	6	9	2	6	8	4	5	9	23	34	57	3	4	4
3	6	9	4	2	6	1	1	2	2	0	2	18	24	42	3	3	3
2	2	4	3	7	10	1	0	1	1	3	4	9	16	25	1	2	2
0	1	1	0	0	0	1	0	1	1	2	3	7	6	13	1	1	1
0	0	0	0	2	2	0	1	1	2	0	2	5	7	12	1	1	1
0	3	3	1	4	5	1	1	2	2	4	6	4	22	26	1	2	2
3	3	6	3	2	5	4	3	7	4	6	10	19	25	44	3	3	3
12	26	38	21	33	54	12	16	20	20	24	44	113	180	293	17	20	19
12	18	30	11	17	28	4	13	17	14	20	34	84	121	205	13	14	13
10	4	14	6	2	8	1	9	10	7	7	14	47	44	91	7	5	6
1	1	2	1	2	3	3	3	6	2	2	4	11	15	26	2	2	2
5	6	11	1	6	7	1	4	5	1	2	3	13	30	43	2	3	3
2	0	2	1	2	3	1	3	4	1	1	2	10	11	21	2	1	1
30	29	59	20	29	49	10	32	42	25	32	57	165	221	386	25	25	25
5	11	16	2	16	18	3	6	9	6	6	12	28	53	81	4	6	5
3	2	5	2	3	5	1	1	2	3	2	5	22	20	42	3	2	3
8	13	21	4	19	23	4	7	11	9	8	17	50	73	123	7	8	8
12	12	24	11	9	20	10	15	25	9	11	20	71	72	143	11	8	9
10	5	15	11	3	14	4	5	9	7	8	15	53	28	81	8	3	5
1	1	2	0	2	2	0	0	0	0	0	0	4	3	7	1	—	—
23	18	41	22	14	36	14	20	34	16	19	35	128	103	231	20	11	14
95	116	211	95	147	242	64	119	183	98	136	234	660	885	1545			
23%	26%	25%	29%	35%	33%	38%	37%	37%	29%	39%	35%				32%	35%	33%
13	22	18	22	22	22	19	13	15	20	18	19				17	20	19
32	25	28	21	20	20	16	27	23	26	24	25				25	25	25
8	11	10	4	13	10	6	6	6	9	6	7				7	8	8
24	16	19	23	10	15	22	17	19	16	14	15				19	12	15

moderate or vigorous extensor movements, however, both these categories are exceeded by static movements, which make up one third of all movement responses. Flexor-passive actions make up only 8 per cent and mixed or conflicted actions make up 15 per cent of M.

Age trends in most of these proportions are not marked. Static actions make up a consistently decreasing proportion of movement responses from 10 to 13 years, after which age they again increase. Extensor movements, combined, increase to a high point at age 12, and thereafter drop to a low point at age 15. Flexor-passive movements vary irregularly, while conflicting movements are proportionally most common at ages 13 and 15 years.

If we consider the projected movements individually, rather than grouping them, a somewhat different picture emerges. We then find that the specific responses of dancing or swinging around predominate at every age except 15 years, when the mixed or conflicted responses of lifting, holding, and carrying predominate. Again it is the age-to-age consistency of distribution, rather than developmental trends, which seems most striking.

If we then consider the second leading individual type of movement response at each age, we note somewhat less consistency. At 10 years of age, the static "sitting, resting, lying, leaning" is the second leading movement category. At 11, the mixed or conflicted "lifting, holding, or carrying" comes second. At 12 as at 10, "sitting, resting, lying, leaning" comes second. At 13 and 14, as at 11, "lifting, holding, carrying." At 15, such static posture responses as "head up" come second, and at 16, "sitting, resting, lying, leaning."

FM   Animal movement responses (FM), in contrast to M, are generally considered to represent natural, unacculturated drives. Piotrowski considers that they indicate

(1) the subject's prototypal role in life which, however, influences overt behavior only in states of lowered integration and in states of diminished consciousness and defective self-control; (2) the prototypal roles in life which were prominent in the subject's past, probably before his sixth year of life; and (3) the approximate degree of physical buoyancy (47, p. 190).

FM, like M, by its nature gives clues as to the degree of activeness or passiveness of the individual's drives.

In the normal adult record the expectation is that M will exceed FM in a ratio of 2:1. In children's records, FM more often than not exceeds M. In our earlier study we found mean FM to exceed mean M at every age from 2½ to 10 years. However, at 10 the two were nearly equal—the average M being 1.70, the average FM, 1.74.

In the years that immediately follow, the balance is shifting, though no definite predominance of M over FM is achieved even by 16 years of age. As Table 6 indicates, mean FM predominates slightly at 10 and 11 years. By 12 years of age, the shift is to a slight predominance of mean M over FM; this continues until 16, when the balance is again about equal.

The variation in mean number of FM responses is considerably less than that of M. Except for 15 years when the mean FM drops to 1.6, the range is only from 2.0 (at 13 years) to 2.5 at 11, its high point.

Considering the sexes separately, the mean FM for boys at 10 years is 2.3, which figure remains essentially steady through 14 years, drops at 15 to 1.3, and returns to 1.9 at 16 years. The mean for girls, starting at the same level as the boys at age 10, declines gradually to 1.6 at 13 years, increases to 2.1 at 14, and, like the boys' mean, drops at 15 and again increases at 16 years.

Altogether, 78 per cent of our subjects give FM responses, the largest usage appearing at 12, 14, and 16 years. Among boys, the most striking age change in percentage using FM is the drop at age 15; among girls a comparable drop appears at age 13.

QUALITATIVE   Animal movement responses have been classified in the same manner as were the human movements. It is interesting to note how much more strongly extensor movements predominate in FM responses. This appears to offer some confirmation of the belief that more spontaneous, less restrained impulses are revealed in FM.

For the total age group, extensor movements make up nearly two thirds of all FM, static movements only about one fourth, and flexor-passive and conflicting movements only 5 per cent each. As in the case of M, age changes in classification of FM responses are not marked, as compared with the over-all distribution. The percentage of static movements declines from 10 to 14 years, increases sharply at 15, then again declines. Extensor movements show a slight over-all increase, with vigorous extensor movements especially predominating at 13, 14, and 16 years. (See Table 12.)

If we consider specific types (rather than general classifications) of animal movement responses, we find again considerable consistency from age to age. At every age but two the vigorous extensor movement of climbing predominates. The exceptions are 13 and 16 where "fighting, quarreling, attacking" lead.

There is more change from age to age in the specific kind of animal movement that achieves second place. Thus at 10 it is the moderate extensor movement of "walking, going, and coming"; at 11, the mixed or conflicted movement "lifting, holding, or carrying"; at 12, the vigorous extensor movement, "fighting, quarreling, or attacking"; at 13, the vigorous extensor movement "climbing"; at 14 and 15 as at 10, the moderate extensor "walking, going, and coming"; at 16, the vigorous extensor "running and jumping."

m   The scoring symbol m, used to indicate inanimate objects in mo-

TABLE 12. PRINCIPAL TYPES OF ANIMAL MOVEMENT RESPONSES:

	10 Years			11 Years			12 Years		
	B	G	T	B	G	T	B	G	T
Static									
Static postures	5	10	15	1	2	3	10	9	19
Sitting, resting, lying, leaning	2	9	11	8	8	16	9	10	19
Standing	3	6	9	8	9	17	4	4	8
Looking, staring	6	8	14	7	13	20	4	7	11
Vocalizing: roaring, shouting, etc.	4	4	8	4	1	5	1	0	1
Other oral activity: blowing, etc.	5	1	6	1	3	4	0	1	1
Expressions: smiling, crying, etc.	3	1	4	0	0	0	0	3	3
Miscellaneous	4	1	5	1	3	4	0	2	2
Total Static	32	40	72	30	39	69	28	36	64
Moderate Extensor									
Individual leg actions: waving, legs out, etc.	3	6	9	5	2	7	4	2	6
"Interpersonal" leg actions: clapping paws, etc.	2	2	4	1	2	3	0	1	1
Walking, going, coming	12	13	25	9	12	21	10	14	14
Eating, drinking	2	3	5	0	1	1	5	5	10
Kissing, noses together	1	3	4	2	6	8	4	3	7
Miscellaneous	13	4	17	7	2	9	4	3	7
Total Moderate Extensor	33	31	64	24	25	49	27	28	55
Vigorous Extensor									
Climbing	16	14	30	16	13	29	21	12	33
Flying	9	7	16	9	8	17	10	2	12
Dancing, swinging around	5	3	8	4	5	9	7	7	14
Running, jumping	7	6	13	5	4	9	5	4	9
Running away from . . .	0	1	1	2	0	2	0	0	0
Running after, charging	1	2	3	5	3	8	3	0	3
Fighting, quarreling, attacking	3	10	13	10	10	20	17	5	22
Miscellaneous	0	0	0	0	0	0	0	0	0
Total Vigorous Extensor	41	43	84	51	43	94	53	30	83
Flexor-Passive									
Flexing: bending down, squatting	0	2	2	1	2	3	0	0	0
Acted on: hanging, falling, tied	5	2	7	3	2	5	6	4	10
Total Flexor-Passive	5	4	9	4	4	8	6	4	10
Mixed or Conflicted									
Lifting, holding, carrying	4	3	7	12	10	22	4	1	5
Pulling, grabbing, tugging	1	1	2	3	0	3	0	1	1
Balancing, bracing	0	1	1	0	2	2	1	0	1
Total Mixed or Conflicted	5	5	10	15	12	27	5	2	7
Percentage of Total Movements									
Static	28%	33%	30%	24%	32%	28%	24%	36%	29%
Moderate extensor	28	25	27	19	20	20	23	28	25
Vigorous extensor	35	35	35	41	35	38	45	30	38
Flexor-passive	4	3	4	3	3	3	5	4	5
Mixed or conflicted	4	4	4	12	10	11	4	2	3

tion, is varyingly considered to be a sign of aggressivity, repressed or overt; as a sign of an intense inner tension, anxiety, or struggle between conflicting emotions; as an indication that the subject feels his inner promptings to be hostile. The nature of the m response can provide clues as to the nature of unresolved conflicts or tensions.

In the first 10 years of life we have found m to occur minimally, its

Number of FM Produced by Each Age-Sex Group

13 Years			14 Years			15 Years			16 Years			Over-all Total			Over-all Percentage		
B	G	T	B	G	T	B	G	T	B	G	T	B	G	T	B	G	T
4	3	7	5	7	11	2	8	10	2	3	5	29	42	71	4%	5%	5%
7	9	16	0	5	5	4	9	13	6	11	17	36	61	97	5	8	6
3	4	7	8	4	12	4	8	12	5	10	15	35	45	80	5	6	5
5	3	8	5	3	8	3	3	6	4	5	9	34	42	76	4	5	5
2	2	4	1	2	3	2	5	7	1	4	5	15	18	33	2	2	2
0	2	2	2	3	5	0	2	2	0	3	2	8	15	23	1	2	1
0	0	0	1	2	3	0	2	2	1	6	7	5	13	18	1	2	1
1	0	1	0	0	0	0	0	0	0	0	0	6	6	12	1	1	1
22	23	45	22	26	48	15	37	52	19	42	61	168	242	410	22	31	27
0	0	0	1	3	4	2	2	4	1	1	2	16	16	32	2	2	2
2	1	3	5	2	7	3	1	4	2	3	5	15	12	27	2	2	2
14	7	21	16	11	27	6	11	17	10	12	22	77	80	157	10	10	10
0	0	0	0	2	2	2	2	4	3	6	9	12	19	31	2	2	2
6	0	6	0	2	2	3	0	3	4	4	8	20	18	38	3	2	2
2	4	6	0	5	5	7	2	9	5	1	6	38	21	59	5	3	4
24	12	36	22	25	47	23	18	41	25	27	52	178	166	344	23	21	22
14	9	23	15	14	29	9	9	18	8	8	16	99	79	178	13	10	11
9	3	12	8	7	15	4	8	12	10	19	29	59	54	113	8	7	7
3	6	9	9	2	11	2	7	9	0	5	5	30	35	65	4	5	4
5	3	8	9	8	17	3	2	5	7	15	22	41	42	83	5	5	5
2	0	2	1	1	2	0	2	2	1	2	3	6	6	12	1	1	1
6	3	9	4	3	7	1	1	2	9	7	16	29	19	48	4	2	3
17	8	25	9	7	16	4	7	11	5	15	20	65	62	127	8	8	8
2	2	4	4	3	7	0	0	0	0	1	1	7	9	16	1	1	1
58	34	92	59	45	104	23	36	59	40	72	112	336	306	642	44	39	40
1	3	4	2	2	4	0	1	1	0	1	1	4	11	15	1	1	1
5	2	7	8	7	15	5	3	8	7	1	8	39	21	60	5	3	4
6	5	11	10	9	19	5	4	9	7	2	9	43	32	75	6	4	5
3	2	5	3	2	5	0	2	2	1	3	4	27	23	50	4	3	3
2	2	4	3	0	3	0	0	0	2	0	2	11	4	15	1	1	1
2	3	5	1	0	1	0	0	0	1	1	2	5	7	12	1	1	1
7	7	14	7	2	9	0	2	2	4	4	8	43	34	77	6	5	5
19%	28%	23%	18%	24%	21%	23%	38%	32%	20%	29%	25%				22%	31%	27%
21	15	18	18	23	21	35	19	25	26	18	22				23	21	22
50	42	46	49	42	46	35	37	36	42	49	46				44	39	41
5	6	6	8	8	8	8	4	6	7	1	4				6	4	5
6	9	7	6	2	4	0	2	1	4	3	3				6	4	5

average ranging from a low of .05 at 2 years to peaks of .5 at 5½ years and .8 at 7 years (1). In the years from 10 to 16 (see Tables 6, 10) it occurs more extensively. Mean scores for 10 to 16 years are as follows: .6, .6, 1.0, 1.0, .8, .5, 1.0. Figures for boys and girls are almost identical.

Nearly half of all our subjects (46 per cent) give m responses. Twelve

TABLE 13. PRINCIPAL TYPES OF INANIMATE MOVEMENT RESPONSES: AGE-SEX

	10 Years			11 Years			12 Years		
	B	G	T	B	G	T	B	G	T
Downward movements: liquids—water	8	2	10	4	2	6	5	6	11
other objects	2	4	6	3	5	8	3	3	6
Upward movements: fire, smoke, clouds	10	9	19	6	8	14	7	13	20
liquids—water, oil	3	4	7	3	1	4	3	8	11
Movements in place: spinning, rocking	1	1	2	0	2	2	5	5	10
Explosions, shooting, sparks	25	14	39	18	7	25	16	10	26
Smashing, broken, split, squashed	14	4	18	8	7	15	13	11	24
Tension: hanging	2	8	10	10	6	16	5	16	21
stretched out	7	2	9	13	4	17	14	12	26
Abstract: conflicts, war symbolism	1	2	3	1	0	1	0	1	1
Miscellaneous	6	2	8	4	5	9	11	8	19
Total primary+secondary m	79	50	129	70	47	117	82	93	175
Percentage of total:									
Downward movements	13%	12%	12%	10%	15%	12%	10%	10%	10%
Upward movements	16	26	20	13	19	15	12	23	18
Movements in place	1	2	2	0	4	2	6	5	6
Explosions	32	28	30	26	15	26	20	11	15
Smashing, broken	18	8	14	11	15	13	16	12	14
Tension—hanging, stretched	11	20	15	33	21	26	23	30	27
Abstract	1	4	2	1	0	1	0	1	1
Miscellaneous	8	4	6	6	11	8	13	9	11

is the high point, 56 per cent of the group giving m. Fifteen is the low point with only 33 per cent.

QUALITATIVE   As with other kinds of movement, we have made a qualitative analysis of the kinds of inanimate movement. Categories used are: downward movements, upward movements, movements in place, explosions, "smashing or broken," tension, and abstract. Both primary and secondary m responses are included in this tabulation. (See Table 13.)

For the age range as a whole, the most frequent kind of m is a tension response—objects hanging or stretched. This response is relatively infrequent at 10 years (15 per cent of m) but increases to over 25 per cent from 11 to 14, and increases again at 15 years (35 per cent), then drops again at 16. Explosions are next most frequent, and this more overtly expressed m response, by contrast with tension m, shows an over-all decrease with age, with its high point at 10, its low points at 12 and 15 years. Upward movements, next in frequency, show no age trend, nor do downward, falling movements. Collision and breaking movements are likewise essentially level except for a proportional increase at 14 years followed by a sharp decrease at 15.

Thus there appears to be an over-all trend from the more openly expressed explosions and outward thrusting movements of 10 years toward the more static, inhibited, tense movements that predominate at 15, with perhaps an increasing openness again at 16 years.

NUMBER OF m, INCLUDING SECONDARY m, PRODUCED BY EACH GROUP

13 Years			14 Years			15 Years			16 Years			Over-all total			Over-all percentage		
B	G	T	B	G	T	B	G	T	B	G	T	B	G	T	B	G	T
2	2	4	3	9	12	3	2	5	5	5	10	30	28	58	6%	6%	6%
6	4	10	2	3	5	2	2	4	2	8	10	20	29	49	4	6	5
6	8	14	4	11	15	4	7	11	4	15	19	41	71	112	9	15	12
3	6	9	1	8	9	1	5	6	3	5	8	17	37	54	4	9	6
0	1	1	0	0	0	1	0	1	2	2	4	9	11	20	2	2	2
22	8	30	11	12	23	8	4	12	14	21	35	114	76	190	25	16	20
10	6	16	12	10	22	2	3	5	3	17	20	62	58	120	13	12	13
10	13	23	9	12	21	10	4	14	9	8	17	55	67	122	12	14	13
9	6	15	7	7	14	9	8	17	9	7	16	68	46	114	15	10	12
0	0	0	0	0	0	1	1	2	2	3	5	5	7	12	1	1	1
7	5	12	3	9	12	6	6	12	5	7	12	42	42	84	9	9	9
75	59	134	52	81	133	47	42	89	58	98	156	463	472	935	100%	100%	100%
11%	10%	10%	10%	15%	13%	11%	10%	10%	12%	13%	13%				11%	12%	11%
12	24	17	10	23	18	11	29	19	12	20	17				13	23	18
0	2	1	0	0	0	2	0	1	3	2	3				2	2	2
29	14	22	21	15	17	17	10	13	24	21	22				25	16	20
13	10	12	23	12	17	4	7	6	5	17	13				13	12	13
25	32	28	31	23	26	40	26	35	31	15	21				27	24	25
0	0	0	0	0	0	2	2	2	3	3	3				1	1	1
9	8	9	6	11	9	13	14	13	9	7	8				9	9	9

MOVEMENT SHOCK

Movement shock, which will be discussed more fully in a subsequent chapter covering all types of shock, was judged to occur only 22 times for boys in the total age range, and only 11 times for girls. Even if we combine these figures with those for tendency to movement shock, which was also noted, we find the aggregate only 47 for boys and 40 for girls.

High points for boys, in the light of these small figures, occur at 10, 13, and 15 years; for girls at 11 and 13 years. Thirteen years is the high point for such a tendency for the total group. From this age on, it gradually decreases for both boys and girls. Thus though movement shock may occur in this age range, it cannot be said to be a usual characteristic of any one age.

Sex Differences in Movement Responses

M   At every age but 11, girls give more M responses than do boys. This consistent difference is all the more conspicuous since the number of M given by the total group does not consistently increase or decrease across the age range. Thus both girls and boys fall off sharply in number of M at 13 and again at 15 years, but in each case, girls still give more than do boys.

The same general trend appears in the percentage of cases giving M.

Though boys and girls are approximately tied from 10 to 12, at all other ages more girls than boys give M responses.

Considering sex differences in quality of response, it appears that there are some consistent sex differences. Girls give a greater proportion of static and moderate extensor movements. Boys exceed in mixed or conflicted responses only.

FM   Sex differences for FM are rather different from those for M. While boys exceed girls in mean FM at the earlier ages of 11, 12, 13, and 14 years, girls increasingly exceed boys at 15 and 16 years.

Girls give many more static responses but boys give more extensor, flexor-passive, and mixed or conflicted FM. This differs somewhat from the situation with human movement, where girls give proportionally more extensor movements.

It is particularly noteworthy that whereas girls and boys give approximately the same total number of animal movement responses (boys 768, girls 780), the girls give many more human movement responses than do boys (boys 660, girls 885). This suggests greater maturity on the part of the girls.

Furthermore, though qualitative differences in M are small and variable, so far as FM is concerned the girls exceed in static movements, the boys in all other kinds.

m   Girls and boys give an almost equal number of m responses at nearly every age. However, though the total number given by each sex is almost equal, there do exist qualitative differences in m responses between the two sexes. Most conspicuous is the difference in upward movements. Thirteen per cent of all m responses given by the boys are upward, 23 per cent of the girls' responses. Boys, however, definitely lead in explosive movements. Twenty-five per cent of their m responses are explosive; only 16 per cent of those given by girls. Boys also exceed girls slightly in percentage of tensional movements—27 per cent in boys, 24 per cent in girls.

Summary

In spite of the fact that interesting and characteristic age changes do take place in the period from 10 to 16 years, by 10 years of age the movement responses in the Rorschach already indicate to some extent what the expectancies in this category will be during the next several years.

The entire age range (10 to 16 years) might be considered as a period of transition with regard to movement scores. With the younger child (up to 10 years), FM responses usually outnumber M responses. From 10 to 16 there is, in general, a balance between M and FM. With the adult we expect M to outnumber FM.

We also see a transition in the quality of the various types of movement. In human movement the extensor actions predominate, with "dancing" or "swinging around" the most frequent type of M. In animal movement, the vigorous extensor subclass is itself large enough to predominate over other classes. Thus animal movement is at all ages more vigorous that human movement, in keeping with Piotrowski's (47) statement that as the child grows older "his prototypal role, his basic attitude toward others in personally vital matters, has undergone a real change since early childhood." Inanimate movement moves from open explosions toward more static tensions.

Starting with the animal movement, we might conclude that concept of role even as at younger ages is definitely active and aggressive. In moving toward greater independence (reflected in the increase in human movement at older ages) the individual, even though less unrestrainedly active, still gives an active expression of role in "dancing" and "swinging around." This may be the individual's means of finding his way toward greater independence and creativity in a social manner as acceptable as possible.

The balance of human and animal movement in general in this age range suggests that the individual is not yet ready to relinquish his dependence, though his independence is making itself felt. This may be the key to the alternation between explosion and tension seen in the inanimate movements. Progress forward in this age range may well be patterned by bursts of activity alternated with periods of refocalization and reorganization. How productive these periods are or become depends to a great extent on the individual's own potential and development. But it also depends on the adequate understanding and employment of this energy by the environment.

Although in other areas (in Content, for example) the individual may well be projecting toward the expectancies of the adult, in the evolution of the movement responses this period of 10 to 16 appears to be a transitional one. The response has shifted from the younger years where animal movement was predominant, to a balance between human and animal movement, but has not as yet reached the period where human movement predominates.

COLOR

Color responses are classified into the three customary categories: FC, CF, and C. FC interpretations are generally considered to be an index of adaptive affectivity or at least a desire for affective adaptation. CF interpretations indicate more egocentric, suggestible, impulsive affect. C responses are considered indicative of nonadaptive, poorly integrated emotional reactions.

In the normal adult record the optimal ratio of color responses has been considered to be about 3 FC to about 1 CF and no pure C.* In our

---

* However, Piotrowski (47) points out that in this country the average ratio more nearly approximates 2:1:0, and that the distribution of 0FC:2CF:0C is a common one.

child sample up to 10 years of age, CF responses predominated at every age except 2 years, when C was the leading color response. FC responses gradually increased in number but were at no age predominant. In our 10- to 16-year-old sample, at every age and for both sexes, CF responses definitely predominate over FC, and FC responses predominate over C.

Close to two thirds of the subjects in our whole adolescent sample give at least one color response of some kind, with somewhat more girls than boys using color. Only at 13 and 15 years do fewer than 60 per cent of subjects use color, while close to 75 per cent use color at 16 years.

In our child sample, the weighted sum of color responses, ΣC, ranged from a mean of .7 at 2 years to 2.9 at 7 years, falling back to 1.5 at 10 years. Mean ΣC in the age range 10 to 16 years is considerably lower than in mid-childhood. For the total sample, mean ΣC is 1.2. While age trends are not marked, less color is apparently used at 11, 13, and 15 years, while 16 shows a definite upswing.

Only about 25 per cent of all subjects give FC responses. The percentage increases consistently from 10 to 14 years of age, drops sharply at 15 years, then rises to its highest point at 16 years. Mean FC fails to show this curve, remaining flat at .3 per child until 16, when it increases to .5.

CF responses are given by very close to half of the total adolescent sample. From age 10 to age 13 a gradual decrease appears in the proportion of subjects giving CF; thereafter there appears a gradual increase. In mean CF, as in mean FC, the curve is again essentially flat from 10 through 15 (between .7 and .9), followed by a sharp increase at 16 years (to 1.2). This jump is entirely caused by mean CF increasing among girls. The girls, like the boys, maintain a level curve from 10 to 15, but while the boys continue level, the girls nearly double in mean CF at 16.

Throughout the 10 to 16 age range, only 12 per cent of subjects give C responses. No particular age trend appears, except that relatively fewer 11-year-olds give C responses, and surprisingly many 14-year-old girls use C (24 per cent). Mean C occurs no more than .1 to .2 per group, except among the girls at 14 years (mean of .3).

COLOR SHOCK   Color shock, considered by Rorschach as a sign of affective disturbance and as a positive sign of neurosis, may be indicated in a number of different ways. On the color cards there may be a sudden diminution of responses, increased response time, or sudden changes in the quality of response. Refusal, dysphoric exclamation, hesitation, long verbalization before response, sudden or excessive turning of the card, all may indicate color shock. Other indicators are complete absence of color responses, interpretation of only pale-colored areas, avoidance of red and orange. When the total number of interpretations given on the color cards is less than one third the total number of interpretations, we may likewise suspect that the response is made more difficult by the color itself.

In the total age range from 10 to 16 years we have classified 13 boys and 17 girls as showing decided evidence of color shock. These figures indicate the rarity of color shock in this period. However, if we include also subjects showing milder evidence of color shock ("tendency to shock"), we find the incidence greatly increased for boys, slightly increased for girls. Out of 350 boys, 55 give some indication of color shock, as do 39 girls out of 350. High points for boys occur at 10, 13, and 15 years, for girls at 13 years. At these ages it seems quite possible that one out of every five subjects might show tendency to color shock. But even though it does occur in this age range, some ages appearing more susceptible than others and boys appearing more susceptible than girls, color shock is not highly characteristic at any age. For the entire period, only about 15 per cent of the boys and about 11 per cent of the girls were seen as showing any sign of vulnerability to color shock.

RED SHOCK "Shock" responses, such as those described above as occurring on Cards VIII, IX, and X, may also occur on Cards II and III, presumably upon introduction of the red areas. Red shock, considered an indicator of repressed hostility along with strong guilt feelings, is sometimes viewed as a precursor of color shock. Incidence of red shock as we have scored it is slightly lower than incidence of color shock, but the ratios for boys and girls are about the same as for color shock. As in color shock, high points for boys occur at 10, 13, and 15 years; for girls, however, the high point is at 10 years. At all ages boys exceed girls in incidence of red shock. Fifteen boys and 12 girls gave definite evidence of red shock, while an additional 37 boys and 19 girls showed apparent tendencies in that direction. Thus 15 per cent of the boys and 9 per cent of the girls gave some indication of red shock in their responses.

Qualitative Considerations

Tables 14, 15, and 16 present a qualitative analysis of FC, CF, and C responses. All responses containing color as a determinent have been tabulated in these tables, regardless of whether in scoring they were considered primary or secondary ("tendency") scores.

FC In the first 10 years of life, FC responses appeared so varied that no tabulation of them was made. However, as Table 14 shows, definite central trends prevail in the years between 10 and 16. For boys, animal responses lead at every age but 10 and 12, when nature responses come first and animals second, and at 15 when objects lead. At other ages, objects come second except for 14 years when they tie with nature, at 15 when animals come second, and at 16 when nature comes second.

For girls, animals come first at every age except 11 and 14 years. Nature leads at 11; objects at 14. These three categories alternate for

TABLE 14. PRINCIPAL TYPES OF FC RESPONSES: PRIMARY PLUS SECONDARY SCORES; PERCENTAGE OF TOTAL IN EACH CATEGORY AT EACH AGE

	10		11		12		13		14		15		16		Total	
	B	G	B	G	B	G	B	G	B	G	B	G	B	G	B	G
Number of primary scores	13	18	14	17	10	23	14	13	15	18	10	17	21	33	97	139
Total number of scores	17	29	20	24	19	35	23	23	19	30	17	31	31	45	146	217
Animals (Snake, butterfly, etc.)	35%	52%	45%	25%	32%	49%	44%	44%	32%	33%	35%	39%	42%	40%	38%	41%
Human details (hair, etc.)	12	0	10	8	0	6	0	0	5	0	0	0	10	7	5	3
Nature: trees, flowers	18	14	10	25	21	9	4	13	11	20	12	23	19	18	14	17
scenes	24	14	0	8	16	6	17	4	16	10	12	10	13	11	14	9
Total nature	42	28	10	33	37	15	21	17	27	30	24	33	32	29	28	26
Food	0	0	0	13	5	9	4	4	11	0	0	0	3	0	3	3
Objects: clothing, bows	0	21	25	21	26	17	13	17	16	23	6	6	0	7	12	15
other	12	0	10	0	0	6	17	17	11	13	35	23	13	18	14	12
Total objects	12	21	35	21	26	23	30	34	27	36	41	29	13	25	26	27

TABLE 15. PRINCIPAL TYPES OF CF RESPONSES: PRIMARY PLUS SECONDARY SCORES; PERCENTAGE OF TOTAL IN EACH CATEGORY AT EACH AGE

	10		11		12		13		14		15		16		Total	
	B	G	B	G	B	G	B	G	B	G	B	G	B	G	B	G
Number of primary scores	40	46	33	39	38	40	34	39	30	46	32	46	39	84	246	340
Total number of scores	58	72	49	47	55	55	49	46	40	52	42	55	52	104	345	431
Animals (butterfly, bird)	3%	3%	6%	13%	9%	5%	6%	11%	5%	10%	5%	7%	8%	11%	7%	8%
Blood, anatomy	19	15	18	17	16	15	22	11	23	19	21	11	17	13	19	14
Nature: flower, leaf, tree	21	13	16	17	22	20	17	24	20	12	24	13	19	15	20	16
scene, grass, water	12	24	16	13	20	11	10	13	5	21	12	25	15	19	13	18
clouds, sunset, rainbow,	3	6	2	6	4	5	2	7	5	6	2	7	6	7	3	6
Total nature	36	43	34	36	46	36	29	44	30	39	38	45	40	41	36	40
Fire, sparks, explosions	21	24	22	19	13	24	12	8	15	8	7	16	6	5	14	14
Food	5	7	2	4	5	7	8	13	3	2	5	4	2	5	4	6
Map	3	1	0	0	2	0	2	0	0	2	0	0	0	1	1	1
Objects	3	3	8	9	2	5	10	9	10	12	10	11	17	12	8	9
Painting	9	8	8	2	7	7	2	0	15	10	12	4	8	7	8	6
Abstract, symbolic (war)	0	0	0	0	0	0	0	0	0	0	2	2	2	7	1	2

TABLE 16. PRINCIPAL TYPES OF C RESPONSES: PRIMARY PLUS SECONDARY SCORES; PERCENTAGE OF TOTAL IN EACH CATEGORY AT EACH AGE

	10		11		12		13		14		15		16		Total	
	B	G	B	G	B	G	B	G	B	G	B	G	B	G	B	G
Number of primary scores	10	8	5	4	9	8	7	6	7	14	3	5	6	5	47	50
Total number of scores	16	8	12	11	9	9	9	9	7	18	3	5	6	8	62	68
Nature: ice, grass, sand	0%	13%	8%	18%	0%	11%	0%	11%	14%	22%	0%	0%	16%	0%	5%	13%
Fire, explosion	44	50	33	36	44	56	44	56	14	22	0	40	16	25	34	38
Blood, anatomy	44	0	33	9	11	11	33	22	29	28	66	20	16	50	32	21
Paint, stain	13	13	8	27	44	11	0	11	43	11	0	0	16	13	18	13
Food	0	25	16	9	0	11	11	0	0	17	33	40	0	0	6	13
Abstract, symbolic	0	0	0	0	0	0	11	0	0	0	0	0	33	13	5	1

second place—animals being second at 11 and 14 years, nature at 10 and 16, objects at 12, 13, and 15.

Thus in general, animals lead, nature tends to come second; then objects; then food or human details.

CF   In the years from 2 to 10, nature is the leading CF category at all ages, flower predominating from 2 to 7 and at 10 years; tree or leaf predominating at 8 and 9. In the present age range, for boys and girls alike, nature responses are the leading kind of response at every age. For boys, fire responses are the second leading category at 10 and 11 years; blood-anatomy at every other age. For girls, fire responses are the second leading category for 10 to 12 years and again at 15. Blood-anatomy comes second at 14 and 16 years; food at 13 years.

Thus, in general, nature responses lead among CF responses; fire responses come second from 10 to 12; blood-anatomy thereafter. Fire responses show a particularly marked developmental trend, dropping from 23 per cent to 5 per cent of all CF responses. Artificial objects and abstract, symbolic responses, on the other hand, make up small but increasing proportions of CF responses. (See Table 15.)

C   As to pure C responses in the first ten years, first paint, then nature, then blood, then fire responses are the leading ones in this category. In the present age range, there is considerable change from age to age in the outstanding kind of C response and also considerable difference between boys and girls. Fire-explosion responses lead or tie for first place in both boys and girls from 10 through 13 years of age and in girls at 15. Blood-anatomy leads in boys at 15 years and in girls at 14 and 16. Blood-anatomy holds second place, or ties for first, in boys at 10, 13, and 14 years; in girls at 13. As in CF, there is an over-all decline in proportion of fire and explosion responses, an increase in abstract and symbolic responses.

Sex Differences in Color

Amount of Color:

FC RESPONSES   More girls than boys give FC responses at every age except 13 years. Also girls give more FC responses than do boys at every age but 11 and 13, when they are equal.

CF RESPONSES   There is somewhat more variability here. An equal number of girls and boys give these responses at 10 and 11 years. Thereafter, more boys give CF at 12 years, more girls at 13, 14, 15, and 16. However, girls consistently give a higher mean CF than do boys at every age except 12 years.

C RESPONSES   Again there is considerable variability. Equal numbers of girls and boys give C responses at 10 and at 16 years. More boys than girls give C at 11, 13, and 15 years; more girls than boys at 12 and 14 years. As to mean number of C responses, boys and girls are nearly equal except at 14 years, when girls clearly exceed boys.

SIGMA C   Mean ΣC for girls exceeds that for boys at every age from 10 through 16 years, the greatest differences occurring at 14, 15, and 16 years. Over all, 60 per cent of boys give some color response, 66 per cent of girls.

COLOR SHOCK   If we combine color shock and tendency to color shock, though the figures are always small, incidence for boys is higher at every age except 11 and 13 years when girls exceed slightly, and at 12 years when they are equal. No girls in our group appear to give evidence of color shock at 14 years.

RED SHOCK   Boys exceed girls at all ages in the combined figures for red shock and tendency to red shock. At ages 14 and 16 only one girl (out of 50 at each age) indicated a tendency to red shock.

Kind of Color:

FC RESPONSES   Animal responses make up similar proportions of the total response in both sexes. Of nature responses, girls tend to give more tree and flower responses; boys are more likely to give total scenes. Object responses, either the second or third leading FC response at every age, are given about equally by boys and girls though girls are a little more likely to give clothing responses.

CF RESPONSES   For the sexes considered separately, as well as when they are combined, nature responses lead at all ages from 10 through 16 years. In the first 10 years of life, girls for the most part gave more CF flower responses than did boys. This situation is largely reversed in the present population, boys giving slightly more CF flower responses than do girls at every age but 11 and 13.

Though boys give more CF flower responses than do girls, girls give more CF total scene responses than do boys at every age except 11 and 12. (This is just the opposite of the case with FC flowers and scenes.) Girls also give more CF cloud, sunset, rainbow responses than do boys at every age.

There is no consistent sex difference in the number of CF fire responses given. However, boys at every age give more blood and anatomy than do girls. Girls give slightly more food responses at most ages than do boys; boys give somewhat more painting responses than do girls.

C RESPONSES   Leading C responses are fire-explosion through 13 years; blood-anatomy from 14 to 16. Girls give definitely more fire-explosion responses at every age than do boys. Conversely, boys give more blood-anatomy than do girls at every age except 16.

Of other outstanding C responses, boys tend to give more paint-stain and more abstract-symbolic responses. Girls give more nature and more food.

Summary

Though the adult expectancy in color response is generally considered to be about 3FC:1CF:0C, in the population we have studied up to 16 years this ratio is never approached. It is true that after 10 years of age the number of FC does increase slightly and the number of C tends to decrease, but CF continues to be the predominant color response. In general, the color response ratio for the ages from 10 to 16 years, with our sample, remains at about 1FC:3CF:0–1C. It is interesting to speculate as to when and if these ratios change later or whether actually, as Piotrowski (47) has suggested, adult expectancies need to be revised.

Some areas of the Rorschach response such as F+% and certain elements of Content appears to stabilize early and to project toward adult expectancies in the age range here studied. Others—the movement responses, for example—appear in the years from 10 to 16 to be in a full transition period. Still others, such as the color responses, appear to change at a much slower rate.

SHADING

Shading responses are those determined by the nuances of gray in the blot. They give an indication of the subject's emotional and intellectual sensitivity; they are an indication of his ability for empathy and the degree of his concern with adapting to others and to the environment. Through them we have some insight concerning the anxieties of the individual—in some instances indications of what may provoke them, and of how he deals with them or how they deal with him.

Shading responses are given by a somewhat larger percentage of our subjects in this age range than in the years before 10. At 10 years of age, as in our earlier study, 41 per cent of subjects give at least one F(C) response. With minor fluctuations, this percentage increases steadily to 16 years when 58 per cent of subjects give at least one F(C) response.

Mean number of shading responses given in the age period from 10 to 16 years exceeds in almost every instance the response in the earlier years. Between the ages of 2 and 5 years, the mean ranges between .2 and .6 only. From 5½ to 10 years, the mean ranges between .6 and 1.1. From 10 to 16 years, the mean ranges between .6 to 1.6. This gradual increase in F(C) response gives us some clue as to the importance of this response in the development of the individual as he progresses toward maturity.

Table 17 presents a qualitative analysis of shading responses. Very definite changes in the way shading is used appear in this age range, as they did in the earlier years between 2 and 10. In the first 5½ years of life

TABLE 17. PRINCIPAL TYPES OF F(C) RESPONSES: PRIMARY PLUS SECONDARY SCORES; PERCENTAGE OF TOTAL IN EACH CATEGORY

Age in years	10		11		12		13		14		15		16	
	B	G	B	G	B	G	B	G	B	G	B	G	B	G
Number of primary scores	27	40	33	31	37	59	50	59	39	77	48	83	59	102
Total primary + secondary	48	66	50	53	63	80	81	87	66	99	67	98	95	158
Diffusion: clouds, smoke	19%	15%	16%	19%	16%	9%	15%	11%	12%	9%	10%	17%	9%	16%
Light-shade: reflections, water, wax, shiny	12	21	16	17	14	18	27	18	15	24	9	27	24	18
Differentiation within blot: eyes, paths	40	29	30	28	35	38	38	32	36	30	21	12	13	16
Texture: hard–stone, etc.	8	5	6	2	6	6	5	1	5	3	13	7	4	9
soft–fur, etc.	19	14	32	23	13	20	11	22	11	12	24	9	22	20
snow, ice	0	2	0	2	0	0	0	0	0	1	0	1	0	1
sticky, slimy	2	8	2	2	0	0	0	0	0	1	0	4	1	5
Total texture	29	27	40	28	19	26	16	23	15	17	37	21	27	35
X-rays, photographs	0	0	1	0	5	4	1	0	2	3	7	3	9	4
Vista	0	8	4	8	11	6	2	15	20	16	15	19	17	11
Total	100%	100%	100%	100%	100%	100%	100%	100%	100%	100%	100%	100%	100%	100%

shading is chiefly used for expressing diffusion (clouds, smoke). There is a variety of responses at 6 years of age, but from 7 through 9 years shading is used primarily for differentiation of details within the blot.

In our present group, with the 10, 12, 13, and 14-year-olds, shading is used most for differentiation of details within the blot. This type of shading response shows an over-all decline in usage, making up 34 per cent of F(C) at 10 years, only 15 per cent at 16 years. Texture responses are second in number at these earlier ages; at 15 and 16 years texture responses definitely lead.

Light-shade responses are notable from 13 through 16 years of age, and vista responses, conspicuously lacking in the younger years, begin to appear in the girls' response as early as 10 years. By 13 years of age, vista is the third leading type of shading response for girls, 15 per cent of their shading responses being in this category. And at 14, 15, and 16 years, for sexes combined, vista response holds third place.

SEX DIFFERENCES   As for most determinants in this age period, sex differences are marked. At every age except 11 years, definitely more girls than boys give shading responses, and the mean number of such responses for girls is noticeably higher, these differences being particularly marked from 14 years on.

Slight sex differences appear in the quality as well as in the quantity of shading responses. At five of the seven ages from 10 to 16 years, boys give more differentiation responses than do girls. At five ages, girls give more light-shade responses than do boys. Vista responses occur sooner in girls than in boys, and for all ages combined, somewhat more in girls than in boys.

Summary

In summary, then, we note through the changes in both the quantity and quality of the F(C) response, the individual's developing emotional sensitivity. We are aware of the increasing demand that his own physical and sensual development make upon him. We recognize his greater ability and concern in evaluating himself and his enhanced consciousness of his relationship with others. The appearance of vista responses would seem to indicate his desire and/or his ability to regard his own reactions, as well as those of others, with increasing perspective.

RESPONSE TO BLACK

Responses scored as FC′, C′F, FClob, or ClobF are all those given to the dark or black parts of the blot in which it is indicated that the black or the darkness conditioned the response. FC′ and C′F are those responses where black is used as color, but without manifestly threatening or unpleasant connotations. FClob and ClobF are noted when the black induces profound dysphoric reactions. Such responses are presumed to indicate an emotional organization that is easily disturbed, an individual subject to strong, often uncontrolled or uncontrollable depressive or morbid reactions.

In the first ten years of life such responses were never frequent, occurring most often at 5½ and 7 years (1, p. 86). Table 18 shows that in the

TABLE 18.   RESPONSES TO BLACK
(FC′+C′F+FClob+ClobF)

Age and sex	Percentage using*	Mean score
10: Boys	6	.06
Girls	10	.10
11: Boys	12	.12
Girls	10	.12
12: Boys	12	.12
Girls	6	.06
13: Boys	10	.10
Girls	4	.04
14: Boys	12	.12
Girls	12	.14
15: Boys	6	.06
Girls	12	.12
16: Boys	2	.02
Girls	18	.18

* Only two children, of the total 700, use more than one of these summed determinants, and they both use two.

years from 10 to 16 such responses continue to be infrequent. Even when all responses to the black are classified as a single group, we have only a range of 7 to 12 per cent of both sexes combined at any one age giving any such response. At no age does the mean score reach 0.2.

Thus we see the infrequency of response conditioned by the black or dark portions of the blot, with or without dysphoric connotations. Hence, we may continue to regard such responses as rare and worthy of refined and critical evaluation in an individual protocol whenever they do appear.

CHAPTER SEVEN

Content

Analysis of content can give us some idea of the intellectual expansion of an individual as well as some insight regarding his emotional tone. Wild, ferocious, predatory animals naturally have a very different connotation from the more friendly, domesticated ones. The various kinds of human beings indicated in the content can also give us some idea of an individual's attitude toward others as well as toward himself; through this category we have some insight as to the maturity of self-identification or ego development. From a survey of the content and the relative proportion of the various responses, we obtain some clue as to an individual's ability to conform to cultural custom and habit, how well he participates in his society, and the relative degree to which he responds to rules and regulations. Certain content ratios may indicate the possibility of anxiety. From content, we have some idea of the general maturity of an individual's concepts. However, as with area and with determinants of response, content cannot be taken out of context, but must always be considered as a part of and in relation to the entire protocol.

The same content categories have been used for this age range as for the first 10 years (1), with the addition of four new categories: explosion, geography-geology, design, mask.

The mean number of times each response is given at each age, for boys and girls separately and for both sexes combined, is found in Table 19. Except for the last five categories (blood, fire, mask, reflection, and abstract), the figures given represent the mean number of times the category appeared as a primary score. Figures for the last five items indicate the total number of times the concept was used as either a primary or secondary score, since "mask" was routinely scored as "object"; "reflection" or "fire" most often as part of a "scene"; "blood" often as part of "anatomy," "animal," or "human" response.

With minor exceptions, the six leading content categories for our present age range, in this order, are: animal, human, object, anatomy, nature, plant. (Exceptions are that at both 12 and 13 years, nature rather

63

TABLE 19. CONTENT: MEAN

	10 Years			11 Years			12 Years		
	B	G	T	B	G	T	B	G	T
Number of									
Animals	9.14	11.60	10.37	9.94	10.30	10.12	11.48	11.12	11.30
Humans	3.58	3.46	3.52	3.62	3.86	3.74	3.76	4.80	4.28
Objects	1.92	2.30	2.11	3.44	2.12	2.68	2.24	3.10	2.67
Anatomy	.54	.54	.54	.86	.36	.61	.50	.86	.68
Nature	.42	.52	.47	.64	.44	.54	.50	.94	.72
Plant	.38	.54	.46	.38	.28	.33	.42	.54	.48
Flowers	.16	.10	.13	.14	.14	.14	.22	.18	.20
Scene	.30	.36	.33	.40	.16	.28	.32	.36	.34
Architecture	.18	.34	.26	.16	.22	.19	.10	.30	.20
Geog.—geol.	.10	.10	.10	.10	.06	.08	.04	.20	.12
Map	.26	.14	.20	.20	.16	.18	.12	.12	.12
Food	.14	.18	.16	.14	.14	.14	.12	.30	.21
Design	.14	.16	.15	.10	.08	.09	.10	.08	.09
Painting-paint	.04	.10	.07	.12	.08	.10	.22	—	.11
Explosion	.20	.10	.15	.22	.12	.17	.12	.10	.11
Blood*	.18	.06	.12	.12	.10	.11	.10	.06	.08
Fire*	.24	.34	.29	.24	.16	.20	.14	.30	.22
Mask*	.18	.10	.14	.16	.04	.10	.04	.02	.03
Reflection*	.04	.16	.10	.20	.20	.20	.14	.24	.19
Abstract*	.00	.20	.10	.08	.02	.05	.06	.04	.05
Mean number of cate-gories per child	5.2	5.2	5.2	5.2	4.9	5.1	5.0	5.4	5.2

* Both primary and secondary occurrence of blood, fire, mask, reflection, and abstract responses are

than anatomy holds fourth place; and that at 15 years, scene rather than plant comes sixth.)

Interestingly enough, these same six categories and in this same order are the leading categories as early as 8 years of age, and also at 9. Even earlier, these same categories appeared prominently, though up through 5½, architecture instead of anatomy was one of the leading responses.

All other content categories listed above occur at least to some extent at every age, but none to the extent of as much as .5 per child. Of these, the most conspicuous at each age and the average extent to which they occur are as follows:

10 years: scene .3; fire .3; architecture .3; map .2.
11 years: scene .3; fire .2; reflection .2; architecture .2.
12 years: scene .3; fire .2; food .2; flower .2; architecture .2; reflection .2.
13 years: scene .3; reflection .3; explosion .2; flower .2; food .2.
14 years: reflection .3; flower .3; scene .3; fire .2; map .2.
15 years: plant .4; reflection .3; map .3; flower .3; abstract .2.
16 years: flower .4; abstract .4; scene .4; reflection .3; explosion .3; geog.-geol. .2; map .2; food .2.

At every age from 10 to 16 the total number of different content categories used by all subjects together is twenty. This shows a definite

OCCURRENCE OF EACH CATEGORY

13 Years			14 Years			15 Years			16 Years		
B	G	T	B	G	T	B	G	T	B	G	T
9.08	10.92	10.00	10.74	12.24	11.49	8.18	10.06	9.12	10.70	11.00	10.90
2.92	4.50	3.71	3.26	6.30	4.78	2.20	4.60	3.40	3.26	4.82	4.29
2.20	3.00	2.60	2.28	3.36	2.82	1.84	2.14	1.99	2.46	2.68	2.57
.60	.62	.61	1.34	1.08	1.21	.78	.68	.73	.98	.68	.83
.68	.88	.78	.66	.92	.79	.34	.88	.61	.62	.90	.76
.36	.66	.51	.28	.64	.46	.38	.34	.36	.36	.64	.50
.18	.22	.20	.18	.38	.28	.22	.34	.28	.36	.48	.42
.30	.30	.31	.16	.38	.27	.22	.54	.38	.16	.54	.35
.08	.22	.15	.06	.22	.14	.06	.22	.14	.06	.20	.13
—	.22	.11	.12	.10	.11	.18	.08	.13	.20	.26	.23
.16	.14	.15	.08	.28	.18	.48	.14	.31	.34	.16	.25
.16	.22	.19	.10	.12	.11	.10	.14	.12	.08	.28	.18
.16	.10	.13	.12	—	.06	.16	.24	.20	.06	.06	.06
.04	.02	.03	.14	.10	.12	.06	.04	.05	.18	.14	.16
.32	.12	.22	.12	.22	.17	.04	.12	.08	.20	.42	.31
.16	.08	.12	.12	.14	.13	.10	.02	.06	.08	.22	.15
.14	.18	.16	.16	.22	.19	.04	.22	.13	.08	.14	.11
.18	.10	.14	.10	.06	.08	.10	.18	.14	.10	.08	.09
.30	.22	.26	.28	.40	.34	.18	.46	.31	.29	.36	.33
.18	.10	.14	.04	.12	.08	.28	.10	.19	.24	.62	.43
5.1	5.5	5.3	5.2	6.0	5.6	4.8	5.6	5.2	5.0	6.2	5.6

tabulated here.

increase in variety of content over the first 10 years when the total number of different categories given by the whole group at any one age ranged from a low of 10 at 2 years to a high of 17 at 9 years.

The average number used by any one child is of course smaller. As Table 19 shows, the average number of different categories per child, *both* sexes considered together, ranges only from 5.1 to 5.6. (At all ages except 10 and 11, girls have a slightly greater variety of content than do boys.) Again, this shows an increase in variety over the first 10 years when the average number of different categories per child ranged from a low of 2.6 at 2 years to a high of 5.2 at 9 years.

As Table 19 indicates, the greatest variety of content is found at 14 and 16 years, for both sexes together and for girls only. Boys have most variety at 10, 11, and 14 years. Least variety occurs in girls at 11 years and in boys at 15.

At every age the median number of different content categories used is 5, and well over half the subjects in every age group use between 4 and 6 different content categories.

Age Trends

The average percentage of animal responses (the most frequent type of response at every age), as in the first 10 years, does not consistently increase or decrease from age to age. Median A% starts high (47 per cent at 10 years), reaches its peak of 53 per cent at 11, and then decreases, ranging between 44 and 47 per cent, thereafter. The very highest point for the stereotypy supposedly indicated by animal response occurs in girls at 11 (56 per cent). The lowest point occurs in girls at 15 and 16 years (41 per cent). In the first 10 years the range was not conspicuously different, being from a low of 41 to a high of 56 per cent. From ages 10 to 16 years, the range of mean A% for the entire group, both sexes combined, is from 44 to 53 per cent.

The actual number of animal responses at each age (Table 19) ranges between nine and eleven. At every age but 12 years, girls give more animal responses than do boys.

H%, unlike A%, showed a definite increase with age in the first 10 years, increasing from an average of 3 per cent at 2 years to 17 per cent at 8 years and remaining at 16 per cent at 9 and 10 years. This increase does not continue into the next age period. For present subjects, median H% is 17 per cent at 10 years, rises to 18 per cent at 11 and 12, drops to 16 to 17 per cent thereafter. Actual median number of H responses per subject is three or four at an age. Considering both sexes together, there is no consistent age trend here. High points for H, both sexes combined and for girls alone, are at 12, 14, and 16 years; for boys, at 10, 11, and 12. Low points for both sexes combined are at 10 and 15 years; for girls alone at 10 and 11; for boys alone at 13 and 15. Girls in general tend to give an increasing, boys in general a decreasing number of H responses.

Of other major content categories, a few tend to show a general increase with age. These are: flower, geography-geology, abstract, reflection, nature. A few, especially architecture and fire, show a general decrease.

Anatomy, object, painting-paint, and mask all follow a pattern of continuous fluctuation from age to age, with lower points at 13 and 15 years than at the surrounding ages. Blood and explosion both show a marked decrease at 15 though not at 13 years of age. Most other categories follow a mixed and ambiguous course as can be seen from Table 19.

ANIMAL AND HUMAN DETAIL   As in the first 10 years of life, we find when we compare the number of whole human figures to the number of human details and of whole animal figures to animal details that whole figures far exceed details in both categories.

For the age range 2 through 10 years, the human detail responses are on the average, all ages combined, 46 per cent as frequent as whole human responses. The average for the years 10 through 16 is a little higher, 55 per cent for both boys and girls, though at no age does the proportion of human detail equal that found earlier at 9 years of age (84 per cent). Animal detail responses are on the average only 19 per cent as frequent as whole animal responses in the first 10 years of life. This figure rises to

26 per cent for boys, 22 per cent for girls in the year from 10 through 16, and at every age from 10 on is higher than at any of the earlier ages.

As Table 20 shows, both age and sex differences are marked. The ratio of Hd:H is highest with boys at 12, 14, and 16 years of age, with girls at 13 and especially at 14 years. Animal details are given most by boys at 14 and 16 years, by girls at 13 and 14 years.

The expected ratio of H:Hd for adults is usually considered to be about 2:1. Human detail responses found in excess of this proportion are generally considered a sign of anxiety. Though averages for both sexes combined notably exceed this ratio in the present age range only at 14 years, for sexes considered separately there are many ages (see Table 20)

TABLE 20. RATIO OF ANIMAL AND HUMAN DETAILS TO WHOLE FIGURES: MEAN FIGURES AND RATIOS OF MEANS AT EACH AGE

Age	Boys			Girls			All
	H*	Hd*	Hd:H	H*	Hd*	Hd:H	Hd:H
10	1.70	1.00	.59	1.68	.80	.48	.53
11	1.94	1.12	.58	2.06	.96	.47	.52
12	1.88	1.24	.66	2.30	1.22	.53	.59
13	1.78	.58	.33	2.18	1.46	.67	.52
14	1.68	1.02	.61	2.76	2.26	.82	.74
15	1.32	.56	.42	2.54	1.10	.43	.43
16	1.62	1.00	.62	2.46	1.06	.43	.50
All	1.70	.93	.55	2.28	1.27	.55	.55
	A*	Ad*	Ad:A	A*	Ad*	Ad:A	Ad:A
10	6.64	1.70	.26	9.60	1.60	.17	.20
11	7.82	1.76	.23	8.00	1.90	.24	.23
12	8.16	2.18	.27	9.02	1.54	.17	.22
13	6.56	1.26	.19	8.28	2.16	.26	.23
14	7.02	2.46	.35	9.02	2.30	.25	.30
15	6.00	1.18	.20	7.50	1.80	.24	.22
16	7.30	2.28	.31	8.28	1.84	.22	.26
All	7.01	1.83	.26	8.53	1.88	.22	.24

* Exclusive of (H), (Hd), (A), (Ad).

when boys especially give more than this expected number of human details.

Whole animal response is generally expected to exceed animal detail response in an even higher proportion than H:Hd. In the present subjects from 10 to 16 years, A response greatly exceeds Ad response at every age and for both sexes. The ratio of A:Ad for the entire group is about 4:1.

(H), (Hd), (A), (Ad) Witches, elves, angels, and such are commonly scored (H), or (Hd) as the case may be; monsters and dragons are scored (A). During the first 10 years, neither (H) nor (A) occurs extensively. Nor does (A) occur more than occasionally between 10 and 16 years.

(H), however, as Table 21 shows, is found frequently in the years

TABLE 21.   (H), (Hd), (A), (Ad): Mean Occurrence for Boys and Girls at Each Age

	10 Years	11 Years	12 Years	13 Years	14 Years	15 Years	16 Years
(H)+(Hd)							
Boys	.88	.56	.64	.56	.56	.32	.64
Girls	.98	.84	1.26	.86	1.28	.96	1.30
Both	.93	.70	.95	.71	.92	.62	.97
(A)+(Ad)							
Boys	.22	.24	.24	.34	.18	.16	.04
Girls	.28	.18	.12	.22	.30	.20	.34
Both	.25	.21	.18	.28	.24	.18	.19

between 10 and 16. Considering both boys and girls together, it reaches the high average of nearly 1 response per child at 10, 12, 14, and 16 years. In fact, (H) is actually half or nearly half as large as H at 10, 12, 14, and 16 years of age. High points for girls alone occur especially at 12, 14, and 16 years; for boys at 10 years. At every age, girls give considerably more of this kind of response than do boys.

Comparison With First Ten Years

A brief comparison between content of Rorschach responses given in the first 10 years of life and those in the present age ranges yields some close correspondences and a few marked differences.

Animals are the chief response during both age periods and occur to about the same extent. Mean A% (2 to 10 years) is 46 per cent; from 10 to 16 years, 48 per cent. Human responses are the second leading content category, but occur more extensively in the later age period. Mean H% in the years from 2 to 10 is 10 per cent; from 10 to 16 years, 19 per cent. However, by 8 years of age the mean H% is already 17 per cent and from this age through 16 years seldom falls below this.

Among the kinds of content that occur less in the years from 10 to 16 than earlier are: plant, tree, nature, architecture, house, paint, and painting. A few kinds of content occur about equally in the two age periods: animal (as mentioned above); flowers; and blood (except for early high points at 4½, 8, and 9 years, not repeated later).

In the case of the majority of content categories, however, there is a marked increase during the age period 10 to 16 over the earlier occurrence.

Anatomy responses occur equally in the present age range and in the years from 6 to 10. (Mean anatomy for both periods is .74.) Fire occurs less than from 6 to 10. (Mean fire 6 to 10 is .34; from 10 to 16, .18.)

Reflection responses, virtually nonexistent in the first 10 years of life (mean of .08 at 8 years, .04 at 9, none at other ages), appear increasingly in the age period from 10 to 16, going from .1 per subject at 10 years to .3 at 16. These responses, suggesting a certain degree of narcissism indicative of the teen-ager's increasing interest in and concern about his self, his role, and how he appears to and compares with others, have been analyzed as to their specific nature.

In boys, we find that animals reflected either in water or in a mirror are the leading reflection responses at every age, and occur increasingly. Scene reflected comes in strongly at 13 years and thereafter. Person occurs increasingly, reaching its peak at 16 years.

In girls, animal reflected predominates at 10, 11, and 13 years. It shares first place with tree and person at 12 years. Person leads at 14 years, scene at 15, though animal comes in again strongly here.

While the gradient of maturity is not clear-cut, animal reflections seem to be the least mature; people reflected—first in water, then in a mirror—more mature; and scenes most mature. An intriguing single item is that persons looking at themselves in a mirror occurs most conspicuously at 14 years of age.

Most conspicuous sex differences are that boys have relatively many more animal than human reflection responses in comparison with girls, boys giving 32 animal and 8 people responses, girls giving 31 animals and 21 people. Girls have more trees and more scenes reflected; they also have more reflections seen in a mirror. Boys in all give 1 animal and 5 persons looking into a mirror. Girls give 4 animals and 10 persons.

In our earlier study, a detailed analysis was made of the *kinds of animal responses* predominating at different ages. Such an analysis was not made for this age range. However, brief comment may be made here about two kinds of responses which while customary on certain cards may be considered somewhat unusual on others. These responses are *bird* and *fish*.

Bird responses occur for the most part on Cards V and X. Nearly half of the bird responses given by boys, more than one third given by girls occur on these two cards. Card I also attracts many bird responses. (There is in boys a steady increase in "birds" from 14 at 10 years to 35 at 16 years. Girls increase in "bird" from 17 at 10 years to 46 at 14, then decrease to 33 at 16.)

Bird responses to most cards, especially to I, V, X, or to the top part of VI are for the most part unnoteworthy. However, "bird" may be considered a somewhat immature response to Card II (where throughout this total age range it occurs in all 23 times in boys, 17 in girls), and extremely immature when it occurs for the black figures in Card III (where it occurs 6 times in all in boys, 4 times in girls).

The response *fish* is somewhat unusual, occurring in all in the present age range only 71 times in boys, 68 times in girls—a total of 139. The response "fish" to some D area of Card X, especially when a total sea scene is given, is not unusual, even though relatively infrequent—given in all 39 times by boys, 29 by girls. This amounts to half of all "fish" responses given. On other cards, however, a "fish" response may be considered rare and unusual. These unusual responses occur most at 10 years of age, and again at 15 and 16 years.

Content Indicating or Implying Interest in Sex

Direct expressions of sexual or reproduction activities appear to be, in this age range, an extremely individual matter and are so few, in our population, that any such expression may be considered evidence of extraordinary and special concern.

In boys at 10 and in girls at 16 there are no such responses. At other ages, such references occur as follows. There are in all three references to reproduction given by girls, seven by boys. "Two mouses put together in their mothers' stomach" (girl at 10); "Looks like a wasp laying its eggs" (boy at 12). Sex-anatomy responses are given by three girls and four boys. Kissing responses or references to love are given by eleven girls, seven boys. There is one direct reference to elimination, by a boy at 15; and two references to intercourse: "Man sold himself to Satan . . . then went out and raped people" (girl at 10); and "Two bats having sexual intercourse" (boy at 15).

In all there are fewer than 50 such references in 700 individual records. Most indications that our subjects are becoming aware of sex or are interested in it must therefore be found, if they exist, in indirect expressions of such interest.

Flower responses, particularly lush flower responses given on the color cards, may conceivably be expressive of sexual interest and awareness. In the present population, means for flower responses increase steadily, tripling during the age range here studied as follows: .1 at 10 years and 11 years; .2 at 12 and 13; .3 at 14 and 15; .4 at 16. Cards eliciting the most of these responses are, in order from least to most: IV, VIII, and IX.

The card that yields the largest number of indirect indications that subjects are concerned with the subject of sex seems to be Card IV. At every age there are, in boys and girls both, many responses that may be considered to have possible sexual implications. Among them are the following:

IN GIRLS:

  10 years: giant (9), tail (4), snakes (2), things hanging or dropping (3), trousers (3), flower (1), anatomy (1), giant's club (3). The chief response at this age is a giant with big feet, and possibly with a tail or club, sitting on a stump.

11 years: giant (3), tail (9), things hanging (4), pockets (1), "rear end" or "bottom" of animal (2).

12 years: giant (8), tail (10), things hanging or hanging out (7), snake (2), things sticking out (2), numerous proportion and vista responses; old, dead, ragged things (4). In four cases, giants and men and animals tend to be in threatening positions. Three girls (more than at any other age but 15) refuse this card.

13 years: tail (9), giant (8), pockets out (2), things in perspective (5), holes (2). Specially suggestive are such responses as "Pockets open, insides dripping out."

14 years: snakes or swan's neck (5), inside of walnut (3), leaves (most of which are dried up or rotted away) (9), anatomy (4), overgrown trees (4).

15 years: snakes (4), anatomy (2), vista or perspective (3), refusals (3).

16 years: tail (3), snake (2), anatomy (4), perspective (6), bomb or explosion (3), cave (1), things that are old, ragged, dead (2). Emphasis on water, especially "running out of a faucet," "limp hands," "trousers with nobody in them," "giant sitting on his shillelagh," "horns sticking out."

IN BOYS:

10 years: tail (4), snakes (2), anatomy (3), old, dead, broken, or ragged things (3), "wet hairy animal" (1), things hanging or dropping (3). Two things are "taking a peek from underneath."

11 years: tail (4), snake (3), trousers (2), old, dead, broken things (3), flower (1), person looking through his legs (1). Trouble with the bottom center of card is suggested by such remarks as: "Not counting that in between there," "This part doesn't make sense."

12 years: tail (2), flower (3), old, dead, broken, or cut-off things (6), things overlapping (2), things hanging (2), things in perspective (2). Giants and men are not, as in girls, threatening but there is more emphasis than in girls on their being headless or having head cut off (3).

13 years: tail (3), old, dead, or broken things (3), flower (2). "Leaf broken off" and "leaf that's dried up and some ripped off" are suggestive.

14 years: tail (3), club (2), things hanging (4), things in perspective (5). Or, "giant with a club or devil with a dagger—sinister."

15 years: walnut shell (1), tail (1), flower (1), "animal going to the john in the woods"; "Underground cave, things hanging from ceiling or coming up from the floor"; "two mooses without their horns."

16 years: flower (2), tail (2), perspective (2), X-ray (2), anatomy (2). "Neck of a chicken, meat chewed off"; "Leg floating in water, looks like a snake."

Another card that may be expected to elicit sex responses is Card VI. In the present age range, however, we found few if any responses that could be undisputably credited as such. "Totem pole," which occurs 26 times in boys, 36 times in girls, for the total age range, may perhaps be considered as a sex symbol, though it may also have group and family connotations. There was only one direct reference on this card to sex or reproductive functions (out of 700 protocols)—"grasshopper laying eggs." Unless one considers the symbolic content of such DW responses as "fly sitting on a flower" or "lighthouse on a rock," there are few such references on this card.

Card VII, however, yields a relatively high number of responses that may be considered sexual in their implication. Such responses are given to the center detail of the bottom tier. Use of this detail is rare among boys, never reaching 10 per cent frequency, but among girls it increases constantly throughout the age range to 24 per cent usage at 15 years. There are 15 responses given in all by boys to this area, 54 by girls. Of this number, 5 in boys and 39 in girls may be considered to have possible sexual implication. These include besides the usual house, church, hinge, or candle responses, such responses as Niagara Falls, passageway between rocks, violin part where you twist the strings, flower petal, stigma where pollen is, candle, waterfall, door in wall.

Sex Differences

Sex differences in content as in other factors are rather marked. Since girls give more responses in all than do boys at every age but 11, it is not surprising that for most content categories girls give more responses at each age than do boys. This is true of the two chief content categories— animals and humans, except for 12 years for animals and 10 years for humans when boys give more responses than do girls. Also median H% is higher for girls than for boys at every age but 10.

For other content categories we have only the mean number of responses for each sex at each age (see Table 18). As this table shows, girls give more object, nature, fire, and food responses than do boys at every age but 11; more scenes at every age but 11 and 13. They give more architecture responses at every age.

However, at some ages and for a few content categories, boys exceed girls as follows: Boys give more anatomy responses than do girls at 11 years and from 14 to 16 years. Boys give more blood responses than do girls at every age except 14 and 16. Boys give more explosion responses than do girls from 10 to 13 years but girls give more from 14 on. Boys give more mask responses at every age except 15.

Summary

In the matter of content, judging from our survey of the first 16 years of life, we find the following:

We can expect that Animal responses will be the highest in any protocol, with Human responses next. Expectancy of A% after 10 years of age (for the middle 50 per cent of subjects) appears to stabilize between 37 and 57 per cent, or slightly higher than the usual adult expectancy. H% tends to stabilize as early as 8 years of age, and in the 10- to 16-year period the interquartile range remains around 10 to 25 per cent, again slightly higher than the present normal adult expectancy. The A:H ratio is about 3:1 as compared with the adult expectancy of about 2:1. A:Ad ratio in the group from 10 to 16 years is about 4:1 and the H:Hd ratio is about 2:1.

An interesting characteristic that emerges in the 10- to 16-year period is the number of (H) responses that occur as compared to the ages before 10 years. Thus, we find it not at all unusual to have at least one "witch," "devil," or "angel" in any given protocol. Such responses were rare at the younger ages (average of about .5 from 5½ to 10 years), and are presumed to be rare in the adult protocol. But in the years from 10 to 16, they appear to be "normal."

After the A and H content responses, we can expect at least two to four other content categories. In fact, over 50 per cent of our group at every age gives from 4 to 6 different categories. Expectancy of 3 to 4 categories, however, was already indicated at 7 years of age, and in the present group the average number of categories per child is rarely less than five.

In our group, the content categories following animal and human responses are such that we can almost predict which ones to expect. For except at 15 years (an age that seems to defy all rules!), the four leading categories after A and H are *object, anatomy, nature,* and *plant.*

Here again, let us indicate that the appearance of anatomy and nature responses in the protocols of subjects up to 16 years of age seems characteristic. Anatomy responses have, in fact, increased in this age range, though nature responses have decreased as compared with children under 10 years. We find anatomy responses appearing on an average of almost one response per child as early as 8 years of age, and in the 10- to 16-year period the range of means is between .5 and 1.2. Means for nature response range in this age group between .5 and .8. Thus *anatomy* as well as *nature* responses remain throughout this age range at least among the expected responses.

So far as content is concerned, we may say that subjects from 10 to 16 years of age (often as early as 7 to 8 years of age) are projecting toward maturity, but they show many characteristics that appear "normal" to adolescence even though deviant from present adult expectancies. In such details, it remains to be seen whether we should revise our adult expectancies slightly, or whether this present type of developmental research needs to be continued into subsequent ages.

CHAPTER EIGHT

Additional Test Factors

Many important aspects of the Rorschach response are not covered in a consideration of form, determinants, or content. These include the following: number of responses, timing, semantics, popular responses, refusals, best- and least-liked cards, card turning, initial exclamations, shock, and nature of adjectives. We shall discuss each of these briefly in the present chapter.

Number of Responses

The average number of responses, both sexes considered together, in the first 10 years of life in our younger group of subjects (1) was found to range from 9.6 at 2 years of age to 18.6 at 9 years.

In the present subjects, median R for ages 10 to 16 ranges between 16 and 20 responses. There is a slight decrease in productivity at 13 and 15 years of age; an increase at 14 and 16 years. The middle 50 per cent of subjects for the total age range give between 13 and 24 responses.

Means are slightly higher, ranging from 18.3 to 23.4 responses per child, but again the trend is the same: a plateau at 10 and 11 years, an increase at 12, decreases at 13 and 15, increases at 14 and 16 years.

SEX DIFFERENCES At every age except at 11 years when mean R for girls and boys is identical, girls give a larger number of responses than do boys (see Table 6). Mean R for boys for the total age range is 18.8; for girls, 22.5. Sex differences are most evident at 14, 15, and 16 years.

Timing

Our earlier study (1) found that timing for total performance increased steadily for the first 6 years of life, from a mean of four minutes at 2 years of age to a mean of 8.85 minutes at 6 years. Timing was not recorded for tests given to 7- and 9-year-olds. Though total time was not recorded in every case for the present study, it was available for 72 per cent of the subjects. Table 22 presents the means and percentile values for boys and girls at each age, as well as the percentiles for the total sample.

TABLE 22. TOTAL TIME
(In minutes)

					Percentiles		
	N	Mean	10	25	50	75	90
10 Boys	33	13.6	8	10	13	16	22
Girls	36	13.8	5	8	13½	17	22
Total	69	13.7	6	9	13	16	22
11 Boys	33	11.4	7	9	10	14	18
Girls	34	13.3	7	9	11½	14	18
Total	67	12.4	7	9	10	15	18
12 Boys	25	11.9	6	7	12	15	18
Girls	35	12.4	7	9	10	15	18
Total	60	12.2	6	8	10	15	18
13 Boys	37	12.5	7	8	10	16	24
Girls	40	13.2	6	8	11½	16	20
Total	77	12.9	7	8	11	16	20
14 Boys	37	13.1	7	8	11	17	22
Girls	36	14.3	6	8	12	19	23
Total	73	13.7	6	8	12	18	23
15 Boys	36	10.7	6	7	10	13	16
Girls	42	12.7	5	7	10½	18	21
Total	78	11.8	5	7	10	15	20
16 Boys	40	13.3	7	8	11	15	25
Girls	42	13.6	6	8	12½	18	22
Total	82	13.5	6	8	12	16	23
All ages							
Boys	241		7	8	11	15	20
Girls	265		6	8	11½	16	21
Total	506		6	8	11	15	20

Median test: Age diff., boys $x2 = 13.51$; $p < .05$
girls $x2 = 2.86$; —
Sex diff., $x2 = 1.06$; —

For the total group the median time was 11 minutes, while the mean was 13 minutes. The finding that 25 per cent of all children took less than eight minutes, and that 10 per cent took less than six minutes for response (including inquiry), is a somewhat surprising one. The median test shows no significant difference between the sexes in total time, and this is evident in the percentile values. The fact that girls' mean values are consistently slightly higher than the boys' indicates that a few girls take extremely long times at each age. The more general finding of no sex difference, however, is especially interesting in relation to the finding that girls give significantly more responses than do boys. Since they give them in the same time that it takes the boys to give their fewer responses, the girls' rate of verbalization must be correspondingly faster.

The median test indicates significant age differences in timing among the boys, with responses being longest at age 10, shortest at 11, 13, and especially at 15. Girls do not show significant age differences on the median test, but their relatively long median time at age 10 and short time at ages 12 and 15 suggests a similar trend.

Because of the negligible sex difference and the relatively small age difference, the over-all percentiles provide a good approximation to those for single groups. That is, the statement that the middle 50 per cent of subjects took from 8 to 15 minutes to produce their Rorschach records applies reasonably well throughout the age span. Two points should, however, be noted, in applying these values to other groups. First is that the total time values include time for inquiry, which was conducted along with initial presentation. Not only does this mean that timing is not directly comparable with that for studies conducting inquiry afterward, but also, less obviously, that "total time" is measuring examiner's tempo as well as the child's. The second point is that the majority of records were contributed by children who had taken the test before—often several times. Though the precise effect of this is not known, familarity with the test may well have had greater effect on timing than on any other test score, and it undoubtedly had the general effect of shortening total time.

Semantics

Among the many different ways in which a child can phrase his response to the cards, the three outstanding are: naming the blot, as for example "a bat"; comparing the blot to the concept as with the use of "looks like"; identifying the blot by use of such phrases as "that is," or "that could be."

In the first 7 years of life, simply *naming* the blot is by far the outstanding method of designation. At 8 years there is a shift—*comparing the blot to the concept,* chiefly by use of such phrases as "looks like," being the leading type of response at 8, 9, and 10 years of age. Naming the blot drops to second place at these three ages (1).

In the age range 10 to 16 years, *comparing the blot to the concept* continues to be the leading type of response (Table 23). The outstanding phrase used for making this comparison, at all ages, is "looks like." Other outstanding phrases are "kind of looks like" or "sort of looks like," "looks to me like," "reminds me," "makes me think of."

Naming the blot ("bat," "butterfly") is the second leading method of identification at all ages from 10 through 16.

Identifying the blot ("that is," or "that might be, could be, would be"), next to the leading type of identification in the earliest years, falls to third place from 10 to 16. Of the various possible types of identification, "that is" leads in the first 7 years. "Might be" or "could be" takes first

TABLE 23.   SEMANTIC ANALYSIS: TOTAL NUMBER OF RESPONSES
OF EACH TYPE AT EACH AGE

	Age in years						
	10	*11*	*12*	*13*	*14*	*15*	*16*
I. Names blot	526	487	664	576	629	625	775
II. Identifies blot							
a. That is	106	143	166	141	145	92	112
b. Extra-positive	3	0	6	1	5	5	7
c. Questions identity	7	4	1	0	2	8	5
d. Might, could, would be	222	281	258	232	271	215	249
e. Maybe, possibly, I guess, think, suppose	18	41	26	44	54	26	24
Total of *c, d, e**	247	326	285	276	327	249	278
III. Assumes reality							
a. I see	10	42	7	0	20	10	8
IV. Compares blot to reality							
a. Sort of, kind of*	50	42	43	46	44	33	55
b. Looks like	766	720	791	728	866	724	737
c. Could, might look like*	35	20	27	31	26	21	19
d. Like, is like	14	14	36	21	21	44	25
e. Looks something like*	49	62	86	70	53	32	21
f. Kind of, sort of, looks like*	83	74	66	78	59	22	21
g. Sort of like*	38	23	41	16	17	10	10
h. If you cut this off*	11	6	8	5	9	5	9
i. Looks to me, reminds me, makes me think of	66	56	26	78	82	78	130
* All qualifying concepts combined	513	553	556	522	535	372	413

place from 8 through 10 years, and continues in first place through 16 years except at 12 when the more positive "That is" once again leads. The extra positive, "With no doubt," or "Certainly" is seldom used in the years between 10 and 16. Nor do children of this age often question identity of their concepts with such phrases as "Could it be?" or "Is it?"

Considering all *qualified* concepts together and comparing them with the number of such concepts used in the first 10 years of life (1, p. 98), we find that there is little use of qualified concepts in the first 4½ years. Such concepts come in rather extensively at 5 and from 7 through 10 years. They continue to about the same extent as at 10 years on through 16. Approximately one fifth of all responses express or imply some qualification or uncertainty as to the accuracy of the response given.

Popular Responses

The responses scored as popular are listed in Chapter 3. All our subjects included at least one of these 16 possible P in their records; all but 10 per cent gave four or more P. The middle 50 per cent of subjects gave between 5 and 8 P, which thus make up a good proportion of the average record (median R=17).

No sex differences appear over-all, nor are the age trends pronounced. The interquartile range of 5 to 8 P is a good approximation to the central trend at all ages. There is, however, a trend toward slight decrease in P with age among girls, with highest mean P at 10 years, lowest at 16. Boys, after an increase in P from 10 to 11 years, show a similar over-all slight decrease in mean P.

These P expectancies are slightly higher than those often suggested for adult protocols (e.g., Klopfer *et al.,* 40; Piotrowski, 47). This is presumably due in part to our relatively long list of P. When an adolescent gives fewer than 5 P, we would want to examine his total record carefully to evaluate the strength of his ties with reality and to determine whether he cannot or does not wish to produce the easier, more obvious responses. When he gives 9 or more P, we would look to see whether these were imbedded in a rich, full record or whether he apparently could feel safe only in giving obvious, conventional responses.

Refusals

Though refusals are not expected in the normal adult protocol, at all but three ages (3½ years, 6, and 7) more than one fourth of subjects under 10 years of age tested by us gave at least one refusal. The mean number of refusals declined gradually from 2 to 7 years and increased slightly thereafter. This number ranged from a mean of .3 refusals per child at 3½ years to a high of 2.4 at 2 years. From 4½ years on, the average refusal per child was in the neighborhood of .5.

In our present subjects aged 10 to 16, there are somewhat fewer refusals than in the years before 10. At four of the seven ages in question, fewer than one fourth of the subjects refuse one or more cards. At only three ages (10, 11, and 15 years) do more than one fourth of the subjects make any refusals.

Also in the present age range somewhat fewer cards are refused per child than earlier. For the entire group, the mean number of cards refused was .3. The greatest number of cards (.5 per child) were refused at 10 years of age, with 11, 13, and 15 years the next high points (.4 per child). Fewest cards were refused at 12, 14, and 16 years, the means for all these ages being .2.

Table 24 gives both the percentage of subjects refusing and the number of cards refused for boys and girls separately and for the sexes combined.

SEX DIFFERENCES Sex differences are not marked, though slightly more boys than girls refuse cards, and slightly more cards are on the average refused by boys than by girls. Thus for the total groups of boys and

TABLE 24. REFUSALS: PERCENTAGE OF SUBJECTS REFUSING ONE OR MORE
CARDS, MEAN NUMBER REFUSED, AND CARDS MOST OFTEN REFUSED

	10 Years	11 Years	12 Years	13 Years	14 Years	15 Years	16 Years	Total
BOYS								
Percentage refusing	30	26	12	22	10	32	22	22
Mean number refused	.6	.4	.2	.4	.2	.5	.2	.4
Card most refused	IX	IV	II	VII	IV	IX	IX	IX, VI
Card next most	VI	VI		III		VI	VII	
GIRLS								
Percentage refusing	26	26	18	24	14	20	10	20
Mean number refused	.4	.4	.2	.3	.2	.3	.1	.3
Card most refused	VI	IX	VI	VI	VI	IV	IX	IX, VI
Card next most	II	VI	IV	IX		IX	IV	
BOYS AND GIRLS								
Percentage refusing	28	26	15	23	12	26	16	21
M an number refused	.5	.4	.2	.4	.2	.4	.2	.3
Card most refused	IX	IX	VI	VI	IX	IX	IX	IX, VI
Card next most	VI	VI	IV	IX	VI	VI	VII	

girls compared, 22 per cent of all boys refuse cards, 20 per cent of girls. The mean number of cards refused per boy is .4; per girl, .3.

As Table 24 shows, though 12, 14, and 16 are ages of fewest refusals for both sexes, and 10 years is a high point for both, other high points differ somewhat for the sexes.

Tables 24 and 25 further show which cards were most refused. As will be seen, Cards IX and VI were most refused by both boys and girls.

Comparing cards most refused with those least liked, all ages combined but sexes considered separately, we find the following: Boys refuse cards IX and VI most often. They like least cards X, IV, and IX. Girls also refuse most often cards IX and VI. They like least IV, I, and IX. Thus neither sex refuses most the least liked cards except in the case of Card IX.

Conversely, comparing the best liked with the least refused for all ages together but sexes separately: Boys refuse least cards V, I, III, and VIII. They like best cards X, V, VIII. Girls refuse least cards I, V, and VIII. They like best cards X, VII, and III. Here again there is little relationship between cards refused least and liked best except for Cards V and VIII with boys.

DISCUSSION Refusals have always been considered suspect in the adult protocol, and we do not wish here to deny their value as a clinical consideration. However, from 4½ to 10 years, approximately one out of three children refuse at least one card. In the years from 10 to 16, there is no age at which less than 12 per cent of the group refuse at least one card —or about one child out of eight.

Thus we are forced to conclude that refusal of one card by subjects up to 16 years of age is not necessarily suspect unless there are other signs to support clinical significance of such a refusal.

TABLE 25. NUMBER OF SUBJECTS REFUSING CARDS

		10 Years	11 Years	12 Years	13 Years	14 Years	15 Years	16 Years	All
Card I	Boys	3	0	0	1	0	1	0	5
	Girls	0	0	0	0	0	1	0	1
	Both	3	0	0	1	0	2	0	6
Card II	Boys	3	1	2	2	1	1	1	11
	Girls	4	2	0	2	1	0	0	9
	Both	7	3	2	4	2	1	1	20
Card III	Boys	0	2	1	0	0	1	1	5
	Girls	3	0	1	1	0	1	0	6
	Both	3	2	2	1	0	2	1	11
Card IV	Boys	2	5	1	1	1	2	1	13
	Girls	2	2	3	1	0	3	1	12
	Both	4	7	4	2	1	5	2	25
Card V	Boys	0	0	0	0	0	0	0	0
	Girls	3	0	0	0	0	0	0	3
	Both	3	0	0	0	0	0	0	3
Card VI	Boys	6	4	1	2	1	8	1	23
	Girls	4	6	4	7	4	2	0	27
	Both	10	10	5	9	5	10	1	50
Card VII	Boys	2	3	1	5	1	2	3	17
	Girls	1	1	0	0	1	2	0	5
	Both	3	4	1	5	2		3	22
Card VIII	Boys		0		2		1	1	5
	Girls	1	0	1	0	0	1	0	3
	Both	1	0	1	2	1		1	8
Card IX	Boys	11	3	1	2	4	9	3	33
	Girls	3	8	2	6	1	3	4	27
	Both	14	11	3	8	5	12	7	60
Card X	Boys	3	2	1	3	0	2	0	11
	Girls	0	2	1	0	1	1	0	5
	Both	3	4	2	3	1	3	0	16
Totals	Boys	30	20	8	18	9	27	11	
	Girls	21	21	12	17	8	14	5	
	All	51	41	20	35	17	41	16	

Best and Least Liked Cards

After the subject had responded to all 10 cards, the cards were spread out before him and he was asked to indicate which one he liked best and which he liked least.

During the first 10 years of life at nearly every age, Card X was preferred by the majority of girls as well as of boys. As to card least liked, there was more variety. Girls disliked most Cards IV, VI, and II; boys, Cards I, VI, and IV.

In the age range 10 to 16 years, Card X continued to be the best liked card, for both girls and boys, at every age. Only for boys at 12 and 15 years does another card, Card V, approach Card X in popularity.

As to the least liked card: girls, as earlier, most dislike Card IV. This card is most disliked at every age except 12 years when Card I is most disliked, Card IV second most; and at 16 years when Cards IX, VI, and IV are most disliked in that order. Boys, as Table 26 indicates, are much more varied in their dislikes. Oddly enough, Card X is most disliked as well as the most liked at several ages.

Table 26 shows by age and sex the most and the least liked cards.

TABLE 26. BEST AND LEAST LIKED CARDS AT EACH AGE

	Best liked		Least liked	
Ages	*Girls*	*Boys*	*Girls*	*Boys*
10	X	X	IV	IV/X
11	X	X	IV	I (IX)
12	X	X(V)	I (IV)	II (X)
13	X	X	IV	X
14	X	X	IV	X
15	X	X (V)	IV	I (IV, IX)
16	X	X	IX (VI, IV)	II/IX/X

TABLE 27. CHOICE OF INDIVIDUAL CARDS AS BEST AND LEAST LIKED: NUMBER OF CHOICES AS BEST AND LEAST LIKED BY TOTAL SAMPLE OF BOYS AND OF GIRLS

	As best		As least	
	By girls	*By boys*	*By girls*	*By boys*
Card I	8	13	51	39
Card II	21	12	24	32
Card III	31	34	10	15
Card IV	8	11	76	48
Card V	16	47	19	13
Card VI	6	14	36	22
Card VII	45	30	23	28
Card VIII	22	42	20	9
Card IX	21	12	39	44
Card X	114	89	22	59

Card Turning

Card turning may be indicative of initiative and spontaneity. It may also indicate resistance, negativism, or a form of passive aggressivity. It is a possible sign of confusion if it occurs constantly, depending on the response that follows. Or it may indicate the kind of individual who likes to look at things from every angle. A subject who turns the cards may be very sure of himself or very unsure. Card turning may sometimes indicate a block in intellectual or emotional processes, or it may be an evasive symptom.

If a subject never turns a card, it is by no means an adverse sign. The concepts of some subjects are so clear-cut and precise that turning the card does not seem necessary for them. Some subjects prefer to solve a situation as it is presented to them and do not particularly feel impelled to search for other possibilities. For other subjects, the Rorschach test may not be as stimulating as various other projective techniques that may provide outlets more suitable to their type of expression. Lack of card turning may, of course, suggest timidity or extreme conformity. But whatever the reason for card turning or its lack, judgments about it are valid only when incorporated into the total evaluation of an individual protocol and supported by additional signs.

However, we are here interested in the amount of card turning that may be expected in this age range, for whatever reason it may occur. Table 28 presents the percentage of subjects, by sex and age, who turned any

TABLE 28.   CARD TURNING

	10 Years	11 Years	12 Years	13 Years	14 Years	15 Years	16 Years	All
PERCENTAGE OF SUBJECTS SPONTANEOUSLY TURNING ANY CARD								
Boys	72	88	72	78	80	68	68	75
Girls	76	82	80	80	76	72	60	75
PERCENTAGE OF SUBJECTS TURNING CARD III								
Boys	28	42	38	46	40	30	32	37
Girls	28	40	40	38	42	32	36	37
PERCENTAGE OF SUBJECTS TURNING CARD VI								
Boys	40	48	50	52	48	42	54	48
Girls	38	52	50	40	44	50	48	46

card spontaneously at least once during the entire test. These figures do not refer to the actual number of times the cards were turned.

As another index of this same variable, we have chosen two cards out of the ten, and again recorded the number of subjects who turned each card at least once. Card III was chosen, in preference to others, as a card that might likely produce little turning because of the strongly predominant single response it often elicits. Card VI was selected as one that might lend itself more readily to turning because of the possible greater variety of interpretations.

The results from the two cards chosen as samples indicate that Card III, though turned less often than Card VI in our group, was turned by 28 per cent of the boys and girls at 10 years and more frequently thereafter. Card VI was turned by 39 per cent of the boys and girls at 10 years, and increasingly thereafter. About 37 per cent of our total group turned Card III; about 47 per cent of our group turned Card VI.

For the total age group, 75 per cent of subjects spontaneously turn at least one card at least once. The range for the boys for the entire group is from 68 to 88 per cent; for the girls from 60 to 82 per cent.

Initial Exclamations

Initial exclamations given as the subject accepts the card may serve, for the subject, a variety of purposes. They may express hostility to the card or to the examiner: "These awful things!" "I hate this one!" They may act as an acceptable delaying device till the subject can verbalize his actual response: "Let's see." They may express feelings of inadequacy: "Oh dear!" "A tough one!" "Oh brother!" They may sometimes be symptoms of shock. Whatever their specific purpose, it is important that they be recorded fully, for they are spontaneous projections of feelings and attitudes that help us to evaluate an individual protocol more completely.

An analysis of initial remarks given by our present subjects reveals interesting sex and age differences as well as a selective response to the different cards. We have classified initial remarks given by our subjects into two categories: First, actual separate exclamations only, words or phrases verbalized in an exclamatory manner and not mere start-offs of sentences—for instance, "Yikes!" "God!" "Wow!" "Eek!" Second, *all* initial remarks of whatever nature, including such merely introductory words as "Well," even though such a word is actually part of the sentence which follows.

BY CARDS Some cards apparently elicit considerably more initial comment than do others. For each sex separately and for sexes together, whether we consider simply "real" exclamations only or include all introductory verbalizations, Card V elicits the fewest remarks, followed by Cards VII and IX.

For sexes separately and together, and again whether we consider only "real" exclamations or include all introductory comments, Card X attracts the most, followed in order by Cards VIII and III.

BY AGE There appear to be clear age differences in amount of initial comment. Considering either "real" exclamations only, or all preliminary comments of any kind, girls give fewest at 13 years. Boys give fewest at 15, 16, and 13 years. Sexes together, the fewest occur at 15, 16, and 13 years, all about equal.

Considering "real" exclamations only, girls separately and both sexes together give the most at 11, 10, and 12 years. Boys only give the most at 10, 11, and 12 years in that order. Including all kinds of initial exclamations, girls only, and both sexes together, give the most at 11 and 10 years; boys alone at 14 and 11 years.

SEX DIFFERENCES As Table 29 indicates, though any such responses are given somewhat rarely, girls give more than do boys at every age but 13, when boys give slightly more. Girls also give more on every card. This is true whether we consider "real" exclamations only, or whether we include such initial words as "Well," followed immediately by the rest of the sentence.

TABLE 29. INITIAL EXCLAMATIONS

	Girls		Boys		All	
	A*	B*	A	B	A	B
BY AGES						
10 years	65	118	60	87	125	205
11 years	84	128	49	97	133	225
12 years	64	105	48	80	112	185
13 years	41	77	45	78	86	155
14 years	58	90	43	101	101	191
15 years	56	93	26	61	82	154
16 years	55	95	30	51	85	146
All	423	706	301	555	724	1261
BY CARDS						
Card I	36	63	26	55	62	118
Card II	45	78	31	56	76	134
Card III	47	73	36	62	83	135
Card IV	48	74	31	61	79	135
Card V	17	46	14	37	31	83
Card VI	44	66	35	55	79	121
Card VII	39	69	26	45	65	114
Card VIII	51	84	36	64	87	148
Card IX	39	67	25	50	64	117
Card X	57	86	41	70	98	156

* A lists include only separate, exclamatory words. B lists include also such merely introductory words as "well," even though they are actually part of the sentence that follows.

Shock

Rorschach found among the population he studied considerable evidence of what he termed "shock" or difficulty with the color cards. He notes:

Some subjects experience an unmistakable shock, an emotional and associative stupor of varying length, when the colored Plate VIII appears after the preceding black ones. These subjects suddenly become helpless though previously they had been interpreting very well. They find the colored plates more difficult to interpret than the black plates, and they react with astonishment or vexation. Such subjects are always "emotion-repressors," neurotics of varying grades of severity. "Emotion-controllers" show the phenomenon to a lesser extent, not showing shock, but scant production with the colored plates. Subjects who are timid in showing their emotions are found between these two groups; interpretations of the colored plates occasionally become hasty and more fantastic after an initial indication of helplessness before the problem. "Emotion-controllers" show a preference for the blue and green figures which is peculiar to this group, and they avoid the red in a striking way (51, p. 55).

Color shock was the only shock response that Rorschach described. But in subsequent studies, investigators have presented evidence of shock in relation to other cards and with other variables, as for example Piotrowski (47), and Phillips and Smith (46).

Thus, among different possibilities, we have initial shock that may occur at Card I. This is thought to indicate possible difficulty with the father figure, or difficulty with or hostility to authority.

Red shock may occur at Card II or Card III. Since this is the first time any color appears, it is often felt to be a precursor of color shock. Red shock is thought to indicate feelings of repressed hostility together with strong guilt feelings. A more positive aspect is that it may indicate an individual with strong feelings of conscience.

Movement shock is usually defined by the absence of movement on Card III where the two figures are usually seen and where movement is most likely to be expressed. Difficulty with this card is thought to indicate some difficulty in self-identification and/or inadequate or insufficient ego development. It implies a reluctance to accept responsibility and may indicate some lack of independence and self-assertion, or a desire to remain dependent and protected.

Dark shock, also termed Clob shock, most often occurs at Card IV, V, or VI. Difficulty with the darker cards may indicate an extremely sensitive individual whose reserves are not adequate enough to protect him from depressive moods; he may be fearful, easily terrorized, and may tend toward melancholy or even the morbid when he is disturbed or emotionally upset.

Space or white shock may occur at Card VII. Difficulty with this card is thought to indicate possible difficulty with the mother figure or with maternal authority. It may also be related to concern with problems of birth and reproduction.

Signs of shock in any area may be such as those implied by Rorschach for color shock: long regard of the card, difficulty in verbalization, diminution of response, expressions of astonishment or vexation, refusal or attempted refusal, poor form response, and in the case of the color cards, avoidance of the red areas. Additional signs may be a sudden or unusual amount of card turning, sudden appearance of only Dd or Do response at the expense of any other.

Rorschach considered color shock to be a sign of neurosis. Shock in other areas that have been described subsequently does not necessarily indicate neurosis, but the implications are in that direction. By virtue of the difficulties each kind of shock is presumed to indicate, it seems probable that if such a difficulty is marked, neurotic symptoms will be present. (Such a diagnosis, however, should be dependent on adequate and complete evaluation rather than on the test results alone. It appears to us that there are still far too many such responses among the normal population and especially at certain age levels similar to so-called neurotic signs for us to assign diagnosis.)

If the term "shock" is to maintain and justify the full implication of its original meaning, then it should normally be rare, even though it may occasionally appear in a so-called normal population. With the multiplication of the possibilities to indicate shock, at present in at least six areas and on practically every card, then it must necessarily be assigned with even more care and caution.

In our group, we never assigned shock except when a constellation of signs was present. If the "emotion controllers" and those "subjects who are timid in showing their emotions," both of which groups often show signs of tendency to shock, had been included, the frequency would have been in some cases a great deal higher. We felt, however, that with the implications of shock such as they are, and with the hazards in the test greatly multiplied, we were not justified in assigning shock except on clear-cut evidence. Thus the figures we give include only those whom Rorschach terms "emotion repressors," or those showing positive signs of shock, and none of those subjects showing merely "tendency" to shock.

As the figures of Table 30 indicate, positive indication of shock is

TABLE 30. NUMBER OF SUBJECTS SHOWING SHOCK

	10 Years		11 Years		12 Years		13 Years		14 Years		15 Years		16 Years		Total	
	B	G	B	G	B	G	B	G	B	G	B	G	B	G	B	G
Initial	2	0	2	1	2	1	0	3	1	1	4	0	0	0	11	6
Red	1	6	0	2	3	1	5	3	1	0	3	0	2	0	15	12
Movement	2	1	1	0	5	2	6	3	2	4	3	1	3	0	22	11
Dark	1	5	4	3	1	4	2	2	2	4	1	2	1	2	12	27
Space	0	1	4	2	0	0	2	1	1	0	1	2	4	0	12	6
Color	2	3	0	4	0	3	4	3	2	0	2	2	5	2	13	17

rare at any age, and for any one type of shock. In our earlier work concerned with children from 2 to 10 years of age, we indicated that at no age do more than 28 per cent of the children give positive indications of any type of shock (1). The highest incidence for any one type of shock in the age range from 10 to 16 years is for movement shock at 13 years. Dark shock is the only category where the frequency line is unbroken, although the range is only from 1 to 7 children here.

Thus, shock in one or several areas is certainly not unknown in the age range from 10 to 16 years in what we consider a normal population, but the group expectancy is never high. In fact, at no age nor for any category of shock can shock be considered an expected tendency, according to the results in our group.

Boys exceed in the totals for all categories of shock at 13, 15, and 16 years; girls exceed at 10 and 11 years; at 12 and 14 years, they appear to be equal. High point for boys for all categories of shock is at 13 years; for girls at 11 years. Low point for boys for total of all categories is at 10 years; for girls at 16 years.

If we look at the totals for the entire age range and for both boys and girls, we note that the boys appear to show more vulnerability to initial, movement, and space shock, while the girls exceed in dark shock.

Although the figures are always small, there may perhaps be some indication here that boys give more evidence of hostility to authority in any form, but have stronger feelings of conscience and feelings of guilt, and perhaps have less conflict over self-assertion than do girls. They also give evidence of slower maturing independence and fewer feelings of responsibility than do girls. The girls on the other hand appear to be more prone to minor, melancholy feelings and seem to repress their emotions more readily than the boys.

Nature of Adjectives

In an attempt to discover age and sex differences in the affect projected into Rorschach records, a classification was made of the adjectives subjects used. All adjectives used at each age were listed and then classified as pleasant, unpleasant, or neutral. Thus such adjectives as *good, gay, nice, fancy* were considered pleasant; *sad, deformed, distorted, diseased* were considered unpleasant; *big, little, young, old, red, blue* were considered neutral.

Certain adjectives, such as *fancy, new,* etc., though predominantly used in a favorable connotation, occasionally seemed to be used with negative meaning. However, we have classified them as they were most commonly used. While exceptions could doubtless be taken to a few assignments of adjectives, they were sorted in the same way at all ages and for both sexes, and it is the group differences that are of interest here rather than the absolute percentages in single groups.

Neutral or nonaffect adjectives were found to predominate at all ages, the number of pleasant plus unpleasant adjectives given at any one age ranging only from 15 to 27 per cent of the total.

Of these affect adjectives, at every age and for both sexes, unpleasant adjectives predominated over pleasant. However, the extent to which affect or emotion-toned adjectives were predominantly unpleasant varied considerably from age to age.

With boys, there appears to be no general over-all trend toward increase or decrease of unpleasant adjectives, but several high points and low points stand out. The largest percentage of unpleasant adjectives is given by boys at 15 years, the next largest at 13. Conversely, 13-year-olds give the fewest pleasant adjectives. At 13 years, there are more than four times as many unpleasant as pleasant adjectives for boys, and at 15 years nearly three times as many. Pleasant adjectives occur most at 11, 12, 14, and 16 years.

With girls, there is an over-all increase in the total number of adjectives given, with low points at 13 and 15 years, also a steady increase in the percentage of adjectives that are emotion-toned. The highest percentage of unpleasant adjectives for girls occurs at 15 years, next highest at 12 and 13. At 13 years there are fewest pleasant adjectives—four times as many unpleasant as pleasant. The high point for pleasant adjectives comes, for girls, at 16 years, at which age only there are virtually as many pleasant as unpleasant.

Table 31 presents these comparisons. Samples of characteristic adjec-

TABLE 31. NATURE OF ADJECTIVES: NUMBER OF ADJECTIVES RECORDED AT EACH AGE AND PERCENTAGE OF ADJECTIVES CLASSIFIED AS PLEASANT AND UNPLEASANT

		Percentage of Adjectives		
Age	*Number of adjectives*	*Pleasant*	*Unpleasant*	*Pleasant + unpleasant*
		BOYS		
10	293	7%	15%	22%
11	320	9	14	23
12	287	8	13	21
13	273	4	18	22
14	249	8	16	24
15	213	7	20	27
16	248	8	15	24
		GIRLS		
10	380	6%	9%	15%
11	385	5	14	19
12	417	5	16	21
13	319	4	16	20
14	434	7	15	22
15	365	5	17	22
16	506	12	13	25

tives used are given in Chapters 10 to 16, in the characterizations of each age level.

CHAPTER NINE

The Individual Cards

The score distributions and age changes that we have been discussing are, of course, based upon and build up from changing responses to the individual Rorschach cards. Responses are not, however, evenly distributed over the ten cards, for the cards differ in their stimulus value and tend to call forth different types of responses. Ranzoni, Grant, and Ives (49) refer to this tendency of the different blots to evoke particular area, determinant, or content responses as Rorschach "card-pull."

To the clinician, a knowledge of the stimulus value of each card is of crucial importance in interpreting any individual protocol. The summation of scores in a psychogram may give him his initial conceptions of the subject's personality structure, but he must always return to the individual responses themselves to confirm these conceptions. The W% in a psychogram, for example, cannot tell him whether the Ws were simple total globals or well-constructed wholes, whether they occurred on the relatively difficult Card IX and X or only on I and V. Such considerations help determine whether the W is to be interpreted as an indication of planfulness, with ability to abstract and synthesize, or of a simple, gross level of perception characteristic of the preschool child.

Until lately, the clinician has had to rely upon wide experience with the test to build up his own subjective norms of what responses are common and what uncommon on the different cards. But Ranzoni, Grant, and Ives (49) have recently presented frequencies for individual scoring categories by cards for their adolescent group, and Klopfer *et al.* (40) and Richards (50) have given qualitative descriptions of what responses the cards facilitate in an adult population.

The findings of the present chapter are based upon detailed frequency tabulations of a great variety of scores and "items" for each individual card. Only the more clear-cut age trends and sex differences are described here, since many of the data proved inconsistently variable and somewhat ambiguous.

Card I

Card I presents an easy introduction to the Rorschach task. Very few subjects fail to respond to this relatively well-defined form; only Card V produces fewer refusals.

A W is the most common response to this card, occurring more frequently by far than normal detail, rare detail, or white space used alone. Three main kinds of W appear: a global W (bird, bat, or butterfly); a WS featuring the white spaces, usually as eyes (face, mask); and W organizing the blot into side and central figures, either as three people or animals or as two side figures acting on the center.

The WS face response is the most frequent at 10 years of age, making up over half of the whole responses. Thereafter it declines in usage, until around 14 years, when it is the least used of the three types of W, though it then increases again at 15 and 16. The decrease occurs earlier and more sharply in girls than boys. For the latter it remains a leading type of response throughout the age range. At all ages, animal face responses are more common than human faces.

The usual adult popular—bird, butterfly, or bat—makes up only 25 per cent of the 10-year-olds' W responses, but increases steadily throughout the age range to about 40 per cent by age 16, again with girls preceding boys in reaching this level.

The organized W, with separate side and central figures, is often a highly revealing response, particularly when these figures interact in a movement response. The curve for this W form mirrors that for the WS face response, with a steady increase in usage from age 10 to 14, followed by a decrease. For the girls this curve is dramatically sharp, increasing from 20 to 40 per cent usage. For boys the over-all trend is similar, but boys give fewer organized Ws and their curve is flatter. (Occurring so early in the test, this re-emphasizes the girls' concern with personal interaction at age 14.)

Though Klopfer indicates that "for subjects who see human figures with any facility, this card should evoke *M* responses. . . . " (40, p. 320), at no age do more than 30 per cent of boys or girls give M responses, nor do more than 16 per cent of boys or 10 per cent of girls give FM responses. Peaks for both of these occur at 14 years in boys, 12 years in girls. Inanimate movement is negligible, and shading responses are rare, but increase with age.

The mention of ghosts, devils, or witches on this card is more common at the earlier ages (10 and 13 among boys, 10 and 12 among girls), and more common among girls than boys. Girls are also more likely to mention the headlessness of the central figure, especially from 10 to 13 years, and they seem in general to place more emphasis on the central part of the blot.

Card II

As with Card I, a W response is by far the most frequent form of response to Card II. The popular form, two persons or animals, is the most common response at all ages and tends to increase slightly with age. Over all, about 70 per cent of girls give this response, about 50 per cent of boys. The "two animals" version of this popular form is more common than the "two persons" version during the early part of our age range for both boys and girls. But while this continues to be true also of the later years for the boys, for the girls "two persons" becomes slightly the more common by age 14 and continues so thereafter. "Two birds" as a variant of this form is not common, but appears to increase with age.

The WS response is far less common than on Card I. Particularly when seen as a single face (the center white as mouth or nose), this has been considered an immature response, and the general decrease in frequency over this age range lends confirmation to that interpretation. Among girls, the WS response is relatively frequent at 10 years (22 per cent for girls), but thereafter drops sharply. It is likewise common among 10-year-old boys, and continues with considerable frequency through 14 years, declining thereafter.

A third type of W response is the total global, usually a bug or butterfly, but occasionally a single animal or even a person (then generally seen ∨). For the whole age range this is given by only about 15 per cent of boys and girls, and seems to show an over-all decline among girls and no defined trend among boys.

Use of white space alone is slightly more common among girls than boys, with peaks at 12 and 14 for the girls, at 13 and 14 for the boys. At even these peak ages it is used by fewer than 20 per cent of the group; at all other ages by fewer than 10 per cent.

The subject's response to the first introduction of color is a significant feature for individual interpretation. It is important to note, therefore, that at no age does more than a third of the group give color responses to this card. Boys and girls give about equal numbers of color responses for the total age range, with neither group showing marked age trends, except that both show low points at 15 years.

The popular response to this card, two persons or animals, is usually enlivened with movement of some sort, and a majority of all subjects give some kind of movement. Among girls this tends more often to be human movement, among boys it is more often animal movement. Over all, M is given by about 40 per cent of girls and 25 per cent of boys, while FM is given by about 30 per cent of both groups.

As judged by the number of children unable or unwilling to respond at all to the blot, Card II is about average in difficulty for the Rorschach series. It does present problems to a few 10-years-olds, however, for seven children fail to respond to it. The number of refusals drops steadily from this point.

Card III

The total number of responses given to Card III is greater than that for Cards I or II, because the number of detail responses increases markedly while the number of whole (including cut-off whole) responses remains about the same. The separateness of the red portions from the rest of the blot apparently facilitates the D response, for D is more common on Card III than on any other of the first seven cards.

The W (or W̸) response, however, remains the most common single response to the card, in the great majority of cases being the popular "two human figures." At all ages this response is given by at least half the group, and the response shows a steady increase with age, being given by about 75 per cent of the 16-year-olds. This trend is more strongly evident among girls than among boys (as seems often to be the case with age trends). Two men are seen far more frequently than two women; two cannibals, and the like, are seen very infrequently except by 16-year-old girls. Two skeletons are somewhat more common, but show a decreasing age trend, appearing most commonly at age 11.

It is interesting that the preschool form of this popular, two animals, is still given by a handful of subjects as late as 16 years. No age trend appears in this curve, which remains level at about 7 per cent of the group from 10 to 16.

Another apparently immature form of perception—the WS response —shows somewhat more of a downward trend. The perseveration of a single WS animal face response on III, following similar responses on Cards I and II, is most characteristic of the 5- to 5½-year level of perception (1), yet a very few of these responses appear in this sample, nearly all at 10 and 11 years. Other WS responses include human, anatomy, and bug responses. Among girls the decline in the WS response is pronounced; among boys the curve is more level, with 20 per cent still giving WS responses at 16 years.

Response to the red areas of the blot occurs in about half the girls, about a third of the boys, for the total age range. The boys' response is a decreasing one, while the girls' response to these details rises to a peak at 14 years and then decreases. The responses are not often color responses, however, for just 10 per cent of the boys and 6 per cent of the girls have primary color scores.

Human movement, on the other hand, is used by a sizable majority at all ages—from two thirds to four fifths of the different age groups. As many authors have pointed out, the absence of movement on this card is noteworthy. FM is much less common than M, and both m and F(C) are unusual on III.

Card IV

Card IV, more of a total unit than Card III, again facilitates a greater proportion of W responses (though not a greater absolute number), and produces many fewer D. Analysis of this blot is interesting because of the clarity with which it portrays the steady decline of a childhood popular, the "giant" figure, and the increase of the adult popular, animal skin.

The animal skin response is an unusual one in the years before 10, and at 10 years it appears in only about 10 per cent of subjects. By 12 years and thereafter it appears in about 35 per cent of subjects. This tends to be a masculine response, being given by nearly twice as many boys as girls at all ages.

The W human (or humanlike) figure, on the other hand, declines from nearly 60 per cent frequency at 10 and 11 years to less than 25 per cent by 15 years. The most common form of this popular is "a person" or "a man," followed in frequency by more depersonalized forms (giant, scarecrow, monster) and then by humanlike animal forms (ape or bear). The sex of the figure is always seen as male or is unspecified; no subject sees it as female. In view of this it is interesting that at all ages more girls than boys give this response, that the response decreases far less among girls than among boys, and that a decided increase in the response occurs among girls at 16 years, with just over half the girls seeing this form (compared with 10 per cent of the boys).

One component of the W human figure response that does not show the over-all decrease in usage is the response "boots" or "feet" alone. In the under-10 age range this is an uncommon response, actually scored Do because of the frequency with which most children generalize the form to a total figure. As the total figure response declines, however, the boots response increases—much more markedly in the case of boys, less clearly so among girls. With boys, the boots response is slightly more common than the whole figure response by 15 years, and three times as frequent by 16. Girls, however, show fewer indications of refining (or repressing) the total figure form, and if they remark on the boots are likely to do so as an elaboration of the total figure.

A third important W response on IV is the bird-bug-butterfly response (often with the card ∨). This response, somewhat more common among boys than girls, shows no marked age trend, but is made by about 20 per cent of the sample at each age.

Card IV is about average in the series for the amount of human and animal movement it calls forth. The amount of human movement given by both boys and girls shows a fairly steady decrease from age 10 to 15, which is not surprising in the light of the disappearance of the human figure. FM maintains a steadier course.

Card IV is second only to VI in the amount of shading produced.

This shows a steady rise from age 10 to 14, when it levels off. Though boys give many more animal skin responses than girls, the number of actual shading responses (which generally relate to this form) is about equal for the two sexes.

A number of factors on Card IV—its darkness, its shaded values, and the unevenness of its edges—apparently combine to facilitate dysphoric responses from many subjects. In the under-10 age range, the qualification of the basic form as being old, ragged, torn, decayed, was fairly common, reaching a peak at 7 years of age and appearing much more often in boys. In adolescence, this same response shows a resurgence, which occurs more often among girls than boys and, surprisingly, occurs later in girls than boys. Such responses are given by boys only at ages 10 to 13, and even at the peak age, 12 years, only about 10 per cent of the boys give this old, dead, broken projection. Among girls the ages covered are 12 to 14 years, with over 20 per cent of girls making this response at 14 years. The highly dysphoric, primitive response, dead, rotted leaf or tree is actually given by 10 per cent of the 14-year-old girls. Such responses are obviously suggestive of body-image problems.

Card IV is the blot least often chosen as liked, most often chosen as disliked by the total sample. It is seen by many subjects as a difficult blot, and is refused more often than any other except IX and VI, though by few children at most single ages. However, 10 per cent of the 11-year-old boys fail to make any response to this card.

Card V

Card V is clearly the simplest blot in the series. It is refused least often of any (by three girls at age 10 and no other subjects) and produces the greatest uniformity of response. Failure to give the winged animal response is an unusual event at all ages.

Of the alternative forms of this popular response, bat and butterfly or moth appear with nearly equal frequency for the age range as a whole, but the bat response declines slightly with age, while butterfly or moth holds steady or increases. Bird is a much less common response, appearing in about 10 per cent of records, while winged bugs, mosquitoes, etc., are uncommon variants at all ages.

Card V evokes the greatest proportion of W responses of any blot. Details, if given at all, are usually given in addition to the popular W response, not in place of it. The only details given with frequency are the center portion alone, most often as a rabbit, and the side projections, most often as crocodile heads. The former response is given by girls mainly at ages 11 and 12, by boys at 11 to 13. The latter shows little age trend, appearing in about 10 per cent of records throughout the series.

A W response that is not common but is of considerable interest is that in which the two sides of the blot, or the two sides and the center, are seen as separate but interacting figures, human or animal. Almost invariably this DW is seen with M, FM, or m determinants, often of a violent nature ("bulls crashing their heads together," "a person crushed between rocks"), as if powerful movement were required to tear this blot apart. Through 13 years this form of response is infrequent, always below 10 per cent incidence, but an increase appears at 14 years that continues at 15, and reaches 18 per cent at 16 years, being more frequent among girls than boys.

Klopfer remarks that, "If the subject tends to see FM at all, it is to be expected here . . . " (40, p. 324). This we do not find to be the case among our adolescent subjects, for the vast majority of the bats and butterflies are simple form responses. About 15 per cent of our subjects use FM on Card V, with the curve showing a gradual decline from 10 to 15 years, followed by an upward turn at 16, among girls especially. The increase in FM at 16 relates more to the girls' increased usage of interacting side figures than to increasing enlivenment of the popular form. The use of other nonform determinants is uncommon, except for a few M given by girls at 16 years.

Card VI

As is true for all the first seven cards, a majority of responses on Card VI are W responses. Use of the top detail alone follows this in frequency; then use of the lower, larger portion of the blot alone. Other details are used infrequently.

Card VI resembles Card IV in that the bearskin response emerges as a popular in this age period. As on IV, more boys than girls give this response. However, the bearskin on VI is a stronger popular than the one on IV, and it had already become common among boys at 9 years. Before 8 years it was almost never used (though a live animal was often seen, and then later a dead animal, which eventually becomes the animal skin). Close to 40 per cent of the 9-years-old boys in our earlier sample gave the bearskin response, and about half as many girls. Over 75 per cent of the present sample of 10-year-old boys give this response, and about 25 per cent of the girls do. Thereafter, the response levels off at about 50 per cent usage by boys and 30 per cent by girls.

No other single W response is very common. Use of the whole blot as a single animal or insect occurs with some frequency at 10 years, but thereafter declines. DW responses, separating and then recombining upper and lower portions ("totem pole on a rock"), are varied in content and are not frequent at any age. An interesting response that appears first with the girls at 12 years and with the boys at 13 is the "landscape" response, given with the card in a side position and the landscape reflected.

Among details, use of the top projection as insect, bird, bat, or animal is the most common. This response is given much more often by girls than by boys. The top D also gives rise to a "totem pole" interpretation with some frequency—slightly more often by girls than boys. It is interesting to see that at 10 and 11 years this response is usually generalized to the whole card. Thereafter, the top detail alone is increasingly discriminated for this interpretation.

Interpretations of the mid-line are infrequent, though a few appear at each age. The most frequently used mid-line responses are bedpost, backbone, and snake.

It is often noted that an important feature of Card VI is its facilitation of shading responses. Klopfer states that, "If the subject responds to shading at all it is likely to be on this card; failure to do so is noteworthy" (40, p. 324). Shading is most often used as texture, generally as part of the animal skin interpretation, but the animal skin response is by no means always enlivened with texture. About half of these P responses are apparently determined by form alone. Use of shading is increasingly common with age, rising from 12 per cent at 10 years to over 30 per cent by 16.* Girls giving shading responses consistently outnumber boys.

Though its importance is not as often noted, m is a common variable on VI. It is nearly as common as F(C), but does not show the consistent increase with age. Rather, it rises to a peak of 25 per cent use at 13 years, then drops again to 15 per cent at 16. Many of these m relate to the animal skin ("stretched out"), but a fair number are explosion or shooting movements.

Among adults, the details of Card VI are found often to facilitate sex responses, in either overt or symbolic form. In our adolescent group, this card produced no mention of sex anatomy and only one direct reference to a sex-related function ("grasshopper laying eggs"). Many responses do suggest the subject's attitude toward sex. Contrast, for example, the solitary "lighthouse on a rock" with either "a dragonfly entering a flower" or "snails trying to crawl out of a pile of dirt." But the interpretation of sex implications in content is sufficiently an individual matter that tabulation of responses having probable or possible sexual significance would be of dubious value, and age and sex trends are not discussed here.

Card VI is one of the most difficult cards in the series, second only to IX in number of refusals elicited. As many as 10 per cent of subjects reject this card at three different ages (10, 11, and 15 years). Whether the problem presented by the card is more a cognitive one or an emotional

---

* This is one of the few points at which our findings appear to differ considerably from those of Ranzoni, Grant, and Ives (49), who report a higher incidence of F(C). The difference may well lie either in different inquiry techniques or different scoring assumptions.

one cannot be decided except in the individual case. However, the fact that the card offers a definite popular form suggests that the blockage is less a matter of a difficult shape to interpret, more one of disturbing implications in the shading values or the sexual overtones.

Card VII

Card VII lends itself most readily to a W or DW interpretation, most often with two persons or animals involved. In the case of animal interpretations the two upper tiers are usually described as the animals, while the third tier is named as the object or natural background on which they are seen. In the case of human interpretations the whole blot is more often seen as making up the human figures. Following this response in frequency is that which uses only the two top tiers as animals or humans in a D response. Only at 10 years are animals seen more often than humans in this form, but both the two animals and the two persons responses reach the criterion for scoring as a popular response.

Though D responses are outnumbered by W's, each tier is interpreted separately by a few children at each age. For tier 1 the most frequent interpretation is person's or animal's head; for tier 2, animal head; while the lower tiers from each side are most often interpreted together as a butterfly or moth.

One other area worth mentioning is the center detail of the bottom tier. Use of this detail is rare among boys, never reaching 10 per cent frequency, but among girls it increases constantly throughout the age range to 24 per cent usage at 15 years. Interpretations for this detail include, besides the usual house, church, hinge, or candle response, such responses as Niagara Falls, passageway between rocks, violin part where you twist the strings, flower petal, stigma where pollen is. It is perhaps here, as much as in Cards IV and VI, that we can look for a reflection of concern with sexual development and emotions.

Interpretation of the center white area alone occurs with about 5 per cent frequency throughout the age range, and incorporation of the center white into a WS response with about 7 per cent frequency. Thus, although it is not frequent, neither is it highly unusual to have an interpretation of the center white space. The content of such responses is highly varied, seldom occurring more than once in 100 protocols.

The determinant category most often used, following F, is M, used by close to 33 per cent of the subjects at nearly all ages and by more girls than boys. After a peak of 30 per cent usage at 10 years, FM drops to 20 per cent usage thereafter. Altogether, very close to 50 per cent of subjects use either M or FM in response to Card VII.

Use of shading increases from about 10 per cent to about 20 per cent over the age range. Although VII is often thought to be readily interpreted by a shading response such as cloud or smoke, only a few such responses occurred in the entire sample. More often, the subject's impression of diffusion and haziness was incorporated into a more formal response, such as two persons in fog or two animals on a cloud. The interpretation of clouds or smoke alone is more characteristic of an earlier period, centering around 4 and 5 years.

Card VIII

Card VIII presents a contrast to all the preceding cards in that D area responses are given more frequently than W's. (This is the beginning of a D trend that becomes more pronounced on each succeeding card.) Some variety of W response is still given by about 50 per cent of the girls and about 60 per cent of the boys, but the number of D's exceeds number of W's at every age.

Probably as important as the introduction of color or the "good articulation" of the subparts of the blot in causing this D emphasis is the fact that the side details actually do resemble animals to a striking degree. A consensual validation of this is afforded by the finding that well over 90 per cent of all our subjects give some sort of animal interpretation to these areas. A subject's failure to do so, particularly if he resists this interpretation when it is later suggested to him, is therefore a decidedly atypical reaction, and one that prompts further inquiry into its cause.

Among the younger subjects in this study, the W trend is still so strong that nearly half of all these animal responses are embedded in a DW response, with the subjects including the center portion of the blot in such responses as animals climbing a tree, a mountain, rocks, or even just "animals climbing something." With age this DW response declines, particularly among girls, indicating their more critical appraisal of the total form. Those DW responses that are given become increasingly sophisticated, such as the "animal crossing stumps and rocks at the water's edge, with his reflection."

The types of animals given fall almost entirely in the mammal category. A few fish, frogs, and lizards are given at each age, but these are all unusual responses. Rather surprisingly, the girls tend to respond with larger animals than do boys. Bears are given twice as often by girls; mice and rats twice as often by boys. Foxes, wolves, mountain lions, etc., are the most common animals given, and are given about equally by boys and girls.

Klopfer reports that among adults, "To see animal figures in the side pink D's and to attribute movement to them is so frequent that absence of this response is noteworthy" (40, p. 325). Among our subjects, almost exactly half of the responses that include this P form are FM responses. There appears to be a decrease with age in FM responses on this card, which decline from about 50 per cent usage at 10 and 11 years to about 35 per cent at 15 and 16. As usual, boys tend to give more FM responses than girls.

Besides this popular figure, the other striking feature of Card VIII is, of course, the introduction of color. Fewer than half the subjects at any age, however, make use of this new feature in a color response, with the exception of the 16-year-olds. In all groups, with this one exception, very close to 25 per cent of subjects give CF responses, 10 per cent give FC, and 4 per cent give C responses. At 16, closer to 50 per cent give CF, though the other color scores do not change. Girls slightly but consistently exceed boys in use of color.

Though the requirement of responding to a colored blot is a new one for the subject, it is not apparently a very difficult one. Card VIII is among the least often refused of the series, no more than one or two children rejecting it at any age. In this respect it stands in sharp contrast to the following card.

Card IX

Card IX, with its vague, overlapping forms and blurred outlines, appears to present the greatest challenge of any blot in the series. No single interpretation is strongly enough suggested by any area to provide a simple, popular response for the subject. The impact of this difficult and often disturbing blot is first to produce a high rate of rejections and second to encourage a great diversity among the responses given.

Outright rejection of the card is more frequent than for any other, occurring in nearly 10 per cent of subjects. Refusal is most common at ages 10, 11, and 15. Fewest refusals occur at 12, 14, and 16 years, ages at which refusal on any card is unusual.

In their attempt to meet the challenge of this blot, it is as if our subjects were thrown increasingly on their own. Intragroup variation is especially wide; age and sex differences are often erratic, varying from group to group. Responses spread out over a wide range of area, determinant, and content categories. Against this background of diversity, the responses of the individual children tend to stand out for their personal quality. Individual responses are less likely to be just run of the mill, because the blot itself offers no strong suggestion of a particular form and the individual must play a more active role in choosing his stimulus. It is apparently for this reason that responses on this card often furnish the most striking clues to the individual's values and self concepts.

In area choice, D responses predominate, W responses continue to decline, and Dd and S become relatively prominent. About a third of the children in the group as a whole achieve W responses. The age trend for W is curvilinear, with about 50 per cent of subjects using W at age 10, dropping to 25 per cent by age 14, and increasing to nearly 50 per cent again at 16. This relates to the fact that the blot itself does not facilitate a simple but good W response; W's tend either to be gross and immature or else well detailed. At 10 years we find a large proportion of the W's made up of such gross forms as "painting" or "child's design," along with a number of W's using positional cues (seen ∨, with the orange as legs— usually a "person dressed up"), though the girls also produce a number of constructed DW ("witches in clouds of mist"). By 16 the positional W's have disappeared and more complex W's increase, particularly natural scenes.

Complementing the curve for W is that for Dd and S. About 20 per cent of all subjects give such responses. A steady increase in use of these areas occurs from 10 to 14 years, followed by a drop at 15 and 16.

Unlike some of the other blots, Card IX permits use of any of the Rorschach determinants, and at each age all the determinants have been used. M and CF are the ones most often used, with about 20 per cent of subjects using each. F(C) and m are each used by about 15 per cent of subjects, and FM by about 10 per cent. FC and C are least often used. Every one of these nonform determinants is used more often by girls than by boys, the difference being most striking in the case of shading. Age trends are largely absent.

The content of girls' responses likewise tends to be more dramatic than that of the boys. Girls produce more scenes and nature responses, including more fire, clouds, and smoke, more reflections. It is interesting that girls' m tends to occur in water forms—fountains and waterfalls— while boys' m more often appears in explosions and eruptions.

Card X

Following the relatively compact, difficult Card IX, with its obscure forms, Card X presents a sharp contrast. Its forms are separated and discrete, brightly colored, well defined. The impact of this card is often striking and is usually stimulating, for it is seldom refused, it calls forth a high output of responses, and it is by far the most often chosen as the best liked card. It is, however, a disturbing blot to some subjects who dislike its scattery quality, and it is chosen by a sizable group as the least liked card.* More girls than boys choose Card X as liked, more boys than girls choose it as disliked.

The number of responses given to Card X by far exceeds the number given to the blot eliciting the second greatest number (Card VIII). The vast majority of responses are normal details, for 80 per cent of subjects

---

* Preliminary research into the Rorschach responses of subjects with particular visual patterns suggests that this card is a particularly difficult one for a certain group of myopes.

give D's and well over 80 per cent of all responses given are D's. Nevertheless, some 40 per cent of subjects still manage to give W responses. This proportion is slightly higher for boys than for girls, and tends to decline somewhat over the age period, but in all groups it ranges narrowly between 33 and 50 per cent.

The most common response to X is a listing of different animal figures. It sometimes seems a short step from this listing to making the generalization that will incorporate the separate animals into a total scene. This "animal scene" is the most common type of W response, followed by sea scenes and then by garden scenes. In general, whole responses on this card tend strongly to be "collection" or "enumeration" W's, a listing followed by a generalization or vice versa. Boys more often give W's, while girls more often simply list details.

The most frequent response on this card, whether in a W, a listing of D's, or alone, is the popular crab form, given by just over half of all subjects. The rabbit's face, considered popular by Hertz (26), Klopfer (40), and Beck (4) just barely achieves the one-in-six frequency criterion. The green worms, considered popular by Hertz and Klopfer, but not by Beck, fall just below this criterion, if tabulated regardless of whether or not color is mentioned. Klopfer (40) considers mention of color necessary for the scoring of this form as P; however, color was mentioned by only about half of our subjects who did give this response.

Surprising to us was the finding that among girls use of the center yellow forms as dogs is second only to the popular crabs response. These dogs were seen by over 20 per cent of the girls, only 7 per cent of the boys. (The generality of this finding rests not only on the samples but on the specific set of blots used, however, since Gurvitz (19) notes that in some editions of the plates the yellow dogs are very faintly outlined.)

It is usual for subjects to use some nonform determinant in their response to card X. Even though more F responses are given than any other type, only 30 per cent of subjects give solely F responses. Use of form only is most common at age 15, when 36 per cent use no other determinant; least common at 16, when only 14 per cent of subjects fail to enliven some response on X.

Though the bright color of this blot is apparently a stimulating factor, it does not necessarily stimulate the subject to give color responses. FM is the most common enlivened response, used by over a third of the subjects. M and m each occur in about 10 per cent of records. CF is used by about 25 per cent of subjects, FC by two thirds as many as use CF.

Part Two

CHAPTER TEN

Ten Years*

16R	65%F	47%A
	92%F+	17%H
52%W		2.0 objects
45%D	2.0M, 2.4FM, .6m	.5 anatomy
3%Dd	.3FC, .9CF, .2C	.5 nature
	.7F(C)	.5 plant
	Mean 2.0M:1.3ΣC	6P
	Median 1.7M:1.1ΣC	

Ten years of age can be viewed as a turning point in the growth of behavior. It is a focal age that both completes one subcycle of development and begins another. Ten is still clearly a childhood age, in many ways culminating the developments of preceding years. Eleven brings a new range of emotions, new stirrings and strivings, which relate more to the adolescent years to come (11).

In Rorschach response, Ten as compared with Nine shows an increased maturity, a calming down, a better equilibrium, an improved critical ability. The 10-year-old seems mature indeed as compared with himself one year earlier. At the same time, Ten marks only the beginning of the cycle of years under discussion here and, as compared with the years that immediately follow, the Rorschach response of the 10-year-old is in many ways strikingly childlike.

Comparing the characteristic response of Ten with Nine, we note the

---

* This chapter and the age chapters that follow present a succession of "composite Rorschachs" for the yearly age levels of our sample. The descriptions point up both central trends and particular features that occur strikingly at a given age, contrasting it with other ages, even though some of the features may not occur in a majority of cases. While our characterization may sometimes sound absolute and sweeping—"Ten does such-and-such"—this is intended only as a device for summarizing important steps in the developmental sequence which we have found with our particular sample.

Heading each age chapter is an "average psychogram." The figures given are medians for the age, except in the case of the enlivened determinants, which occur with low frequency. For M, FM, m, FC, CF, C, and F(C), mean scores are given.

following major changes. Though total number of responses is about the same, the balance of areas chosen for response is quite different. At 9, D% definitely predominates over W%. At 10, mean W% is 51 per cent, mean D% only 41 per cent. At 9, color responses definitely exceed movement. At 10, the mean M (2.0) is greater than the mean ΣC (1.3). Thus the 9-year-old response is characteristically extratensive and detailed. Ten is more global and, for the first time, introversive.

Along with increased introversivity comes apparently a lessening of disturbance areas. Thus, as compared with 9 years of age, Ten shows somewhat fewer shading responses, fewer Clob responses, fewer small details, relatively fewer Hd, lower C. Greater critical ability is suggested by an increased F+%.

When compared with the years that immediately follow, the 10-year-old response is seen to be considerably more global than it will be later. At 10, animal movement continues to predominate slightly over human, though this will not occur conspicuously hereafter. Though human movement responses predominate over color here as at other teen and pre-teen ages, ΣC at 10 is relatively higher than in the years that follow until 16. (Also, the percentage of subjects giving some color comes nearer to that giving some human movement than at any other age but 11.) Shading responses, on the other hand, are far lower than in the succeeding years. A% fluctuates but tends to decrease after 10; H% also fluctuates but tends to increase slightly.

Though leading content categories do not change conspicuously during the age period 10 to 16, we find such categories as architecture, design, blood, and fire higher at 10 than they will be at most subsequent ages, while reflection, objects, anatomy, flower, nature are lower.

Compared to that of the following ages, we find Ten's Rorschach response to be somewhat restricted. Mean R of 19 is lower than at any following age except the extremely restricted Fifteen. Only at 15 is mean M lower, and only at 11 is F(C) lower. Furthermore, there are more refusals of blots (mean .5) and a higher percentage of subjects giving refusals (28 per cent) than at any subsequent age. Both A% and number of popular responses are high.

Perhaps the outstanding aspect of the Rorschach response at 10 years of age is the difficulty many children of this age seem to have in defining and in expressing what they see. There is much indecision, qualification, changing of mind. But at the same time a very large proportion of response, especially in girls, is popular response. Thus the 10-year-old goes through a great deal only to come out in approximately one out of three responses with a merely popular response.

Uncertainty and inability either to identify blots or to express that identification clearly are seen more in boys at this age than in girls, but they occur in both sexes. There is some giving of response followed by outright denial: (IX) "Fiery people and the way they look." (Fire?) "No. I said it but I changed my mind." More frequently, however, we get alternative answers, vague answers, an inability to say exactly what is meant, rather than outright denial. Thus there are a great many simple alternate responses given: "Moth or bat," "Two cats or a lamb or a bulldog," "Skeleton or a bell." At later ages, two such alternatives are often allowed to stand. At 10, most often the earlier concept is denied: "Looks like a bug or something. Not a bug"; "This part looks like a rabbit. Or no, maybe a child with a horse's tail (hair)." Or "Bears. Not bears. Sort of like bears."

There is a great deal of difficulty in giving an exact description, and much reliance on the phrase, "Or something." Thus "Ant or something"; "Looks something like a cave or something"; "Two bats or ghosts trying to get into whatever this thing is in the middle."

Even greater vagueness is shown in such characteristic statements as: (II) "Looks like someone's, looks like, uh, some kind of face in there. Not actually a face. Looks like some kind of a design or an animal"; (III) "Well, this looks sort of like a person with a funny . . . well, it would be kind of hard to explain, but they look sort of like something."

Some subjects state plainly that this is only a guess, or that they don't really know: "A couple of boys arguing on a stone. They don't really look like them but that's my best guess"; "Well this isn't correct I know, but it reminds me of Tom Corbett's adventures with robot things." In others, uncertainty leads on into form contamination: "Let's see now, it could be, I think it could be a, I don't know, well, only thing I can think of is a cottage. Has wings and chicken feet with walk around."

General uncertainty may lead the subject to confuse human with animal forms: (VII) "This would be an animal and this would be their dresses and blouses"; (VII) "This looks like some person's head. Like a dog's head, boxer type"; (II) "Two people, no two bears. Two people changed into bears. I changed my mind"; (IX) "This looks like a person with his—an elephant with a sword on instead of a trunk—standing up— he doesn't have two feet. Like a person with two arms and an elephant's head."

A similiar kind of vagueness is expressed in the mention of people or things not actually seen in the cards: (III) "Two men holding a bag with a bomb in it and police have a gun on them, and they're supposed to drop it and it will go off. That's even better than the electric chair." (Police?) "Oh, you can't see them. It's just the men are standing so queerly." Or, (III) "Looks like they're getting ready to kill the man and boil him for dinner." (Man?) "Oh, he's not in the picture."

Perhaps a little surprisingly, after all this hesitancy, groping, and considerable expenditure of effort, responses when finally achieved and settled on are as indicated above very often merely popular responses. Girls give more populars here than at any other age (mean 6.8; median 7). Boys give fewer than girls, but still an appreciable number (mean 5.1, median 6).

Thus Ten seems on the one hand to be rooted in the utmost clarity and reality and even banality, and on the other hand to be lost in confusion, uncertainty, and the unreality of things half human and half animal, or of things not really there. Even popular responses now often have an original twist. Ten frequently sees a popular figure but gives it an unusual connotation, as "A dragon rug," or "A dinosaur's clothing," or "A wet bear rug" on IV; or "A cat holding up a bearskin" on VI. At 11 and 12 years of age, many subjects start with a popular response and then elaborate it into a DW. This trend has already started to some extent here at 10.

A similar ambivalence is suggested by the numerous rather childish scenes of horror and violence, but at the same time the giving of many comments that suggest that Ten is firmly rooted in reality. Thus he still gives such fancifully violent responses as: (VIII) "Scary one. Corpse of a girl and two squirrels climbing up here. Might be inside of a tomb. Pulling her hair." Or (III) "Some ogreish monster. Two. With I don't know, doesn't sound right, but babies hanging from ropes. One of them has his kidneys out." But at the same time he explains his sources as "Butterfly. I caught thirty this summer"; "I saw it at a museum"; "We study them in school"; "I saw it in a book."

Ten seems appreciative of the need to conform to the group and to identify himself with reality and with the group (high P, mean A% of 49 per cent, higher H% than at earlier ages, very low m), and yet he shows a good deal of interest and belief in magic and superstition (high number of (H) and (A) figures).

In everyday life, 10-year-olds appear prepared to meet the world in an essentially conforming, accepting manner, without the automatic oppositionality of the early adolescent. Ten's Rorschach response likewise shows many indications of conformity. But both in manner of response and in forms given it also shows a strain of nonconformity, opposition, resentment, even secretiveness.

Opposition is suggested by the high number of WS responses (mean 1.0), higher than at any other age in this range. These are particularly noteworthy as they occur frequently on the first three cards—more by far than at any succeeding age. On Card I, for instance, more than half the subjects begin with a WS response. Ten also appears to resent having seen the cards before. Resentment may also be expressed in the high number of refusals that occur at this age, a further way of expressing opposition.

Some secretiveness is suggested both by the actual nature of responses

—one of the highest ages for both "mask" and "map"—and also by the child's manner as he responds to the test. Tens seem to resent questioning and inquiry more than do subjects of almost any age. They may become silent or moody with inquiry. Some also at this age seem to be especially conscious of and resentful of a recorder or an observer stationed behind the one-way screen. A few make such remarks as: "Would you tell those women in there to stop peering at me?" "Somebody is watching me. Here comes that hand again!" At the younger ages, one seldom encounters this attitude; and later a recorder is accepted as routine, often without comment. But at 10 the examiner is quite conscious of the child's reaction and his sudden tension once he suspects that he is being observed, or when he is questioned about his response.

It rather seems as though Ten experienced a sense of inability to cope with the environment, even though he appears amenable and reasonably easy to get along with. Rorschach signs that indicate restriction have already been discussed. One expansive sign is seen, however, in the relatively high number of color responses (mean ΣC, 1.3), somewhat higher than in the years that follow, until 16 years, though considerably lower than at any preceding age since 4 years. Analysis of color responses shows that at most ages that follow, the more conforming and adaptable FC response occurs to about half the extent of CF, whereas at 10 years CF is three times the number of FC. Furthermore, pure C is used by twice as many subjects as at the following age.

This somewhat unconforming nature of color responses, the many responses suggesting horror and violence, the fairly high number of headless creatures (especially in boys), the comparatively low number of shading responses, as well as the general tendency to restriction of responses, suggests a personality less open and conforming and more guarded and perhaps more violent than our surface impression of the 10-year-old might lead us to expect.

Even though unpleasant adjectives are used more frequently than pleasant ones by subjects at all ages from 10 to 16, at 10 the number of pleasant adjectives used is relatively high in comparison with other ages. Girls especially use a high number of pleasant adjectives (see Table 31). Characteristic positive adjectives at this age are: pretty, strong, colorful, good, fine, golden, civilized. Less pleasant concepts are often described as: scary, terrible looking, wild, distorted, crazy. A certain flatness and shallowness, however, which is noted in the emotional response of the 10-year-old in everyday life (11), is hinted at here in the fact that in girls there are fewer affect adjectives than at any other age; though in boys more than at most other ages.

Shading responses are relatively few at this age, but their quality

reveals one further example of the opposite extremes apparently characteristic of the 10-year-old's Rorschach response. Both vague diffusion responses and the more specific and detailed differentiation responses reach
relatively high points at this age. Vista and reflection responses, which seem
to increase along with an increased awareness of and interest in self as
the subject grows older, are here at their lowest points.

The foregoing description of Ten as revealed by the Rorschach conforms closely to our description of this age in a preceding Rorschach study
(1), even though some of the figures differ slightly from one group of
subjects to the other. However, in the earlier study we had only the oppor-
tunity of comparing Ten to younger ages. Now that we can see him with
either a backward or a forward look, our interpretation of some items
(anatomy responses, color responses) changes slightly. In looking at Ten
in the light of the ages that precede and follow, we find perhaps the most
outstanding characteristic, one that sets the key for subsequent ages but
appears here for the first time, to be the predominance of movement over
color responses. For the first time, the child appears to be more introversive
than extratensive. This, along with the relatively high number of anatomy
responses (mean .5), indicates a stronger sense of self than we have seen
at earlier ages. But when we examine some of the supplementary details,
we find a considerably less mature concept of self and a less discriminating
self-awareness than we shall see at subsequent ages.

Even though the type of reactivity is introversive, animal movement
still exceeds human movement. And although ΣC is lower than it has been
since 4 years of age, CF is still the predominant color response, occurring
in higher ratio to FC than at later ages, and with "blood" and "fire" responses relatively prominent. Thus, though his role is more stabilized than
it has been up to this age, the 10-year-old still shows an immature buoyancy
and impulsiveness, a drive to immediate gratification of wishes.

From our present data we can draw an integrated, composite picture
of our typical 10-year-old. We see him as someone who wants to be on the
safe side, one who is protecting himself as much as the forward thrust
of development will allow. As he does this he is like a man on a seesaw.
He protects himself negatively by restriction of output (low R), by refusals, by his defensiveness in inquiry or in being observed, by dealing very
little with specific detail (low Dd%) or with nuanced reflective reactions
(low F(C)). He protects himself positively by high generalization (high
W%), by sticking to reality (high F% and references to undisputed experiences, "I saw it in a museum," "We study them at school"), and by
being very precise about that reality (high F+%). He conforms and does
things the easy way (high P, high A%) and he strongly identifies with the
group (high H%), which is at the same time the most satisfactory way of
affirming his self.

When his first line of protection breaks down, the most characteristic 10-year-old response is revealed in vagueness ("map," "or something"), in withdrawal ("mask"), in denial of response or readiness to change response, form contamination and unpleasantness of concepts, as well as the giving of responses indicating ideas of magic or attitudes of superstition. Here we see him caught in the middle of the seesaw. Many of these characteristics are indicative of his general immaturity; we have seen most of them more strongly at earlier ages.

It is interesting to note, though difficult to document, that this is one of the last ages where the characteristics of the age seem to stand out in most protocols as prominently as the individual, personal characteristics. In relatively few instances throughout our entire group at 10 years did we find strikingly personalized and individual protocols. This may be another indication of the 10-year-old's remaining on the "safe" side. By revealing less of himself, he is protecting himself. We shall see this picture change as we progress through subsequent ages.

Ten years, then, seems to mark a terminal point where, though introversivity appears predominant for the first time, the child is mobilizing his reserves before a new drive toward maturity gives him a more positive and personalized direction. Protectiveness and safety seem to be the keynotes.

Individual Determinants

Number: The mean R of 19.2 is slightly smaller than at any other age in this range except Fifteen.

Area: The response at this age is primarily global. Mean W% is 51.4 per cent; mean D, 41.3 per cent; mean Dd, 7.3 per cent.

Form: Mean F% is 62 per cent. Mean F+, 91 per cent.

M, FM, m: Mean M is 2.0, exceeded slightly at other ages except Fifteen. Mean FM is 2.4. Mean m is .6.

As at every age but Fifteen, the specific "vigorous extensor" M responses of dancing or swinging around predominate. The "static" sitting, resting, lying, leaning comes second.

As at every age, "vigorous extensor" FM leads, especially climbing. The "moderate extensor" FM walking, comes second.

Among m, explosion movements lead.

Color: Mean ΣC is 1.3, very slightly higher than at any other age but Sixteen. CF responses (mean .9) definitely predominate. Mean FC is only .3; mean C, .2.

Of FC responses as at other ages, animal responses predominate. Of CF, nature responses lead; of C, fire and explosion.

Shading: Mean F(C) response is only .7, less than at any other age in this range except eleven. Differentiation of details within the blot is the leading type of shading; texture comes second.

FC', C'F, FClob, Clob: Fewest subjects of any age but Thirteen use these responses—8 per cent. Also mean score (.08) is lowest of any age but Thirteen.

Content: Total number of different categories used at this age is 20.* Average number per child is 5.2. A% is 48.5 per cent; H% is 18.9 per cent.

Animals are the leading content category; humans come next; then objects. Anatomy, nature, and plant follow in that order.

Characteristic Adjectives: pretty, fairytale, strong, normal, colorful, good, fine, golden, civilized. Also scary, terrible looking, wild, distorted, crazy.

Length: This is one of the three ages for girls, one of the two for boys, when records are longest.

Total Time: Only at 14 years is total time equally long. Here the mean is 13.7 minutes.

Semantics: Comparing the blot to reality by means of the phrase "looks like" is the leading means of identification. There is less use of qualifying phrases than at other ages except Fifteen and Sixteen.

Best and Least Liked: Girls and boys both like best Card X. Girls like least Card IV. Boys like least IV and X.

Refusals: More subjects than at any other age (28 per cent) refuse at least one card. Card IX is most refused; VI next most.

Populars: At this age the mean for popular responses is 6.4; median 6.5.

Sex Differences

The responses of boys are more global at this age, the responses of girls more detailed. Girls' responses are considerably the more restricted: mean F% in boys is only 60 per cent, in girls 65 per cent. However, girls may be more accurate: mean F+% in boys 90 per cent, in girls 92 per cent.

Girls give more responses than do boys (boys, mean R of 18; girls, 20). Girls give more M, more FM, a little more shading.

Girls are not only more restricted, but have a higher A% and a high P%. Girls give more architecture, fire, reflection, and abstract responses. Boys give more human, explosion, blood, and mask responses.

The Rorschach response of the 10-year-old is in some respects paradoxical, rooted in clarity and banality but at the same time often lost in confusion, uncertainty, unreality. Girls seem to emphasize more the banal side of the age, boys the confused side.

Comparison of Rorschach and Developmental Findings

DEVELOPMENTAL	RORSCHACH
Conventional.	High A%.
	Many popular responses.
In general, well adjusted, uncompli-	Less shading, fewer Clob, fewer Dd,
cated, direct, straightforward.	lower C than at 9 years.

---

* This is slightly larger than the number reported in our earlier study (1), since in the present analysis we have added four new categories: geography-geology; explosion; design; mask; though we also combined several that were previously separate.

Comparison of Rorschach and Developmental Findings

DEVELOPMENTAL	RORSCHACH
Some restriction and inability to cope with the environment.	Mean R lower than at ages that follow. Many refusals. Tendency to red shock and to color shock, especially among boys.
Ambivalent: conforming yet oppositional.	High P but WS higher than at any other age in this range. Most refusals in this range and more subjects refusing.
Introversive.	2M:1.3ΣC; ΣC smaller than at any preceding age since 4 years.
But still warm, buoyant, childishly impulsive.	Mean FM > M; CF much exceeds FC.
Mostly good-natured, even-tempered.	Relatively large number of pleasant adjectives used as: pretty, strong, normal, colorful, fine, golden, civilized.
But a certain lack of emotional depth.	Fewer affect adjectives, in girls, than at any other age in this range.
Responsive to others, interested in people.	High H%.
But rather secretive, though not withdrawn.	Highest age for "mask"; one of highest for "map." Resents inquiry and observation.
Hypochondriacal, self-concerned though not self-critical or self-analytical.	High number of anatomy responses but fewest reflection responses of any age. Shading least of any age in this range; virtually no vista.
Vague, find it difficult to specify.	Much use of "or something." Confusion of animals with humans. Low Dd; W% exceeds D%.
Superstitious, interested in magic.	High (H): witches, devils. Tendency to dark shock.
Cautious, evasive, balances responses: "Sometimes I do, sometimes I don't"; "Maybe, maybe not."	Protects self by refusal, by restriction of output, by lack of specific detail, by lack of F(C), by high generalization and low Dd, high F%, the precision of high F+%. Or in his phrasing: "Looks like a bug. Not a bug"; "Bears. Not bears. Sort of like bears."

Sample Record of 10-Year-Old-Boy M.R.

RESPONSE	INQUIRY		SCORING		
I. How do they do it? Blot ink? A devil or someone who's mad or a cat.	(Whole.) ? "Because he's mad and his eyes are up like that."	WS	M	(Hd)	P
	(Whole.) ? "Ears and eyes and nose —witch's cat."	WS	F+	Ad	P
(Anything else?) No.					
II. I had the same ones last year, so you can compare them, I see. Elephants touching trunks together, if you took out the red.	(Black only.)	D	FM	A	P
<Can you take half? It could be sort of a bear sniffing along.	(One side black only.) ? "This. I'm not doing it by the color you understand."	D	FM	A	
III. How many are there? Ooh! Men trying to pull something up. (Demonstrates pulling.) And cowboy boots.	(Two usual figures.)	W	M	H	P
> V It could be a mouth—looking into the mouth. That would be the nose here—that would be the holes of the nose.	(Whole with use of white spaces.) ? "Just the mouth and nose."	WS	F±	Hd	
IV. > ∧ V Giant sitting on something, with two big feet—a stump, I should say—his arms.	(Whole.)	W	M	(H)	P
V. It's a bat—that's what I said last time. Do you want to check? A butterfly!	(Whole.)	W	F+	A	P

RESPONSE	INQUIRY		SCORING		P
VI. This could be a comic strip—like giving a wolf the hot seat. Those are his legs. The head gave me the idea mostly.	(Whole.)	W	FM	A	
Can you cut out certain parts of it? (Covers portion with his hands.) Looks like a man sleepwalking with his hands out in front of him. (Leans over and takes another card from Ex.)	(One side of lower D.)	Dd	M	H	
VII. ∨ ∧ Does it matter which way you give it to me? (Pause) Two rabbits! That's all I guess.	(Whole.) ? "Skirts on, little paws and turning around looking at each other."	W	FM	A	P
VIII. > ∨ < ∧ (Now almost twirls card.) (Long pause) You'd have to cut out almost everything here, and then you'd have a jet plane with exhaust here.	(Blue and gray as plane with exhaust leading from blue toward red and yellow. Plane not in movement. But mention of "exhaust" gives some idea of suspended movement.)	D	↗m F+	object (mid-line)	
IX. I don't know. > ∨ ∧ (Makes face.) (Pause) Without this and without that, this is the atom bomb blowing up—mushrooming! Water coming up.	(Pink and center only.)	D	m	explosion (mid-line)	

Sample Record of 10-Year-Old-Boy M.R. (Continued)

RESPONSE	INQUIRY		SCORING
X. $<$ V $>$ ∧ (Tends to twirl card.) Two sea horses.	(Green center. Form)	D	F+ A
Rocket and jet plane again. That's all.	(Top gray.) ? "I don't know—that straight thing."	D	F+ object

Card most liked: VIII. "The color, I suppose."
Card least liked: III and X. "This (X) is all spread out and nothing is there." "This (III) doesn't look like anything. It's not supposed to anyway, but . . . ."

R:15   Time: 13 minutes

6W   6F =40%F   6A
3WS=60%W   5F+, 1F± =92%F+   1Ad =46%A
5D =33%D   4M, 4FM, 1m   2H
                                    (→1m)   1(H)
1Dd =7%Dd   4M:0ΣC   1Hd
                                                                    1(Hd) =33%H

                                                                    2 objects
Succession: None   1 explosion
Shock: None (?→Color)   7P

The following remarks and those that follow each of the other sample records are not intended to be exhaustive analyses of the individual protocols. The cases were selected to be reasonably representative examples of normal subjects at each age; the comments point out some of the ways in which the protocols typify the age characteristics and some ways in which a knowledge of developmental trends can aid in individual interpretations.

COMMENT In his approach to the total Rorschach situation, this boy shows a conformity, a desire to do the correct thing, typical of many 10-year-olds. He expresses a polite interest: "How do they do it?" He asks permission before taking any liberties: "Can you take half?" and even seeks reassurance a second time. He is interested in his previous response and accepts the situation equably. He is not verbally expansive, and inquiry does not bring any extensive elaboration except to help identify the area. In many of his scores he is very close to the medians for boys of his age, particularly in number of responses, in area balance, in form accuracy, and A%.

In other elements he departs from the typical response of 10-year-old boys. Purely mechanically we can select the scores in which he differs from the middle 50 per cent of subjects. Elevated scores, those at or above the 75th percentile, are M, FM, m, and H%. Scores at or below the 25th percentile are F%, CF, and ΣC. This already gives a picture of a boy with rich inner living and an active search for self, with a restriction and control of spontaneous response to the environment.

He conforms and responds to social demands on a par with others of his age, but seems to have more emotional depth than the typical 10-year-old. This boy is not only strongly introversive, but much of his effort is devoted to strengthening his idea of self and to assertion of himself. He appears to depend on himself for answers rather than on others or on the environment. In fact, the (H) response and the absence of color, plus the tendency to color shock (longer time on color cards, much manipulation, grimacing, only four responses, dislike of III and X) and the fact that the m and the m tendency appear only on color cards suggest some distrust of others and somewhat aggressive feelings toward the environment.

The animal movements projected seem generally to indicate a basically gentle and co-operative nature—"elephants touching trunks," "bear sniffing," "rabbits looking at each other." An exception ("like giving a wolf the hot seat") has m elements, and resembles in nature his m responses, "jet exhaust" and "atom bomb blowing up." These inject feelings of sometimes being imposed upon by others and reveal hostile impulses of his own that he cannot fully accept. Such feelings contribute to his distrust of others.

His human movements include "devil . . . who is mad," "men trying to pull something up," "giant sitting," "man sleepwalking." Here there is more variety than in the FM. In spite of his agreeable nature, he has the potential for various adaptive reactions as the situation may demand. His energy pattern is such that he can easily vary between well-defined, productive activity and more passive response, but there appears to be a reserve of power and force behind it. There is a sense of stilled strength in all four M. The "man sleep-walking" is certainly a most original response and perhaps the one most expressive of his present state of emotional and intellectual activity: that of actively looking for something without knowing what, or why or how he will find it.

This boy's intellectual functioning is most adequate, though his intellectual horizon is perhaps somewhat restricted. He prefers situations where synthesis and coherence are apparent and is disturbed by ones where he must make his own synthesis with discrete elements (see cards best and least liked). Such situations induce feelings of insecurity in him that are often unwarranted, for his response is often better than he feels it to be (see reaction to III and response at III).

This boy appears to have real potential and rather well-unified basic reserves, and an ability to find answers for himself. His self-control is almost too great. It will be interesting to see if at another age these restraints are somewhat released.

Sample Record of 10-Year-Old-Girl U.G.

RESPONSE	INQUIRY		SCORING		
I. I said it last year and I'll say it this year—it's a mask.	(Whole. White as eyes.)	WS	F+	object	P
(Long regard) It does—sort of— looks like someone with feet and arms and a very big head. Not very much.	(Whole. Indicates side proj. as arms, feet at bottom. Head is quite vague.)	W	F±	H	
II. (Sighs) Two elephants fighting.	(Whole.) ? "Bashing together. Don't look friendly. Look furious."	W	FM	A	P
∨ Two Scottie dogs.	(Black only.) ? "Their noses and ears." ? "Kind that has square nose."	D	F+	A	
I don't know what this is. (Bottom red.)					
III. All the same since last time I did it. Let me see—two cannibals. And that's a bone, and these are two other bones. I don't know what this is—I guess a pot. They're cooking. Just bones maybe from animals.	(Whole. Center and side red are bones.) ? "Cannibals and bones go together." ? "Just all twisted like bones." (Bones could be scored separately, but she conceives them as a logical part of the total picture.)	DW	M	H	P
IV. Oh yes! Guess only thing this looks like is a rug. Looks like a dragon's rug—head does. Rug made out of a dragon, if there is such a thing. Eyes, nose, just his feelers. Head is only part that looks like	(Whole with head at center bottom.)	W	F+	(A) object	P (0)

Sample Record of 10-Year-Old-Girl U.G. (Continued)

RESPONSE	INQUIRY		SCORING		
a dragon—rest doesn't look like anything.					
V Like a dragon this way too—a small, flying dragon, wings flapping.	(Whole. But rug concept has disappeared. Now an active animal.)	W	FM	(A)	P
V. A bat. That's all.	(Whole. Form)	W	F+	A	P
VI. (Holds at arm's length. Sighs.) Well, I guess it's a rug—a tiger rug. That's all I see, because it's so flat. Nose and things coming out of its head. Body, two hands and feet. Don't know what happened to his tail. Two whiskers.	(Whole. Form.)	W	F+	A object	P
VII. This is the hardest one. Well, only thing it really looks like is two rabbits sitting on the very edge of a stone—their ears.	(Whole.)	DW	FM	A	P
VIII. I hate this one. It doesn't make much sense, 'cept these look like two animals. I guess they could be climbing a tree and a pretty rock.	(Whole. Usual animals with tree in center and rock at bottom.) Rock? "Looks like one when you collect rocks. Boy next door collects ones like that, colorful and bumpy."	DW	⟋CF, F(C) FM	A	P

RESPONSE	INQUIRY	SCORING			
IX. They get harder and harder as you go along, don't they? Well, this in itself looks like something—pink—looks like a statue, doubled on the other side.	("Pink" is used to identify area.) ? "Of a man. Moustache, forehead, nose, chin, waist. Nothing else."	D	F+	object	
Well, this doesn't make too much sense, though it could be someone peeking through some leaves—two eyes—but not very possible because how could you see the eyes and nothing else. Leaves for him to hide behind.	(Eyes are shaded dark spots in green at left. Green is "leaves.")	D	$\nearrow$CF / M	Hd	
X. Oh yes. I shall call this "Under the Sea." Well, these are two crabs, horseshoe crabs. Coral. These two look something like heads of sea horses—hiding behind rocks—only heads show. I guess all the others are just rocks. Coral or pink seaweed.	(Whole. Details blue as crabs, pink as coral, center blue as heads of sea horses. But all parts are included in scene. Color is most important determinant.)	DW	$\nearrow$FM / CF	Scene	P

Sample Record of 10-Year-Old-Girl U.G. (Continued)

Card most liked: X. "Pretty and makes sense."
Card least liked: VIII. "Doesn't make any sense." Also dislikes IV and VI. "No sense and not very pretty."

R:14   Time: 14 minutes

6W   7F = 50%F   5A
4DW   6F+, 1F± = 93%F+   1(A)
1WS = 73%W   2 A object = 57%A

                        2M, 4FM
                        1CF   2H
3D = 27%D   (→1FM, 2CF, 1F(C))   1Hd = 21%H

                        2M:1ΣC   2 objects (2A objects)
                                                      1 scene

                                                      9 P

Succession: None
Shock: None

COMMENT This girl, like the 10-year-old boy, has many scores close to the typical values for her age. Statistically, she departs from the average only in W%, FM, and P, which are high (at or beyond the 75th percentile), and D%, which is low (below the 25th percentile).

This girl is more actively aggressive in her rapport with the examiner than was the boy just described. She is more expansive verbally than he, but still maintains the somewhat restrictive reticence of her age.

She is much more ambitious than most of her peers, and her intellectual functioning is most adequate, though her intellectual horizon seems somewhat restricted, as did that of the boy. It is interesting to contrast the difference between the types of intellect in the 10-year-old boy and girl. He was disturbed by blots with discrete elements, while she likes X best because it is "pretty and makes sense." Since she is responsive to social and cultural demands, and probably complies easily to rules and routines (9P, 57%A), she undoubtedly makes social and intellectual adaptations more readily than the boy.

Her projections toward independence are mixed with more childish attitudes. The FM surpasses M by 2:1. The FM, "elephants fighting," "flying dragon," "rabbits sitting," "animals climbing," with the tendency to FM, "animals hiding," all give evidence of a variety of basic reserves and idea of role, but with no unified direction. There are aggressive attitudes, power motives, passive and dependent reactions, ambitious desires, and very timid responses. The M reveals "cannibals cooking" and "eyes peeking." Here we may have identification with somewhat savage (?cruel) human beings and even though it may not be manifest in her activities or her overt behavior, the "cannibal" response combines with others ("fighting," "flying," "climbing," high W%) to indicate ambition, perhaps even somewhat predatory, and a desire to dominate. Such a drive alternates with the timid, "hidden" approach in the "eyes peeking." This may also be indicative of a feeling of being spied upon, of being too much restrained. Her reaction to the first color card is "I hate this one." This indicates some aggressivity toward the environment, which she apparently overcomes in the actual response given, an agreeable one. One has the impression from all these factors that this is a child with a strong drive to dominate, but her own inhibitions, her response to social pressures, plus the complexity of her basic drives, operate effectively to deflect or restrain this drive at present.

We have described the 10-year-old as protective of himself. This is an interesting example of the way in which the age operates through the individuality. In spite of the impression given here that this is an aggressive child with a strong desire to dominate, there is a protective mechanism operating that shields her both from herself and from society. It will be interesting to observe, when and if the basic drives are somewhat more unified, the way in which the more independent reactions will be exhibited.

CHAPTER ELEVEN

Eleven Years

16 R	63%F	53%A
	93%F+	18%H
46%W		2.7 objects
47%D	2.2M, 2.5FM, .6m	.6 anatomy
4%Dd	.3FC, .7CF, .1C,	.5 nature
	.6F(C)	.3 plant
	Mean 2.2M:1.0ΣC	
	Median 2.0M: .9ΣC	7P

Eleven-year-olds in everyday life situations behave in a manner often strikingly different from their own 10-year-old selves. Tens characteristically appear easygoing, friendly, well adjusted, but shallow. They accept the world about them in a docile and equable manner.

At eleven, in girls especially, there comes a marked breakup in the 10-year-old calm. Disruptive forces are at work. Parents often describe their 11-year-olds as proud, belligerent, highly verbal, argumentative, rude, unco-operative, though outsiders may find these same children to be sincere, confiding, unguarded, extremely communicative, exuberant, and expressive. Eleven seems to be engaged in an active search for self, and he often seeks to define that self through conflict with others (11).

The 11-year-old in his Rorschach response, even though many of the major Rorschach determinants occur to about the same extent as at 10, shows much of this conflict with the environment.

Eleven's talkativeness is shown, first of all, in the fact that though the total number of scored responses given is fewer than at subsequent ages (except Fifteen), records are longer than at any following age except Fourteen—in individual instances extending to three and a half closely typed pages (as recorded; recorder did not get every word).

Though actual scores to some extent reflect the qualities of the age, as will be described later, much of the character of Eleven is revealed by the child's behavior and verbalization as he reacts in a strongly personal manner to the examiner and to the ink blots.

First of all, there are more initial remarks here than at any other age. The quality of these remarks varies considerably from enthusiasm ("Whee oh ee! That's pretty!" "Wow! That's a pretty one!") through perplexity ("Oh gosh! Now what's this?") to outright criticism ("Oh dear!" "Not this again!" "Good grief!"). Some remarks seem to suggest a mixed reaction: "Oh brother!" "Oh boy—this is a dilly!" "Egad!" All serve both to express the verbal exuberance of Eleven and at the same time to delay an actual response.

Next in many come comments about having seen the cards before. Of repeat subjects, nearly half (both boys and girls) make some comment about earlier tests. Some of this is of a negative and complaining nature, but much indicates a friendly familiarity with the situation: "Oh! I remember this one!" "I think I told you this last year" or "I've got my answer already."

Once launched on his actual responses, Eleven sets up with the examiner a frank, friendly, extremely personal situation. He laughs, he jokes (sometimes on the verge of rudeness), he answers back, he asks if he may turn the cards, he explains his own mental processes—how he came to certain conclusions and how his mind is working. He tells about outside experiences that led him to see what he is seeing. (In fact, in girls especially, some of the verbalization approaches a stream of consciousness report.) He comments on the examiner's recording, tells examiner how to spell words and what they mean, asks what the cards really represent. (He also wriggles and twists, tips his chair, yawns, coughs, hums, waves his hands to illustrate action seen on the cards.)

An example of the more or less stream-of-consciousness response typical of this age is found in this abbreviated record of one girl's reaction to several of the cards:

(She smiles) (Card I) You mean what kind of a person or what kind of a thing it is? Well certain parts of it look like one thing and others like others. They look like pumpkin eyes to me. Maybe crabs. To me it just looks crazy, that's all. (II) Mmh! well maybe it looks like a butterfly; maybe I'm wrong. Never saw a butterfly with antlers. Well, a butterfly with shoe ears. (III) Well this looks like a little easier to tell. Eyes in there and a silly looking head and the part turning. Kind of a butterfly in between. (IV) These are getting harder and harder. Mmh! It looks like one of those scary things which might jump out at you at a costume party. I never heard of a person with crooked feet. (VIII) Well this one looks kind of easy in a way; these two things look like animals of a type. . . . Not a very good guess. (IX) Now I'm really puzzled. Gee I don't know what to say this is. (Laughs) It looks like some kind of monster. Brother! Golly I don't know what this is standing on. I've never seen anything like this . . . probably a wild guess. (X) Looks more like a bunch of splattered paint except for these things. I don't know what kind of a bug it is up here climbing a post—never heard of a bug standing on three feet.

Comments to examiner in regard to the recording and meaning of the test are frequent: "Oh, this is pretty—I seem to say the same things I said last year. You write down every time I turn. I don't like it. Do you write down my actions too?" "Klu Klux Klan. You don't spell it that way— you spell it with a K."

A very similar warm, frank, friendly interpersonal relationship with the examiner is set up by 11-year-old boys, though in general their responses are not quite as lengthy as are those of girls, and it seems to be the more advanced boys who present this picture. All the things we have described as occurring in girls are seen in the responses of these advanced boys. There is especially a good deal of questioning as to whether or not it is all right for them to turn the cards, much reference to having seen the cards before, and a good deal of self-protection in the prefacing remarks, "This may sound silly," or "This may sound a little funny." Like girls, they are very communicative, asking questions and explaining their own perceptions. Thus:

(I) I never did know what this one was—let me think a minute. It could be a mountain and a tunnel. What do you do, put ink blots then fold over? . . . Hm! This could be somebody who was decapitated. (III) I'd like to ask you how you can possibly analyze my results, they're so far-fetched. Here's a very distinct picture of a butterfly. . . . Have you ever read Mr. Magoo? This is Mr. Walrus, his friend. These are two Negro girls back to back, kicking at some sort of stones. Behind them is a bat. Negro girls because of shape of mouth, big lips and the color of them. Also no suggestion of hair so I take it to be very frizzy and short. Do my results change from year to year? I remember what I've said on many of these. (V) Were these ink blots chosen out of a large batch because of their interest? Chosen by whom? Hoping this would work out the way it does? Merely a bat. Nothing else. I'll look at it sideways. Nothing.

Both the extremely personal and the lively emotional nature of Eleven's responses (especially in the case of girls) is found in their expression of their reasons for choices of best and least-liked blots. Though as at other ages many like cards because they are "easy" or "look more like something," Eleven may choose Card I "because it looks like a cat and I like cats." Or, III, "I like the mystery of the red and white and black and it's so pronounced." Or, in the detailed, wordy, manner of eleven, one explains her choice of III: "I thought that was quite cute. But after that I thought they were a man and woman but they didn't show any difference because they were skeletons. And maybe their hearts were going out and shaking hands. Maybe they were man and wife! Red is hearts shaking hands just before they died."

Cards are disliked most because they are "hard to figure out," or "make no sense," but also because they (IV) "scare me," (I) "sort of scare you. A vicious cat," (I) "Seem to glare out at you," (VIII) "I hate that one. It doesn't look decent."

Considering the length of responses and the large amount of energy put into them, it is something of a surprise that not only is R no longer than at the preceding age (and smaller than at following ages), but that there is here a very large occurrence of popular responses. Boys give more populars here than at any other age (mean 6.8), and for boys and girls together the mean is 6.7. Thus one in three responses given is a popular one.

Actual verbalization is highly enlivened. The 11-year-old seems to have an unusually lively manner of expressing himself. Even his popular responses appear lively, as in the case of the girl who sees Card I as "a cat with glaring eyes and a great big grin on his face."

Another sign of enlivenment appears in the movement responses which, though not greater in quantity than at surrounding ages, are of an extremely vigorous if not violent quality. The percentage of static movement responses drops considerably from 10, in M; and somewhat in FM. Among FM there is a slight increase of vigorous extensor movements over 10. In fact, Eleven is one of the two highest ages for fighting, quarreling, arguing, battling movements. These plus running, chasing are the second leading kind of M responses at this age, second only to dancing.

As to FM responses, this is next to the highest age for running after, charging, fighting, and quarreling, which together nearly tie with climbing for first place. And this is the highest age by far for mixed or conflicted FM, there being more than twice as many such responses as at 10. Among m responses, tension and explosion responses tie for first place.

Thus to Card I: "Two witches on two sides and they're tearing apart a girl and taking her head off"; (IX) "Dragons spitting at each other with fiery tongues"; (II) "Bears hitting each other, hands all bloody"; (II) "Two bears being shot because they were fighting and the blood squishing out of their claws and the reflection of blood in the water." At the same time, this is the highest age for things being acted upon, i.e., hanging, falling, pushed, tied.

Color responses are fewer than at 10, though like movement somewhat violent. Blood responses make up 18 per cent of CF (exceeded only at one age); fire responses comprise 20 per cent of all CF and are now more frequent than at any subsequent age though fewer than at 10. Thus (Card II) "Panther's claws that have just been killing something," or "Siamese twins, both got shot—all bloody."

Further enlivenment comes from the fact that though the number of popular responses is high, frequently a simple popular response is expanded into a DW. Mean DW of 1.9 is highest here for any age. The manner in which a popular response is elaborated into a DW is shown in the following response to Card VIII.

Well this looks to me like two pink baby mice walking over some puddles of oil that make these funny little colors when the sun shines on them. And then when you look at it this way it might be a reflection of one of his forepaws. (Baby mice?) I've seen baby mice up at the zoology lab up at the college and they were pink and had fur on them. Some things take shape immediately, and others are fantastic deductions. But you tell me to see what I see, so I see them.

Elaboration may become confabulation:

(X) Here comes the last one! I don't like these small things as well. They're too hard to find. . . . Two peacocks leaning together and some prankish boy for some reason has thrown a paper cup stuffed with confetti and then it is going to come down and fall all over the peacock's tail and he won't be able to move and will die. Just the green.

(IX) I have something worked out and I'm not quite sure how to tell it. You remember in the Brementown musicians and they climbed up and scared the robbers away. This might be these. Musicians (green and orange). I think this one (pink) is a musician too. When they're climbing up against the wall they have to be outside the wall, yelling or singing. Little window.

Records are lengthened in some cases, even though not enlivened, by the large amount of qualification found especially in boys at this age. Less than at 10, there is still a tendency among 11-year-olds to give a response and then deny it: (VII) "Looks like some mountains. Not mountain but clouds"; (II) "I was going to say a human stomach but no. It doesn't look too much like a human stomach."

This denial is often combined with an initial refusal. (I) "Mm! Can't make much out of that. It might be a boy having cotton icecream at a circus. No, it's Paris and that's the Eiffel tower. Probably. I'm not too sure." The initial refusal of the card is often longer than the final response. (VIII) "Now what will they think of next? I don't understand that one. I can't find a single thing out of that I really can't. ∨ Might possibly look like a bathing suit."

Boys' responses tend to be both vague and uncertain: (I) "Kinda reminds me of persons swinging around something, tree or something"; (IV) "Well I can't say much. All I can say is that these look like boots I guess."

There are more qualified responses at this age than at any other. Boys most, but girls also outstandingly express this qualification by the frequent use of such words and expressions as "might be," "could be," "maybe," "possibly," "I guess," "looks something like," "kind of," "sort of." Simply naming the blot without any qualification occurs less here, in both sexes, than at any other age.

Boys also make remarks strongly resembling what we find later, in presenility (2). Boys of 11 say, "Wait a minute!"; confirm their own responses with "Yeah!"; ask "How am I going to know if these are right?" Or, like the 4-year-old (1), an 11-year-old may comment of a "crab" which he sees on IX, "Ouch! he just pinched me!"

Thus the 11-year-old boy may refuse the blot; may refuse initially but quickly overcome this refusal; may give a response and then immediately deny it; may suggest changes in the blot, or may give a rather vague and indefinite response. An occasional girl also gives an initial refusal and then overcomes it; or denies her own response: (I) "Could be a bridge. No, it couldn't. Yes it could"; (VII) "Sheep. No it doesn't. Butterfly." But such responses are not characteristic of girls at this age.

Something of the nature of Eleven's relations with other people can be seen if we consider the relatively high H% (the median H% of 18 is not exceeded at any age), the interpersonal engagement with the examiner that we have described as taking place during the giving of the test, and the large amount of fighting and quarreling in movement responses. Unable to stay out of touch with other people, Eleven is not always able to maintain good interpersonal relations.

Oppositional and critical, antagonistic tendencies are shown in the large number of refusals (mean .4) exceeded at only one age; in the unusually high number of WS responses—mean of 1.9, more than at any other age and especially noted on Cards I and II; in initial refusals later overcome; and in the large amount of criticism of blots ("Well it's all crazy; doesn't make any sense; just a blot of ink") and suggestions for changing of blots.

Strong and for the most part rather violent and unpleasant interpersonal reactions are expressed on both Cards I and V, when the different parts of the card are seen as acting on each other: the two sides acting on the center, or (on V) two sides meeting violently in the middle.

The somewhat unpleasant and critical attitude of Eleven is also suggested in his use of adjectives. Girls give three times as many unpleasant adjectives as pleasant, and in both boys and girls such censorious adjectives as queer, weird, awful, nasty, strange, crazy, silly, predominate.

For all his use of qualified phrases—"This might be," "kind of like"—Eleven frequently expresses a certain unmodulated positiveness and a certain flatness of assertion, often seen at earlier ages (1). Asked in inquiry to tell why he gave a certain response, he may reply, "Because it looked like one." He characteristically explains that he likes certain cards because "I just do," and dislikes others because "I just don't like it too much." The many definite terminal remarks, "That's all," "Can't see anything else," "Nothing else," "All I can make of that," give an impression of "And that's that!"

The total aspect of the response at Eleven, in spite of the large amount of enlivened verbalization, is primarily one of flatness. The actual scores— the high A%, the large number of object responses, the high P%, and the lowest mean ΣC of any age but Fifteen—all contribute to this appearance of flatness.

In actual scores, Eleven appears to be little different from Ten. There is one important change, however, which begins here and continues till 15, and that is the increase of D and Dd% and the decrease of W%. This increase in D and Dd is an indication of Eleven's increased practicality and his ability to deal more adequately with facts, to be more precise. The W:D:Dd ratio between the ages of 2 and 10 years fluctuates a great deal. Throughout the entire age range to 16 years, in the groups that we have studied, mean W% always exceeds mean D% except at 9 and 14 years. But at 11 years for the first time median D% is higher than median W%. Eleven seemingly marks a point of departure toward greater maturity in the Area ratios and all that this implies interpretively.

Signs of characteristic immaturity at eleven (at least as compared with present adult expectations) are reflected in the scores themselves. FM responses still exceed M; CF exceeds FC; F(C) is low; and the number of popular responses is high. Changes toward maturity are seen in all these factors (except in the predominance of CF over FC) in the years that immediately follow.

A growth spurt at 12 throws the relative immaturity of Eleven into relief. This spurt is suggested by the following changes: mean R at 12 rises from 19.5 to 22; W% declines further; mean F+% rises from 90.3 to 92.4; mean M rises from 2.2 to 2.6 and exceeds FM: mean F(C) increases from .6 to .9; and A% decreases slightly.

The nature of content, though immature in relation to subsequent ages, is however beginning to change. Reflection responses have doubled their mean since 10 years. Median A% reaches its peak here. After this it begins to decrease. Blood, fire, and mask have decreased slightly from Ten. Plant is lower than at any other age, as is the category geography-geology. Scene is lower than at any age except Fourteen.

It will be noted that one of the outstanding characteristics of Eleven is the marked difference in quality between the response of girls and that of boys. Some individual boys, certainly, give responses similar to those of some individual girls. But so far as the group as a whole is concerned, girls are more inclined toward a warm, interpersonal, stream-of-consciousness wordiness. Boys, rather more like the 10-year-olds, are inclined to qualify, to refuse initially, to use the phrase "could be," to give a response and then change or deny it. Twice as many girls as boys give the first kind of response; five times as many boys as girls give the second.

There is something of a paradox, however, in this matter of sex differences at Eleven. Though qualitatively the records of the two sexes tend to differ conspicuously, so far as the actual scoring is concerned they are closer together than at most other ages. Thus we find that at every age but 11, girls give more M, more F(C), more total responses, more populars than do boys. At 11, these figures are equal or boys exceed slightly. Also at this age, unlike other ages, for most determinants boys are more variable than are girls.

In summary, a look at the qualitative changes that occur at this age gives us a definite, individual picture of Eleven, even though the actual scores for most determinants have changed very little since Ten.

Eleven is the age of paradox. The verbal exuberance and liveliness, that are so characteristic and unmistakable, contrast with often flat and uninspired final scores. Eleven talks constantly, and it is interesting to listen to him, but he may actually say very little. He is swept away in the wonder of his own verbalization, and the recorder often trails far behind. He is so expansive that, as we have noted, he even spontaneously verbalizes his termination with "That's all," or "That's about it," or "Nothing else." But in contrast he has "shot his bolt," by the time he arrives at inquiry, and resorts to "Because it looked like one," or "I just did," when questioned about his response. In spite of all his earlier elaboration, he feels no need to give a specific reference as Ten often did.

This verbal productivity accompanied by a warm, friendly, good-humored attitude often seems to produce its own deterioration. Eleven's stream of consciousness often leads him into confused and poor form response. He begins to use unpleasant and censorious adjectives. He criticizes the blots and suggests changes for them; he qualifies, denies, and stalls with his verbalization.

His criticism of the environment does not often extend to himself, but though F(C) responses are low, reflection responses have doubled since Ten. This does not necessarily mean that Eleven is being critical of himself. On the contrary, he is probably more or less enamored with himself. But at the same time this increase in reflection provides a basis for greater sensitivity to criticism from others. And the amount of Clob, though the figures are small, is higher here than elsewhere. Thus in spite of his criticism and aggressivity, he may not yet have the reserves to protect himself from occasional depressive reactions.

Eleven appears willing to leave Ten's protective balance to launch out into more active engagement with others. Eleven adopts a more dynamic, aggressive role than does Ten, as seen in the amount of fighting, quarreling, arguing, and battling that appears. Though dancing and swinging around rank first as activity of any type, the active engagement in arguing, battling, fighting is next. Eleven also appears more ambitious than Ten (climbing ties with fighting for first place in animal movement), but is still not ready to relinquish his dependence. And though his argumentativeness appears to have increased, he also shows a projection toward or a desire for adaptive inhibitions (tension movements lead in m, explosions come second; blood and fire have decreased slightly from 10).

Ten is restricted and cautious, protective and balanced. Eleven is highly verbal, exuberant, critical, argumentative, and ready to launch into greater activity with others. But Eleven, as we suggest, is an age of paradox. Thus in spite of these characteristics that seem most typical of Eleven, we also see increased sensitivity to criticism, and projection toward more adaptive inhibitions. Eleven battles and argues; and at the same time, conformity and response to the pressures of the group reach a new high at this age. Girls and boys seem very different from each other at Eleven in the quality of their response, and yet the sexes are more alike here in formal scoring than at any other age. Eleven seems to be full of fantasy and can embroider a concept delightfully, and yet this age marks the beginning of the tendency toward the giving of more practical and precise concepts, a realistic step toward maturity. Eleven talks a great deal, but the final scored record may appear little different from that of Ten. Paradox seems to be the key; and the verbal exuberance of the 11-year-old record sets it off clearly from the response at other ages.

Individual Determinants

Number: There are fewer responses here than at subsequent ages except Fifteen —mean of 19.5.

Area: Mean W% is 48 per cent; mean D%, 44 per cent. For the first time, however, median D% (47 per cent) surpasses the median W% (46 per cent). This continues to be true of the medians until 15 years when median W% again exceeds median D%.

Form: Sixty-two per cent of responses are determined by form alone. F+% is 90 per cent, a little less than in the years that follow.

M, FM, m: Mean M is now 2.2; mean FM is 2.5; mean m, .6. The "vigorous extensor" M of dancing, swinging around, predominates. The "mixed-conflicted" responses of lifting, holding, carrying come second. Among FM, the "vigorous extensor" movement of climbing comes first. The "mixed-conflicted" movements of lifting, holding, carrying come second. However, as a general class static movements lead among M; vigorous extensor among FM. Among m, explosion and tension responses tie for first place.

Color: ΣC is slightly lower here than at other ages except Fifteen, a mean of 1.0.

As at other ages, CF responses predominate. FC comes next, then C. Of FC responses, animals of some kind lead; of CF, nature; of C, fire and explosion.

Shading: There are fewer shading responses here than at any other age—a mean of .6. Texture responses are the leading type.

FC', C'F, FClob, Clob: At only one age, Fourteen, do more subjects use Clob, or is the mean score higher. Here 11 per cent use Clob and the mean score is .12.

Content: As at other ages, 20 different content categories in all are used. The average number per child is 5.1. Mean A% is 50 per cent, highest of any age. Mean H% is 19 per cent, one of the highest ages for this.

Animals is the leading content category, followed by humans, objects, and anatomy, in that order.

Characteristic Adjectives: queer, weird, awful, nasty, strange, crazy, silly.

Length: One of the ages for girls when records are longest.

Total Time: Total time less than at preceding ages, mean 12.4 minutes.

Semantics: The leading kind of identification is comparing the blot to reality by means of the phrase "looks like." There is less simply naming the blot than at any other age, and more use of qualifying concepts than at any other age.

Best and Least Liked: Both sexes like Card X best. Girls as at most ages like IV least. Boys like I and IX least.

Refusals: Still a good many subjects (26 per cent) refuse at least one card. Card IX is most refused; Card VI next most.

Populars: One of the three high points for popular responses. Mean for populars is now 6.7; median, 6.5.

Sex Differences

Though at this age the records of boys and girls seem more different from each other than at most ages, so far as scores for the main determinants are concerned the two sexes are actually more alike than at most ages. Girls' responses tend to be longer and more detailed than those of boys, to express much interpersonal engagement with the examiner, and to contain a good deal of more or less "stream of consciousness" material. Fewer boys have his kind of response. Also, boys more than girls make qualifying remarks, give vigorous M and FM responses, fire responses, WS responses, and have the two sides acting on the center of Card I.

However, in spite of these conspicuous qualitative differences, we find that while at every age but 11 girls give more M than boys, more shading, more responses, more populars, longer records, at 11, scores for the two sexes for these items are almost equal. Thus boys and girls are actually more alike at this age than at other ages in this range. The only conspicuous scoring differences are that girls give more D and Dd responses than do boys and have higher F+, A%, and H%.

Comparison of Rorschach and Developmental Findings

DEVELOPMENTAL	RORSCHACH
Antagonistic, oppositional.	High WS, more than at any other age.
	Many refuse blots; refuse initially; or give response and then deny it. Mean refusal exceeded only at 10.
	Much criticism of blots.
	More turn cards than at any other age.
	Space shock not marked, but higher than at most other ages.
Quarrelsome, argumentative.	Nature of movement responses: the percentage of static movement drops from 10. One of two highest ages for fighting, quarreling, battling, in both M and FM.
Highly responsive to people even though quarrelsome.	Relatively high H%. Many fighting, quarreling responses.
Tends to be unpleasant and critical of others.	Girls use three times as many unpleasant adjectives as pleasant. Typical adjectives: queer, weird, awful, nasty, strange, crazy, silly.
	Tendency to dark shock is greater for girls than at any other age.
Low in self-criticism and in critical evaluation.	F+% lower than at any other age in this range.
	F(C) less than at any other age in this range.
Expansive.	Records are wordier than at surrounding ages.
	Mean DW higher than at any other age.
Behavior stereotyped and predictable in spite of expansiveness.	Boys give more populars than at any other age. A% higher at this age than at any other.
Tends to go on and on in conversation in endless detail.	"Stream of consciousness" type of response to the blot.
	Median D up to 47 per cent. Dd% higher than at 10 years.
Finds it difficult to make a clear, specific statement.	More qualifying expressions used at this age than at any other.
Unmodulated expression of emotions.	CF responses predominate. Of these, blood responses make up 18 per cent, exceeded at only one age; fire responses make up 20 per cent, more than at any age following.
Girls more mature and show more breakup of 10-year-oldness than do boys.	Qualitative sex differences here, in this same direction.

Sample Record of 11-Year-Old-Boy M.S.

RESPONSE	INQUIRY	SCORING			P
I. Couple of pelicans that are mad at each other and aren't looking at each other.	(Two side figures, looking outward. Large side proj. are beaks.) Reminded you? "I don't know—big beaks—don't have wings yet—not speaking."	D	FM	A	
(Anything else?) Well, in the middle looks like a woman beetle and looks like she got shot.	? "Figure looks like a woman—hole in it. Top, of a beetle. Hole might be an open mouth—women's mouths usually are open, but I think a hole (in the beetle)." (Inquiry reveals two concepts. He sees central figure as woman. Area, center to top, as beetle. But he has difficulty in disentangling them in his perception. Strong tendency to contamination.)	D { D	F+ m F+	H A	
A couple of snakes with mouths open are over top of her.	(Two top center proj. Separate concept. His expression is a means of identifying the area rather than relating concepts.)	D	FM	A	
II. Looks like a couple of bears rubbing noses—and they've been shot—see—that's all blood.	(Black plus bottom red as "blood.")	W	↗CF FM	↗(blood) A	P
Oh, coming out of the top of the head, there's a couple of hands	(Top red.) ? "Well, see, they're coming out of the top of the bear's head."	D	↗CF M	↗(blood-paint) Hd	

Sample Record of 11-Year-Old-Boy M.S. (*Continued*)

RESPONSE	INQUIRY		SCORING		
pointing up—all bloody, or else they're painted red, I don't know.	More like human hands making a fist, pointing up.				P
The noses look like they have sort of space ships on the end of them.	(Center black.) Part of bears D or separate idea? "I'm not too sure—could be either way—might be glued to 'em. Look like they're part of the noses, but you can't tell well." (Scored as separate concept but again difficult for him to separate from original response.)	D	↗m F+	object	
III. Oh! This looks like a couple of guys bowling—at each other, by the way.	(Usual figures.)	W	M	H	P
In between the two bowling balls, looks like sort of a bat—guess it got shot.	(Lower center gray. He indicates the holes in the center for place where it was "shot.")	Dd	↗m F+	A	
And this looks like two baby kangaroos falling down from up above—something like that.	(Side reds.)	D	m	A	
And in between the two men is a butterfly.	(Center red. Form.)	D	F+	A	P
IV. Hm, well—looks like two bear's feet	(Usual boots.) ? "A little too big for human's feet—unless they're the boy-who-lives-across-the-street-from-me's feet."	Do	F+	Ad	P

RESPONSE	INQUIRY	SCORING			
—with looks like a bug in between 'em—oversize bug. Can only see half of him though.	(Lower center. Form.)	D	F+	Ad	
Up above 'em is a flower just opened.	(Top half of blot, above boots.) ? "I don't know—just looks like a flower just opening." ? "I don't know, just looks like a flower." (Original expression and explanation in inquiry must credit inanimate movement, since it did not seem possible to pursue inquiry further.)	Dd	↗?F(C) m	plant	
Oh, a couple salamanders coming out from the side.	(Usual arm proj.)	D	FM	A	
V. Well, first of all looks like a bat—big bat.	(Whole, except for side proj.)	W	F+	A	P
(Lifts eyebrows.) And it's got crocodile's heads sticking out from the ends of its wings.	(Side proj. Form. Identification of area. No relation to bat.)	D	F+	Ad	
VI. ∨ Well, looks like a bear rug with two heads.	(Whole.) ? "Four legs and all that."	W	F+	Aobject	P
∧ Looks like an Indian headdress up at the top	(Top D.) ? "Looks like feathers."	D	F(C)	object	
and coming through the headdress is two fists.	(Small detail, top center of top D.) Fists? "I can't tell—looks like two arms with fists on the end coming through—just punching their way through."	Dd	M	Hd	

Sample Record of 11-Year-Old-Boy M.S. (Continued)

RESPONSE	INQUIRY		SCORING		
∨ In between the two heads, looks like sort of a bug with long hands reaching out.	(Small, gray, lower center detail.)	Dd	FM	A	P
VII. Well, looks like two Indians that are sort of walking away from each other, but they're looking at each other—must be in love or something (disgusted tone), but I can't tell.	(Whole.)	W	M	H	
And there are these two big boulders with a church in between them—that's about it, I guess.	(Lower tier, with light lower center detail as church.) ? "So big and oddly shaped and all that—look like twin boulders like you see out west."	D	F(C)	scene	
VIII. ∨∧ Well, here we go—looks like two—raccoons, climbing up a hill	(Usual animals.)				P
∧ and there's a backbone going right down through the hill	(Mid-line. This is interpolated without break in his explanation of the raccoons and his description of the hill.)	DW	FM	↗scene A	
∨∧ and the hill has sort of—what would you call these things—sort of—there's a ledge and another ledge up above, so if it rains it acts as a sort of roof.	(Top gray as "roof," with blue center as "ledge.") ? "Looks like they're (raccoons) gonna go on top of the roof."	Dd	F+	anatomy	
				elaboration	
And looks like a butterfly underneath the second ledge—a big one.	(Lower pink and orange.) ? "Just looks pretty and all different colors—two different colors."	D	FC	A	

RESPONSE	INQUIRY	SCORING

IX. (Pause, frowns.) Well, the top part here looks sort of like a witch, laughing. — (Orange.) — D M (H)

This looks like—what do you call those things on the floors of caves that stick up? Oh, a stalagmite rock sticking up. — (Mid-line.) — D F+ ↗m nature

Oh! Looks like a big green pig, with instead of a tail, he's got claws. — (Green, each side. Claws are incorporated as confabulatory detail and indicated as "tail of pig," because of position.) ? "Not a green pig." — D F± A

Well, down here, looks like a red sunset. — (Pink.) ? "Just looks like clouds, you know." — D CF ↗F(C) nature

X. ∨ Well, the blue spots look like two tarantulas with a couple of extra legs. And it looks sort of like a cavern in between two mountains. And on it there are two dinosaurs, and they're pushing their heads together—looks sort of like they're fighting. Two beetles on a stick, holding up the two mountains. On the other (Two mountains are pink. Dinosaurs are center blue. Beetles and stick are top gray. Side brown is "cow-kangaroo"; side yellow is "yellow fire" the "cow things" are breathing. Center green is "bug" with "sea horses for his arms." Tarantulas are incorporated into the total confabulation, though original concept seems discrete. Side green is their "dinner.") — DW FM ↗CF ↗m scene A (P)

(confabulation)

Sample Record of 11-Year-Old-Boy M.S. (Continued)

RESPONSE	INQUIRY	SCORING
side of the mountains, away from the dinosaurs, looks like a couple of—sort of cows—with a cow's head and a kangaroo's body—big long horns—and they're running down the mountain. Coming down between the mountains, about to land on top of the dinosaurs, looks like a bug with two sea horses for his arms. And the tarantulas, they're holding onto some dinner or something—I don't know. Oh, and the cows are breathing yellow fire.		

Card most liked: III. "Because I like bowling and those are two men bowling."
Card least liked: IX. "I don't know, just sort of—uh—I don't know why—just don't like it—can't describe why."

R:31

3W		13 F = 42%F	13A
2W		11F+, 2F± = 92%F+	3Ad
2DW = 23%W			1Aobject = 54%A
18D = 58%D		5M, 7FM, 2m	3H
		1FC, 1CF	1(H)
		2F(C)	2Hd = 20%H
5 Dd			
1 Do = 19%Dd		(→5m, 3CF, 2F(C))	

5M:1½ΣC

3 objects
1 plant
2 scene (→2)
2 nature
1 anatomy
(→2 blood)
(→1 paint)

9–10P

Succession: Orderly
Shock: None

COMMENT See page 142.

COMMENT   If Eleven can be said to be critical, argumentative, to carry a chip on his shoulder, this boy has certainly hit the age hard (or vice versa). His exuberance and expansiveness are not only products of his relish of the situation but result too from his attempts to amaze and confound the examiner. Where many Elevens are often vague, his responses become downright confused. Where expansiveness leads some to confabulation, it leads him to contamination at times. He sees things shot and bloody, hands or fists emerging from heads, backbones appearing suddenly in a peaceable landscape, cows with kangaroo bodies breathing yellow fire, in what can only be termed a surrealistic fashion. The parts are all good, but the combinations are amusingly indifferent to reality. Yet this "stream of consciousness" reaction does not seem to disturb him. He engages himself intellectually and emotionally with a breathtaking immediacy, leaving the environment to trail along in his wake.

While his manner of production may be an exaggerated picture of Eleven's response, his scoring is hardly the typically "flat and uninspired." He scores beyond the 75th percentile in R, D%, Dd%, M, FM, m, FC, F(C), ΣC, and P, and falls below the 25th in W% and F%. There is ample evidence that this is a bright, imaginative boy whose contact with reality is quite sound. He certainly has an individual viewpoint, and he tends to get lost in nonessentials. In fact, he may "get stuck" with his initially good perceptions, being able neither to incorporate them satisfactorily into other perceptions nor to release them. But he can accept readily the usual cultural ideas and demands and can comply with social and daily routines, though undoubtedly in a highly individual manner. He is less inhibited than many at his age, as is indicated not only by the number of responses, the low F%, the number of content categories, and the extent of movement and color responses, but also by "much humorous antagonism, grimacing, dramatic, startled expressions," noted during the testing.

While M is high, FM is even higher, indicating the pressure toward direct gratification of impulses. His awareness of these impulses is much greater than his actual acting on them, as the relatively low CF shows, and much of his activity is clearly "just talk." His FM movements reveal many opposing tendencies: there are antagonistic fighting, predatory, ambitious, demanding, friendly, timid attitudes all implied in the activities of the animals. Thus, he does not seem at all certain about a unification of impulses in a role concept, though aggressiveness seems to satisfy him most. It is interesting to see that the animals exhibiting the only friendly gestures have just been shot. One may suspect that he distrusts friendly overtures!

His "menagerie" is also interesting in this regard. There are definitely dangerous animals in the record, tarantulas and dinosaurs, crocodiles and cow-kangaroos breathing fire. But in general his animals, though not particularly domestic, are benign and harmless. The use of innocuous animals in aggressive attitudes suggests some element of bluff.

The m responses, especially "baby kangaroos falling down" and the two "shot" responses, indicate a sense of insecurity, of vulnerability to attack, even of abandonment, which throws some light on the aggressiveness. But whatever its source, he undoubtedly presents to the world an antagonistic-hostile attitude, only partly softened by humor. The "two guys bowling—at each other," the "witch laughing," the "hands pointing up, all bloody," and the "two fists punching their way through," indicate a mistrustful attitude and show that he believes a good attack is the best defense. His "two Indians walking away from each other—must be in love," indicates that he is conscious of social, heterosexual relationships, even intrigued by them, but not fully accepting of them as yet.

The color response is balanced between FC and CF, "butterfly" and "sunset." Both are agreeable responses and indicate that his reaction to the environment can be pleasant and satisfactory. The secondary CF elaborations of blood, paint, and fire are indicative of less adaptable, less mature reactions, more impulsive and egocentric. The shading responses here indicate his sensitivity to the nuances of the gray as well as a beginning awareness of perspective. This reveals a perceptiveness and sensitivity to his own feelings and to those of others not suggested by his surface brashness.

Thus, this boy has a gamut of emotional and intellectual drives and energy which, though not well organized at present, provide him with a potential for highly productive and warmly satisfying activities and relationships. He is subject to and undoubtedly subjects those around him to much confusion and highly personal involvement. He does not know the limits, and it is up to others to draw them, but he is able to make an adaptation once it is demanded of him.

At present he is a boy of extremes: highly adaptable contrasted with superficial, egocentric, impulsive behavior; thoughtful, self-critical reactions contrasted with abandonment to emotional impulses and reactions; independent urges combined with feelings of dependence, even insecurity; aggressive and cocky attitudes, yet ability to follow rules in an agreeable social fashion; factual, realistic perceptions used in highly personal, often incongruous combinations; interest in others, yet mistrust of them. This boy certainly shows the "paradox" of Eleven, in his own highly individual manner.

Sample Record of 11-Year-Old-Girl A.G.

RESPONSE	INQUIRY	SCORING			

I. Looks like a couple of guards holding a man—see, those would be his hands. Ready to take him. Or it might be in a circus doing a balancing act, holding onto a pole. Shape of a lady—those two are the men.

(Whole. Two side figures acting on center in each concept.)

DW   M   H

V This looks rather amusing. These look like a couple of lions, chasing up a tree. Both want something up there. Jumping. Arm, arm, standing on one leg. Awful big tail.

(Whole. Lions are somewhat misshapen, but she sees them clearly. Tree is center.)

DW   FM   A   O

II. Oh, I remember this one! (Frowns.) Might be two robbers, rope tied there. Light gray going right between there, tied by a stick, planning what they're going to do while the man calls the cops. Instead of wearing black and white hats, they wear striped red hats. Might be when they got shot, they were twin brothers, Siamese twins. Maybe if they were shot in the same place—drop of blood.

(Whole. Men are tied together at center black. She is quite conscious of the nuances of gray, as well as of the red shadings. Movement is the most important determinant here, but shading and color are strongly incorporated. "Blood" is lower red.)

DW   /FC /CF   M /F(C)   H   P   (confabulation)

RESPONSE	INQUIRY	SCORING			
V Looks like a couple of divers going in for a swim—chain—chain divers. They go in together—chain divers—going in. That splash might be where someone else had swum and the water had quieted down. Maybe going awfully fast—drops of water from the vibration in the air.	(Whole. This time the figures are attached at the bottom center. She incorporated the red this time as m and not as color.)	DW	↗m M (confabulation)	H	0
III. Oh these are two hotsy-totsy gentlemen, see? Their coats! Could it possibly be at a party? Could they be talking to one another while they held a chicken over a pot of water?	(Usual figures.)	DW	M (confabulation)	H	P
Bow tie. What could that mean? Could it be—might be an outdoor party and they were wearing costumes, going to put on a play.	(Center red. She actually incorporates the tie and the apron in the total confabulation, but they are given as separate concepts.)	D	F+	object	P
This is an apron ready if there should be a couple of maids in the play.	(Side red.)	D	F±	object	
V Oh, I see something beautiful. This is a forest. Tree. Couple of	(Each side black is a tree, with perspective seen through the center. She in-	DW	↗CF F(C)	scene	

Sample Record of 11-Year-Old-Girl A.G. (Continued)

RESPONSE	INQUIRY		SCORING		
log limbs. This might be something left in the way. Somebody left a couple of red paper wrappers in the road.	corporates the red this time as debris left in the road.)				
IV. Oh, I remember this one. This is an awful big bear sitting on a tree stump. Funny kind of bear; very, very thin arms, but rest of him is awful big. Boots, heel. Begging for honey.	(Whole.)	W	↗M FM	A	P (0)
V Turn it upside down, might be if you went to Savin Rock. Two of the eyes. That would be the tail. These would be the two big wings that hold him up. Two extra legs for walking.	(Whole. Savin Rock is local carnival. Evidently sees this as a carnival figure. Eyes on usual lower center animal head. A stationary figure, but wings give idea of suspension.)	W	↗m F+	Aobject (0)	
V Oh this is a bat. V A bat both ways.	(Whole. Form.)	W	F+	A	P
VI. Oh, this is a funny one. This one I like. Cat, whiskers, ears. Must be looking upward for something. Wild cat. Guess that's it. Tail— even split the tail.	(Whole.)	W	FM	A	

RESPONSE	INQUIRY	SCORING		
∨ What would it be upside down? Did you ever watch the Riley show? Has a friend named Gillis. The two might be doing a pogo act together—pogo stick. Their coat. Seamstress wasn't very careful—left a little part out.	(Whole with pogo stick top D, figures on each side.)	DW	M	H 0
VII. Oh, I remember this one! This lady was vain. Very vain. She used to stare at herself in the mirror. As a matter of fact, it might not be a lady—it's a bunny, not a lady. Very careful. Getting dressed up to go somewhere. Staring at herself in the mirror. Her ear. Bunny lady. Not ready to go yet. Just anointed her face with dark cold cream, smeared all around. ∨ What would that be upside down? Not so easy. I don't like turning them upside down. I get one thing established and I don't like to turn it.	(Top two tiers only.)	D	∕FM, F(C) M	∕H A P (reflection)
VIII. I like this one. This is a little girl with pigtails. I guess it must be a skeleton from a prehistoric age. See, those are her ribs and her	(Whole. Head and pigtails are top gray. Usual ribs, center backbone. Center blue is sweater. Usual animals. Sees center figure first, but then incorpo-	∕WS DW	FM	∕scene A P (0)

Sample Record of 11-Year-Old-Girl A.G. (Continued)

RESPONSE	INQUIRY	SCORING
backbone. Her sweater. I don't know how the sweater managed to stay, but it's rather ragged. These are two squirrels. The two squirrels are climbing up, exploring her. They never got close enough to a human being to see what it was before.	rates animals in confabulatory whole.)	
IX. (Long regard.) I have something worked out and I'm not quite sure how to tell it. You remember in the Brementown musicians—they climbed up and scared the robbers away. These might be those. Musicians. (Indicates green and orange.) I think this one (pink) is a musician too. When they're climbing up against the wall. They have to be outside the wall, yelling, or singing. Little window.	(Whole. Donkey, dog, and cat, one standing on back of other. Center and white is wall and window.)	↗WS DW FM ↗A scene O (confabulation)
X. Oh, I remember this. This is animal land Two high cliffs. This animal land is funny. The animals can fly around in the air. They	(Whole. She details the most popular elements. Pink are cliffs. Ducks are center blue; dogs are center yellow; caterpillars, center green. Bone is top	DW ↗m FM ↗A scene (P) (confabulation)

RESPONSE	INQUIRY	SCORING
don't necessarily have to hold on to something. They are double-jointed. They seem to be able to do so many things. Usually we can't stretch ourselves around into such queer shapes. Those are two ducks. Dogs dressed up in costumes. Caterpillars. Everything is suspended in the air. Oh, this is a bone—separates like a leg bone. And these two animals are trying to get it. This—baby octopus. This might be a crab. These might be cliffs.	gray with animals on each side. Side blue is octopus. Side brown is crab. Original determinant is FM, though there is the element of m with the expression of "everything suspended." Additional score is given to "bone" since the content is so different from the total, but it is really incorporated into the total scene quite logically.)	D F+ anat.

Card most liked: IV. "The bear."
Card least liked: VII. "I feel sort of sorry for her. Don't like vain people."

R:18   Time: 18 minutes

4W	5F = 28%F	8A
10DW = 77%W	4F+, 1F± = 90%F+	1Aobject = 50%A
4D = 23%D	6M, 6FM, 1F(C)	5H (→1H) = 27%H
	(→2M, 3m, 1FC, 2CF, 2F(C))	2 objects (1Aobject)
	5M:0ΣC	1 anatomy
		2 scene (→3)
		(→1 blood)

Succession: None
Shock: None

8P, 4-7 O

COMMENT See page 150.

COMMENT The outstanding characteristic here is the confabulation. This provides also for the great number of secondary scorings, as was also the case in the 11-year-old boy. The quality of the confabulation, however, is quite different. The girl has surmounted the confusion shown by the boy. It is evident from the high W% and the way she incorporates all the details in the blots that she likes complete concepts. She does not neglect details, even though D% is low, but includes in her well-embroidered DW's such perceptions as "water vibrating," "red paper wrappers," and even comments on missing details, which a careless seamstress must have left out.

She appears to be a born story-teller. Instead of leaving unrelated facts, she combines them in a charming total concept, weaving a story around them to support any incongruities that may appear. Yet, for all the elements she brings in, few of the actual scoring variables are notably elevated. Only W%, M, and FM score beyond the 75th percentile for 11-year-old girls, while D%, F%, CF, and ΣC score at or below the 25th. The combining, creative elements are strong, the more practical responsiveness less apparent.

Her use of scene and perspective is indicative of the tendency seen more frequently at later stages in the developing adolescent, though somewhat characteristic of the entire period. It seems to represent a search for self and for an idea of self in relation to others. Her self concepts appear active and ambitious. She appears to have few doubts about her ability at problem solving or in adapting to a situation. All FM are active, moving upward, doing something. But there is a feeling of restraint or inhibition imposed on her. Even a note of pathos may appear at X when she projects her feelings in regard to her dependence: "The animals can fly around in the air. They don't necessarily have to hold on to something. . . . They seem to be able to do so many things." Her "menagerie" is composed of agreeable domestic animals as a rule. The lions, the most aggressive animals employed, are termed "amusing."

The M shows the restraint she still feels in translating her activities into a more independent, responsible role. Her first interpretation is that of guards holding a man, which quickly becomes a balancing act, with a lady held between two men. Two robbers are shot and tied by a stick, and they become still more dependent when she refers to them as Siamese twins. Next appear divers, chained, and finally two men working together on a pogo stick. All these responses give the impression of being restrained by and dependent on the actions of others. There is also a well-defined feeling of the role of authority. She seems to have a sense of the interdependence of human relationships, an unusually mature concept, and perhaps unduly restraining to a girl of her age.

Only at III is there a more relaxed, social interpretation in the idea of a party, with the men wearing costumes, talking, getting ready for a play. But she seeks a good deal of reassurance for becoming so daring and spontaneous.

The interpretation at IX is interesting in that it represents accomplishment despite possible feelings of inadequacy. The Brementown musicians were animals who outwitted the robbers. While she shows again that co-operation is needed, and in piling one animal on top of another suggests a feeling of working against heavy odds, the weak do overcome the strong by means of their wits. She may feel at present restrained and cautious, but her natural ability and drive are generally ambitious and optimistic.

She has some insight into her own mental processes, as she shows at VII by the comment, "I don't like turning them upside down. I get one thing established and I don't like to turn it." However, up to this time she has methodically turned each blot and given a most adequate response. One would surmise that she has methodical work habits and orderly thought processes. She shows both independence of thought and action and willingness to accommodate. But when a situation becomes one where her moral judgment comes into play, she may revert to a less adaptable and more rigid approach. She comments, on VII, "I feel sorry for her. Don't like the vain people." Is this critical self-evaluation? Is she hard on herself? Or does she have a highly developed sense of moral and ethical values that exercise a strong restraint on her intellectual and emotional processes?

Although this girl exhibits characteristics of the age, such as verbal facility and expansiveness, she shows her own individuality. She is observant, original, empathic, adaptable, energetic, has a wide range of intellectual interest and emotional activity, and seems in some ways "wise beyond her years." Her ethical sense exercises restriction which she escapes in charming and highly intellectualized confabulation.

CHAPTER TWELVE

Twelve Years

19R	63%F	46%A
	93%F+	18%H
42%W		2.6 objects
48%D	2.6M, 2.2FM, 1.0m	.7 anatomy
4%Dd	.3FC, .8CF, .2C,	.7 nature
	.9F(C)	.5 plant
	Mean 2.6M:1.2ΣC	7P
	Median 2.3M:0.9ΣC	

Ten years of age seems to mark a breathing point in the course of development, a temporary period of consolidation and organization terminating the complex period of change that takes place in the child's behavior between 5 and 10. At 11, a new cycle of behavior starts with the breaking up of 10-year-old smoothness. This period of disequilibrium is, however, relatively brief in many and by 12 is in most children more or less completed. Twelve takes a long stride toward approaching maturity. Many 12-year-olds seem almost suddenly to have reached a new plateau of expansiveness and of easy functioning, in which many forerunners of more mature behavior make themselves seen for the first time (11).

In considering the Rorschach response of the 12-year-old, it will be interesting to see whether or not there are reflections of increased maturity, equilibrium, expansiveness, enthusiasm, and readiness for new experience that we characteristically observe in the overt behavior of the 12-year-old. With the Rorschach as with any other single test, we cannot hope to discover all that more extensive observation and testing will reveal about any individual or group. However, the Rorschach may show us facets of Twelve that are not revealed in overt behavior; or it may give us new interpretations of what we already know of him.

Eleven was expansive but querulous; active, and vigorous but critical and argumentative. Twelve seems to emphasize all the good points of Eleven and to have resolved many of Eleven's difficulties. He is even more expansive than Eleven, but seldom as complaining. His activity and vigor have taken an even greater surge, a more positive direction, and he is seldom critical or quarrelsome.

The continued expansiveness of Twelve is shown in the Rorschach, first of all in the marked increase of the number of responses given. The 12-year-old gives more responses than at any age to date, namely a mean of 22, median of 19. Only at later ages, Fourteen and Sixteen, are as many responses given.

In keeping with this tendency toward increased response, the 12-year-old seems to see many possibilities at once, and frequently gives multiple responses to one card or area in a card, one concept following the other immediately. Thus: "Cat's head or a mask"; "Head of a cat or a dog"; "Two dogs chasing a rabbit or could be a bat"; "Could be a butterfly. Wait a minute. Might be a bow tie." Since these multiple responses are often given in a single score, depending on inquiry, the record is even more expansive than an actual counting of scores might indicate.

Twelve may even give a choice of action as well as of content. Thus: "A dog or a fox chasing or running toward a rabbit." The large number of DW responses (discussed later) is a further example of the "bursting out all over" quality of age Twelve.

Furthermore, only about half as many subjects give refusals as at 10 and 11, and only about half as many cards are refused. At Twelve, only 15 per cent of subjects refuse any cards; mean number of refusals is only .2.

Twelve not only gives more actual responses than does the just younger or just older child, but he also gives a response that is indicative of a considerably more vigorous and enlarged activity in many areas. Human movement responses occur here more than at any other age in the first 16 years. Both the median (2.3M) and the mean (2.6M) bear this out. This great increase of psychic vigor and inner drive characterizes Twelve perhaps more accurately than any other single Rorschach factor.

Not only are mean and median M strikingly high at this age, but 84 per cent of subjects, considerably more than at earlier ages, give M responses. That the 12-year-old actually carries out a more active role, and does not merely see himself as active, is suggested by the fact that at 12 years of age for the first time, mean M exceeds mean FM. This is perhaps the clearest indication that the Rorschach gives us of the strong thrust toward maturity that occurs at Twelve.

It must be noted here, however, that at no age in our group is the adult expectancy of a 2:1 ratio between M and FM attained. By the age of 10 years, M and FM are at a ratio of about 2:3 and throughout the entire range to 16 years, M and FM remain nearly equal. But at Twelve for the first time M responses are greater than FM.

Another tendency that emphasizes Twelve's activity and vigor is the fact that WS whole card responses are beginning to give way to whole responses made up of two side figures. This occurs especially on Cards I, II, and III (see Chapter 9 for discussion on separate cards). This interest in twoness, implemented by the frequent use of the word "two," suggests not only the balance and symmetry of Twelve's thinking and perception, but indicates to an even greater degree his increased tendency toward movement responses.

The 12-year-old not only gives more movement responses than at other ages, but he also tends to give more vigorous movement responses. Twelve has a larger percentage of "vigorous extensor" M (29 per cent) than does any other age. "Flexor passive" M occur here less than at surrounding ages and least of any class of movement given. The outstanding single kind of movement, as at all ages in this range except Fifteen, is the vigorous "dancing, swinging around," which reaches a peak at Twelve.

Animal movements, as at other ages, are of a generally more vigorous nature than are human movements. The class "vigorous extensor" predominates here as at other ages. The single kind of FM that occurs most is climbing, followed by some kind of fighting or quarreling response. At Eleven, quarreling and fighting were equal to climbing, but at Twelve climbing takes the lead.

Not only is Twelve the high point for M responses, but for m as well. The median 1.0 m found here is higher than at most other ages in the first 16 years. Mean m is the same—1.0. This would indicate a potential of unemployed energy and could be an area of difficulty. But explosions have coutinued to decrease and tension movements are definitely predominant. This is more indicative of greater restraint and stronger inhibitions, which can be an asset as well as a liability. The configuration of the results for the total group at Twelve indicates many stabilizers that counterbalance this possible area of difficulty.

Color responses, too, though less so, are increased at Twelve over surrounding ages (mean ΣC is 1.2). Also, a slightly higher percentage of subjects than at any other age gives color responses, many more than at the age that follows. As at all ages in this range, CF predominates. Leading CF responses are various kinds of nature response. Pure C occurs a little more frequently at Twelve than at surrounding ages. Color used as fire is higher here than at any other age except 10 years. Color used as blood and in anatomy responses is low among both CF and C responses, and color used in explosion responses has decreased. Twelve is certainly egocentric, but probably not more so than the other age groups in our range, since CF is always the predominant color response. The fire responses indicate the possibility of warm interpersonal clashes, but they are not as chaotic and diffuse as they were earlier. The subject now has enough reserve to feel that these may be resolved satisfactorily. For fire, although destructive, is also productive.

In the matter of type of reactivity or experience balance, the 12-year-old appears to be more introversive than extratensive, as at every age in this range. At this age only four subjects (three girls and one boy) give an equation of $0M:0\Sigma C$, as contrasted with the following age, when 13 subjects give such an equation. At Twelve, with some subjects, the number of human movement responses rises as high as 9M.

The number of shading responses has increased over 10 and 11 years, but is by no means as high as it will be later. Also fewer use shading (42 per cent) than at the ages that follow. Reflection response remains about the same as at Eleven, with a mean of .2. Responses suggesting awareness of vista are still very few. There appears to be less conscious effort to evaluate self and to see self in perspective than at the years that immediately follow. Sensitivity and perception of the subtle nuances of a situation are improving but are still immature.

One outstanding characteristic of Twelve's Rorschach response is his strong conformity. The mean for popular response is high, especially for boys (6.7P). No sex differences exist in either mean or median scores for populars, but for girls the peak age for popular response is earlier, at 10 years. With a mean N of 22 this gives, on the average, over one fourth of all responses as popular; and in some individual cases, nearly every single response is popular. The sample records for this age (pp. 164–170) suggest just how banal the response of the 12-year-old can be.

Perhaps one of Twelve's greatest charms is that he seldom recognizes his own banality. He is delighted with what he feels to be his unique performance: "I don't see how you can make anything out of this. I have such a terrific imagination!"

This high conformity suggests that though the typical 12-year-old is ready for rather full experience, he is perhaps not ready for particularly individualized experience. Being isolated or separated from the group may provide one of Twelve's greatest difficulties.

Twelve very much enjoys the common experience of the group and his identification with it. Because of this, his responses are perhaps more predictable than they will be at later ages. And though the peak for A% was reached at Eleven, the 49%A response we find here supports Twelve's pleasure in conformity.

In his desire to conform, Twelve likes to know whether there are right and wrong "answers" to the blots, though in somewhat more sophisticated terms than earlier: "Is there anything that's supposed to be in it?" "Are they supposed to look like something?" And he is also interested in comparing his response with that of others, in knowing how he compares with the group: "What do most people think?" "Does anyone else ever give the same answers I do?" Overcoming initial refusals is also evidence of his desire to comply.

An interesting combination of the conformity and the expansiveness both seemingly characteristic of this age is seen in the relatively high number of DW responses, which decline in number hereafter, and occur here more than at any other age except Eleven. Mean DW at Twelve is 1.8, nearly two such responses per subject. Often these DW are built up from a single popular response. Thus we find a drive for a more generalized and inclusive experience stemming from the old and tried. Even the DW responses show much similarity from one to the other, another indication of the homogeneity and conformity at Twelve. On Card III the two side figures are in action with the central figure, or all combined with top red (decorations) to be at a party. The idea of "party" is a very prevalent concept at Twelve. Or the two top figures on Card VII are sitting on rocks. Or the "animals" on VIII are climbing over rocks or across streams. Typical DW responses are:

III: "Two butlers sort of lowering a wash tub. They may be at a ball with chandeliers."
IV: "Giant walking into a tree. Going to kick it out of his way."
VIII: "Two bears trying to see who can get there first. Getting out of a forest fire. Going to a lake."

At Twelve, the subject's desire to combine is such that he may combine two major details of a card even though there may be no logical relationship: "Looks like a Mayfly and a totem pole" (VI); or "Goose head stuck in a boot" (IV).

Twelve is occasionally able to mention parts without combining as Eleven did, with such comments as "These don't look like anything in particular," or "That could be a butterfly, but I don't know what relationship it has to the rest of it." But in general, his need to include all parts into some kind of a whole is so strong that it may even surpass his ability to make this combination successfully, and may end up in rather unusual combinations as cited above, or even in contamination and confabulation.

Contaminations or near contaminations include: "A rabbit with wings or a deer with wings" (V); "Goat with rabbit ears"; "Worm with cat head or bat head"; "Lady unicorn" (VII); "Moose-ass" (IX); "Antenna coming out of head of turtle" (VI); "Two rabbits hanging onto a bird; bird may be part bullfrog because he's got two eyes" (I); "Rabbit bird" (V).

Confabulations include:

VII: "Two ladies backing into each other. Then a man who's cutting a hedge (center bottom) . . . there were two young ladies across the street and he's watching them and he made a figure of ladies in the hedge—absentminded I guess."
VII: "Well those are two Edwardian ladies. Obviously behaving very badly for time they are living in. Probably trying to be like deer. Oh excuse me, that's one Edwardian lady trying to look at herself in a mirror. She is

trying to be like a deer and she doesn't know what she looks like so she is turning herself completely around to look. Those are her horns and that's her ear. By the way, change the deer to unicorn."

VII: "I guess those are two little Indians. Their faces. Their feathers are coming out. Two pillows below. Just finished a pillow fight."

This inclusiveness and strong need to generalize is also seen in a tendency to perseveration at this age. Frequently a subject gives the same response to several cards, though maintaining good form. Several seem to have a feeling of perseverating even when they do not actually do so. Thus they may remark, "Butterfly—they all are", "Everything looks like butterflies to me"; "Two more witches; I don't know why everything should impress me as witches"; "I've got elephants on my mind"; "Don't know why I'm getting all these poodles today," even though they actually give only one of any of these responses. Or even more diffusely, and suggesting a real block, a subject may remark, "Ink blot—to me they all look like ink blots." We might possibly ask whether this is an age where stereotypes and prejudices are adopted on slight evidence. One obvious fact is often enough for Twelve to build up a whole structure even though the result is not always satisfactory. But his original premise is usually sound. This characteristic of his intellectual functioning certainly has many implications for our educational handling of the 12-year-old.

In spite of Twelve's easy ability to generalize, his interest in detail and his ability to observe more carefully are shown in the continued increase of D and Dd%, a tendency that was begun at Eleven. Although mean W% is higher than mean D%, the ratio is closer than it was at Eleven, and the median D% surpasses median W% by a greater margin than at Eleven. The fact that F+% has continued to increase also gives evidence of Twelve's ability to handle facts with precision. It is also shown in the way he responds in inquiry. Ten frequently gave a reference for his response: "I saw it in a Museum"; Eleven felt that "I just did" was sufficient reason for a response, though he also presaged the characteristic that comes more into prominence at Twelve when he said, "because it looked like one." Twelve is more certain of shapes and forms and usually compares his response to reality with, "The way it is shaped," or "Well, it just sort of looks like a boot."

He may even show a good deal of doubt about his response, but his complacency and his willingness to accept a situation may still allow an interpretation to stand, in spite of his doubts. Thus he characteristically remarks: "I don't really think they look like that"; "I don't know what they're doing there"; "Looks like it, but it doesn't"; "Bears don't have tails"; "I never saw a butterfly quite like that"; "I don't know what a wishbone is doing with a lot of animals"; "It might be guinea pigs except guinea pigs don't have such long tails—don't have tails"; "Animal's face sort of like, too small really for ears, though these are ears"; "Elephants, but wouldn't be very good elephants."

Because Twelve is so factual and realistic about things that he does know, he uses more qualifying phrases than at any other age but Eleven (see Table 23). Subjects say, "It might be," or "It could be." The phrase "Looks something like" is used here more than at any other age in this range, as also are "sort of like" and "sort of looks like." Boys use many more qualifying expressions than girls. This tendency can lend a feeling of uncertainty and a lack of positiveness to his response when he qualifies too extensively. But in general Twelve uses qualifying phrases because he is realistic and practical.

Eleven was often content to characterize a blot rather diffusely as "Design," "Modern art," "Abstract painting." Twelve often goes on to explain: "A kindergarten person just scribbling and making something up. Like my sister does. She just takes a paint brush and blots. Some kindergartener just splattered paint all over."

Twelve is curious. He seeks to enhance his knowledge. He often asks about the blots: "Are these done with water colors?" Who made these?" "Where did they come from?" "What are these anyway—ink spots on paper?" "What do they do—just drop ink on it?" He may also show a wish to compare his own response with that of others, when he asks, "What do most people think?" "Does anyone else ever give the same answers I do?"

Twelve's interest in other people is high and his own sense of self is strengthening, as indicated by the high H% (mean H% of 18 per cent is equaled only at one other age, 11), plus the fact that for the first time human movement surpasses animal movement. As to other characteristics of content not already mentioned, it should be noted that "mask" reaches its lowest mean incidence at this age; reflection and abstract responses are about the same as at Eleven; blood is at its lowest incidence except for 15 years; and food is definitely at its highest incidence for the entire age range. One of Twelve's major interests and needs is undoubtedly in the area of nourishment!

It is interesting to note here the sudden increase of (H) and (Hd) response, especially for girls. This is evidence of feelings of magic and superstition in regard to others. Investing others or even one's self with supernatural or superhuman characteristics may well be related to the onset or imminence of puberty. And group relationships may also have some aura of magic and mystery for Twelve. It may be one of the group's drawing powers for him. This is, for example, the age when individuals are often accepted into the rites of the church. Whether it is a reflection of the cultural rites or of his own developmental needs would be difficult to determine, but the increase of (H) and (Hd) is noteworthy.

Twelve shows oppositional tendencies in the fact that S responses reach a mean high of .8 here. However, WS responses are equal to the S responses, having a mean incidence of .8. Even the opposition is often inclusive, and he tries to use it adaptively. And though S alone occurs as frequently as WS, since the reactivity is in general introversive we might surmise that Twelve turns his aggressivity more in upon himself than outward upon society.

Opposition is also shown in the tendency toward initial refusal, but Twelve's desire to conform is so great that this refusal is overcome almost at once. Thus he may say, "Doesn't look like anything—a dog"; "Doesn't remind me of anything—these could be eyes or something"; "That doesn't look like anything—might be two buffaloes up there and a man riding a goat."

Concern with sex and feelings of ambivalence or fear about it may be expressed by the rather large number of responses that portray animals or people as "headless," "heads cut off," "chopped off heads," "without any body," "cut off, might be on one foot." In addition to being headless or having other parts missing, a conspicuous number of things are described as being cut open or split open, especially on Card VI, even though some of these responses are given as seemingly harmless concepts: "Well now, that looks delicious. Looks like a hot dog split open and flattened out from here to here." Such concepts indicate at least feeling of incompetence or inadequacy, and that such feelings might be related to sex seems entirely possible.

Adjectives used by the 12-year-old to describe his perceptions are, as at all ages in this range, predominantly unpleasant. But at this age girls give three times as many unpleasant as pleasant adjectives; boys only one and a half times as many. Among characteristic 12-year-old adjectives used by girls are: funny-looking, snooty, strange, scary, ragged, torn, droopy, skinny, weird.

In conclusion, we may note that at 12 years of age as much as at any age to date, responses from subject to subject are enough alike for us to obtain a rather clear picture of the expected response. This homogeneity makes it much easier to identify individual variations and protocols that seem already to mark the individuality of certain subjects. Though at earlier ages it was quite possible to draw up a picture of the age, the homogeneity was less marked and thus individual deviations were not as clearly revealed. The structure of the age picture at 12, however, is such that an individual subject can at the same time express his adherence to this common picture, and nevertheless show himself clearly as an individual.

At the very earliest ages, though the Rorschach response could tell us something both of the age and of the individuality of the subject, it told us less than at later ages about either. Group averages up to 10 years give us a reasonably clear picture of the age, but fewer individual protocols than at 10 fit closely to this picture. At 10 years of age, responses seem so uniform from child to child, but at the same time Ten is so restricted, that the Rorschach tells us a good deal about the age but perhaps less about the individual personality. But by 12, both the age and the individuality stand out clearly.

We should expect, as the subject matures chronologically toward adulthood, that his Rorschach will tell us increasingly more about his individuality than about his age group.

What then does Twelve tell us about himself in the composite picture of the age offered by the Rorschach results?

We know that he has taken an important step toward maturity in his apparent willingness to relinquish his dependence and to assume a more independent, active role. He has a much stronger sense of self and his horizon is enlarged in many directions. He continues the expansiveness of Eleven but without many of Eleven's difficulties.

He is vigorous, assertive, ambitious, self-assured, and yet his relations with others are in general productive and pleasant, for he has learned the value of inhibition and restraint and he attempts to use his oppositional tendencies adaptively. He is egocentric and may well have warm interpersonal clashes, but his reserves are such that they can often be resolved satisfactorily. He is not immoderately responsive to the subtle nuances of a situation but in general appears to enjoy himself and others.

He is developing rapidly in many directions, but his equilibrium is maintained to an admirable degree. His greatest stabilizer is perhaps his conformity. His identification with and participation in group activity, his enjoyment of rules, regulations, and routines, his acceptance of the demands of the culture and his understanding of the common cultural information, all contribute to his steadiness. He likes to know how he compares with others, what other people think. He is compliant and easy to work with.

Twelve is realistic, down to earth, matter-of-fact, practical, and precise. But he is also a great combiner and enjoys multiple possibilities in the intellectual as well as the emotional realm. Total structures may sometimes appear wishful and unsatisfactory, but original premises are usually practical and sound.

There is some evidence of feelings of incompetence and inadequacy, possibly in relation to sex, and there is a resurgence of ideas of magic and superstition. When Twelve has difficulties, he may resort to food as a substitute satisfaction. For food appears to be one of his highest interests.

Eleven is the age of paradox where the developing individual seems to be trying to reconcile opposing tendencies. Twelve appears to have resolved many of these paradoxes. Twelve is a golden age of equilibrium keynoted by conformity.

Individual Determinants

Number: There are more responses per child at this age than at any preceding age—mean of 22. This number is exceeded only at Fourteen and Sixteen.

Area: Whole responses still predominate slightly over detail responses. Mean W% is 47 per cent; mean D%, 45 per cent; mean Dd%, 8 per cent. Again median D (48 per cent) surpasses the median W% of 42 per cent.

Form: Mean F% is 61, a little lower than at other ages. Mean F+% is 92, slightly higher than earlier.

M, FM, m: Mean M of 2.6 is a little higher than at other ages. Mean FM of 2.2 is very slightly less than at preceding ages. Mean m of 1.0 is highest of any age to date and only equaled in this range at 13 and 16.

As at other ages, "vigorous extensor" M of dancing or swinging around predominates. As at Ten, "static" sitting, resting, lying, leaning comes second. As earlier, among FM, the "vigorous extensor" movement of climbing comes first. Fighting, quarreling, or attacking comes second. Among m, tension responses lead.

Color: Mean ΣC is 1.2. CF continues to lead with a mean of .8; FC comes next with a mean of .3; then C, with .2. As at preceding ages, animal responses lead among FC responses; nature among CF; fire and explosion among C.

Shading: There is a considerable advance here in shading responses, the mean being 1.0, the highest of any age to date except Seven, though lower than at ages which follow.

FC', C'F, FClob, Clob: Slightly fewer subjects use these categories, and the mean score is slightly lower than at the preceding ages. Nine per cent use Clob here; the mean score is .09.

Content: As at preceding ages, there are twenty different content categories used in all, five per child. Mean A% is 49 per cent; mean H%, 19 per cent. Leading content categories are: animals, humans, nature, anatomy, objects, in that order.

Characteristic Adjectives: funny-looking, snooty, strange, scary, ragged, torn, droopy, skinny, weird.

Length of Records: Records for both boys and girls are slightly shorter than at Ten and Eleven.

Total Time: Total time is steadily, though slightly, decreasing. Mean here is 12.2 minutes.

Semantics: Comparing the blot to reality by means of the phrase "looks like" continues to be the leading means of identification. This is one of the two leading ages for the use of qualifying phrases. However, it is also one of the two leading ages for identifying the blot simply by naming.

Best and Least Liked: Both sexes like Card X best, though boys also like V. There is considerable variety as to the card liked least. Girls like least I and IV; boys, II and X.

Refusals: Fewer subjects refuse cards than at surrounding ages. Only 15 per cent refuse any cards. Card VI is most refused; Card IV next most.

Popular Responses: This is the highest point for popular responses. Mean number of popular responses is 6.7; median 7.

Sex Differences

Sex differences, both qualitative and quantitative, are actually much greater here than at 11. Girls' records are, on the average, more expansive than those of boys. Thus girls give more responses than do boys, and more detail responses; have a lower F%, more movement, and slightly more color responses, more shading responses. H% is higher in girls; A% is higher in boys. An increased expansiveness is one of the most outstanding characteristics of Twelve, and thus girls more than boys express this trend. Girls more than boys use predominantly unpleasant adjectives characteristic of the age. Girls and boys give about equal numbers of the popular responses so characteristic of the age.

In many respects, however, boys give more fully than do girls the kinds of responses that appear characteristic of Twelve. Refusals are fewer in boys, DW responses increase more in boys than in girls from 11 to 12, and more are given by boys. Boys give more of the typically vigorous M responses than do girls and also have a higher percentage of quarreling and fighting responses. Boys give more qualifying responses than do girls, and also more WS responses.

Thus some of the kinds of responses most characteristic of this age are given most by girls; others by boys.

An interesting sex difference occurring for the first time at this age is that here girls give considerably more M than FM, whereas in boys, mean FM still exceeds mean M.

Girls' responses are much more variable than are boys'.

Comparison of Developmental and Rorschach Findings

DEVELOPMENTAL	RORSCHACH

Expansive.

More responses than at any age to date.

Multiple responses to single areas of the blots.

Only about half as many refusals as at 10 and 11.

Energetic, enthusiastic, ready for new experience; vigorous drives.

Response more enlivened than at surrounding ages. Higher M than at any other age to date. Also more subjects give M than earlier.

Larger percentage of vigorous extensor M than at any other age in this range.

Responsive to environment.

Mean ΣC higher than at 11 or 13 years.

Subject carries out an active role, does not merely envisage such a role.

Mean and median M exceed FM by more than at any other age in this range.

Emotions strong but unmodulated and shapeless.

As at other ages, CF the leading type of color response.

C slightly larger than at surrounding ages.

Fire and explosion responses prominent.

Confabulation and occasional tendency to contamination.

High interest in others.

Mean H% of 19 per cent.

Less self-evaluation than in later teens.

Vista and reflection responses very limited.

Subjects more alike, fewer individual differences, than at later ages.

More popular responses than at any other age in this range. On the average, one fourth of all responses are popular.

Higher mean A% than at any age which follows.

Combination of banality and expansiveness.

More DW than at any other age in this range but 11. However, many of these are based on popular responses.

Factual, down to earth.

Virtually no abstract responses.

Belief that own concepts are right or wrong.

Great interest in eating.

More food responses than at any other age in this range.

Sample Record of 12-Year-Old-Boy J.F.

RESPONSE	INQUIRY		SCORING		P
I. (Delay.) Looks like a face—eyes, mouth, nose.	(Whole.)	WS	F+	Hd	P
II. Looks like two ladies fighting, with red hats.	(Whole.)	W	M ↗FC	H	P
(Else?) Two animals' heads without top—can't see what the top could be.	(Black only. "Without the top," indicates that the red is eliminated.)	D	F+	Ad	P
III. That looks like two monkeys.	(Usual figures.)	W	M	A	P
(Else?) Butterfly in the middle.	(Center red. Form.)	D	F+	A	P
(Else?) No.					
IV. Pair of boots.	(Usual boots.)	D	F+	object	P
Hands.	(Usual side proj.)	Do	F+	Hd	
Whole thing looks like a bat, upside down.	(Whole. Form.)	W	F+	A	
V. Now that looks even more like a bat, or a swallow, a bird. Looks like a butterfly. About all I guess.	(Whole. He includes all the possibilities, but all with the same content.)	W	F+	A	P
VI. ∨ That looks like a tree with grass growing around the bottom.	(Whole, with top D as grass. Inquiry reveals no other determinant except form, though there is possibly some perspective here.)	W	F+	plant	
Pelt of animal being hung out to dry. Face at top—reminds me of	(Whole. Is conscious of shading at midline.)	W	m ↗F(C)	Aobject	P

RESPONSE	INQUIRY		SCORING		
VII. a raccoon I once saw—with legs out and a line down the middle. Oh brother! Looks like two ladies. I don't know what they're doing. Dancing, to tell the truth. Guess that's all.	(Whole.)	W	M	H	P
VIII. Well, I know what that looks like. > Hold it this way, it looks like an animal walking along rocks on the shore of a stream and reflected in the water.	(Whole, usual animals.)	DW	FM	A (reflection)	P
IX. Only thing I can think that looks like is a volcano. Green is trees on side not burned off yet by lava. Orange could be lava. And top is the volcano.	(Pink is omitted. White center with top formed by orange proj. is volcano.)	D	↗m CF	nature	
X. ∨ Well, can't see much of anything in that except it's pretty. Oh, yes, crab with one big claw.	(Side blue plus green. Form.)	D	F+	A	P
Looks like a picture of the seashore with rocks and fish and snails.	(Includes all parts. Shapes of fish and sea animals.)	DW	↗?FC F+	scene	
Black thing at top could be an old dead tree that fell in the water with roots and trunk.	(Top gray. Indicates nuances of gray. ? some tendency to use of black as color.)	D	F(C)	plant	

Card most liked: X "is the prettiest."
Card least liked: VIII. "Doesn't look too good."

Sample Record of 12-Year-Old-Boy J.F. (Continued)

Time: 6 minutes

R:17

7W
2DW = 58%W
1WS

6D   = 35%D

1Do = 6%Dd

Succession: None
Shock: None

10F = 58%F
10F+ = 100%F+

3M, 1FM, 1m
1CF, 1F(C)

(→2FC, 1F(C), 1m)

3M:12C

6A
1Ad
1 Aobject = 47%A

2H
2Hd = 24%H

2 plant
1 nature
1 scene
1 object(+Aobject)
   (1 reflection)

11P

COMMENT   This is a good example of the prosaic, banal, conforming, and adaptable Twelve. Almost every response falls into the popular category, hardly one popular is overlooked. This boy's scoring profile approximates very closely that of the average 12-year-old for most variables, particularly R, the area scores, F% and F+%, color, and A%. His scores are high (at or beyond the 75th percentile) on M, F(C), H%, and P, and are low (at the 25th percentile) only for FM.

His matter-of-fact "looks like," heightened occasionally by "I know what that looks like," plus his termination with "Guess that's all," or "About all, I guess," are typically forthright and realistic. He appears sure of himself, satisfied with himself, desires to do well, and yet appears to have no desire to do anything that is unlike the group or out of the ordinary. His attitude toward others appears frank, trustful, straightforward. He generalizes quickly though he can and does perceive details accurately.

He appears independent and responsible (3M:1FM) and is undoubtedly kind, considerate, and moderate in his demands. He tends to accept situations as he finds them, and does not seem to become too involved either emotionally or intellectually in them.

The m response, "Pelt of animal being hung out to dry," presumed to reflect a feeling of inhibition or restraint, is so common at this age that one must ask if it is not an index of equilibrium and adaptability. It seems to denote an ability to use restraint and inhibition when they are required, as they often are, by society.

The CF response of "volcano" at IX indicates the explosive, impulsive potential of Twelve. Twelve-year-olds are conformists, realists, matter-of-fact, easy to work with, but their amount of energy often calls for a sporadic outburst. These blow-ups may surprise the 12-year-old as much as they do those around him.

In spite of his frankness and candor, this boy shows a sensitivity to his newly developing physical and emotional sensations as well as to the feelings of others. The quality of the shading and reflection responses plus the higher than usual H% indicate this. In the response at VI, one suspects that this sensibility is heightened by his sexual growth (probably pubic hair growth) and his concern about it. This same tree symbol is old, dead, fallen, and black, by Card X, suggesting a decided anxiety in physical growth and ideas of damage. He tries to avoid his worries and fears by social conformity in a sort of "protective coloration," but they must certainly give him difficulty at times.

Though 12-year-olds seem not to have a care in the world at times, to be exuberant and balanced, we find that there is often a great seriousness in their inner reflections and in their efforts to channel their feelings in socially acceptable forms.

Sample Record of 12-Year-Old-Girl K.P.

RESPONSE	INQUIRY		SCORING		P
I. Looks like a wolf's face—see the same thing each year.	(Whole, with white spots as eyes.)	WS	F+	Ad	P
V This looks like a crown or something—take off this part right here.	(Whole minus part of wing proj.) ? "We're studying kings and queens in school."	W	F+	object	
II. Well, these two faces look like two dogs or two lambs together, looking at each other.	(Black only.)	D	FM	A	P
V Look something like a butterfly—hasn't the right kind of wings—has antenna, swallow tails.	(Whole, including reds.)	W	F+	A	P
III. This looks like two skeletons over a pot.	(Usual figures.)	W	M	(H)	P
With a butterfly flying over them—between them.	(Center red. No connection with figures.)	D	FM	A	P
V Looks like the head and upper part of a body of a lizard or—ambush bug, I think they're called.	(Head is lower center black; rest of black is legs and body of bug.)	D	F+	A	
IV. This looks something like a bearskin rug or something.	(Whole.) ? "Colors in it, and looks like a head with two ears." Colors? "Shaded—looks like fur."	W	F(C)	Aobject	P
V. V Looks a little like a butterfly too. Nothing the other way up.	(Whole. Form.)	W	F+	A	P

RESPONSE	INQUIRY		SCORING ↗F(C)?			
VI. (Squints. ∨ Pause.) Right down here looks like the front of a storm coat, where you zip it.	(Mid-line only, center of lower D.) ? "The straight line."	Dd	F+	object (mid-line)		0
VII. As I said before—two bunnies arguing. One pointing north, one pointing south, or vice versa.	(Top two tiers only.)	D	FM	A		P
VIII. This is the one I usually can't identify. These both look like mice or something—or a musk-rat. I guess they couldn't be mice.	(Usual animals. Form.)	D	F+	A		P
IX. This looks like two witches making a spell over some gas coming up from the ground. Big, bony hands, and like the middle of a Bunsen burner here.	(Includes whole. Witches are orange; gas is mid-line; green is ground; pink is "underneath the ground.")	DW or WS	↗m M	(H)		
X. Are these done with water colors? Thes e look like crabs.	(Side blue. Form.)	D	F+	A		P
The se two look like cocker span-iels—begging.	(Center yellow.)	D	FM	A		
This looks a little like the coast of California.	(Inner edge of R. pink.) ? Curved and San Francisco in here.	Dd	F±	map		
This looks like a wishbone. I guess that's al l.	(Center orange. Form.)	D	F+	object		

Card mo st liked: II. "Doesn't look as gruesome as the others."
Card least liked: (Long pause.) "I don't know." Makes no choice.

Sample Record of 12-Year-Old-Girl K.P. (Continued)

R:17

5W
1DW $=41\%$W
1WS

8D $=47\%$D

2Dd $=12\%$Dd

Succession: None
Shock: None

10F $=59\%$F
9F+, 1F± $=95\%$F+

2M, 4FM, 1F(C)

($\rightarrow$? 1F(C), 1m)

2M:0ΣC

9A
1Ad
1Aobject $=65\%$A

2(H) $=11\%$H

3 object (+Aobject)
1 map

9 P
1 0

COMMENT   This is again a protocol that seems typical of Twelve, though there does not seem to be the equilibrium here that we saw in the 12-year-old boy. Statistically, most scoring variables show values in the middle 50 per cent range. This girl tends to exceed the typical 12-year-old girl (scores at or beyond the 75th percentile) in Dd%, FM, F(C), A%, and P. She scores low (at or below the 25th percentile) in m, ΣC, and H%.

This girl is certainly conforming and obedient to rules and regulations but she appears to be less confident of others and of herself than most of her age group. The only two movement responses are those involving "skeletons" and "witches." In one case there is a dehumanization of the figures and in the other, superstition-induced and supernatural beings are indicated.

She shows initiative and independence in her spontaneous turning of the cards until Card VII. The sudden inhibition of card turning after VII may imply some difficulty with maternal authority and with environmental stimulation. When environmental demand impinges on her too much, it tends to inhibit her spontaneity and she becomes somewhat mistrustful, doubtful of her responses, and evasive. This may make her interpersonal relations somewhat unsatisfactory.

Although she is ambitious, she shows some dependency and her image of self is not strongly integrated at present. The animal movement varies from passive to dominating-active to mildly aggressive to ingratiating activity. Both the human movement responses are active but seem to lack direction.

There is sensitivity here, relating to physical sensations, probably some tendency to worry, possibly a tendency to psychosomatic complaints. She is easily disturbed (in choosing card she liked best, she implies that all the other cards are "gruesome"), and there is a search for security that at present she attempts to stimulate or attain by inhibition and restraint, but her search for self and self-evaluation is not highly developed. Her emotional and intellectual terrain seems limited at present, and the high A% plus the higher than usual Dd% may indicate a kind of obsessional "busy work" individual.

It would be very interesting to follow the progress of this girl's emotional and intellectual development in longitudinal study. We should like to know whether or not there will be spontaneous integration of her energy potential, thus providing the possibility for greater independence, self-assurance, and productivity than seems at present indicated. Perhaps we are witnessing an evolution of processes, for this protocol may illustrate the conformism and adaptability of Twelve blended with the withdrawal and retreat of Thirteen. Because of the rather unusual combination of traits, however, we are inclined to believe that much of what we see has an individual basis.

CHAPTER THIRTEEN

Thirteen Years

17 R	66%F	47%A
	94%F+	16%H
42%W		2.6 object
49%D	2.1M, 2.0FM, 1.0m	.6 anatomy
3%Dd	.3FC, .7CF, .1C,	.8 nature
	1.1F(C)	.5 plant
	Mean 2.1M:1.1ΣC	7P
	Median 1.5M: .5ΣC	

Typical Twelve is blithe and outgoing. Thirteen is more reflective; he tends to withdraw into himself. There seems to occur at this age an inner mobilization of forces with a tendency to pull things together, to inwardize, to think about things. This narrowing down and compressing produces a great deal of energy, though whether or not this energy is used constructively depends on the individual. The boy or girl of this age seems to need to discriminate, to select, to discard. Less enthusiastic and less exuberant than at twelve, he may at times be sullen, morose, secretive, pessimistic, moody. He is a worrier, and is beginning to worry about and be concerned about himself. He is particularly aware of and concerned about his intellectual abilities and inabilities (11).

The Rorschach response reflects the withdrawal, inwardization, and restriction that the 13-year-old shows clearly in other life situations. The number of responses given to the Rorschach cards increased steadily between 10 and 12 years. At 13, it declines to a median of 17. Refusals are more frequent. Not only do more subjects refuse cards (23 per cent) than at surrounding ages, but more cards are refused (mean of .4). "Mask" is a prominent response. There are fewer initial comments than at any age to date, and qualifying remarks are limited.

Furthermore, the median F% is the highest of any age to date, 66 per cent. This high form response gives us the most restricted record thus far. Only at 15 years of age is there greater restriction. The response at 13 is more restricted by far than at the surrounding ages of 12 and 14.

The withdrawal characteristically seen in the 13-year-old is expressed in the Rorschach not by an increase in M responses as might be expected, but by a diminution of response so far as both movement and color responses are concerned. The 13-year-old appears to show not only less response to environmental stimuli, but also less inner drive than do subjects at some other ages. Mean experience balance is reduced to 2.1M:1.1ΣC (median 1.5M:.5ΣC). A good many individual subjects of course are even more restricted. Thus 23 boys and 20 girls have an equation of only 1M:1ΣC or less, and of these, 9 boys and 4 girls give 0M:0ΣC. In records containing only 10 or 12 responses, these extremely restricted equations are perhaps not surprising. But they also occur in records that contain as many as 20 or 30, or in one instance 73 responses. And some subjects, in inquiry, go so far as to deny any color influence when asked about some apparently obvious color response they have given.

Thus for total number of responses, for average amount of movement, for average amount of color, we get a substantial falling off at 13 years. The only major determinant not reduced is shading, whose mean (1.1) is higher than at any earlier age except 7 years. Also more subjects (57 per cent) give shading than earlier. We thus have the interesting picture of an age where shading occurs about as fully as do all color responses together, and where the mean for shading response is over half that for human movement. In fact we have seven cases where the only determinant except form is shading. (Four boys and three girls give only shading and no movement or color response; and others give as many shading as movement and/or color responses.)

With shading the second leading (and in individual cases the leading) determinant (excluding form), we have a picture of an individual less responsive to external stimuli, less concerned with expressing his own inner drives, and more occupied with a somewhat anxious evaluation of the finer nuances of a situation. He is responsive to his own emotional, physical, and intellectual processes and he is sensitive to the reactions of others. There seems to be a change from the frank, direct interpersonal relations we saw at 12 to a more contemplative search for deeper, less evident causes and effects. Thirteen is beginning to worry, is particularly vulnerable to inner doubts and misgivings, is seeking new answers for his own reactions as well as those of others.

Since they are outstanding at this age, an analysis of Thirteen's shading responses may be revealing. Thirty-five per cent of all shading responses are based on interpretations that indicate fine differentiation within the blot. Such responses often give evidence of careful scrutiny of a situation, a sensitivity to less apparent forms, and thus may be indicative of a somewhat worried, anxious attitude. (This interpretation is reinforced by the fact that at 13 there is a great deal of card turning. Many ask to turn the card. Others are conscious of the various angles and preface their response with "this way" and "that way." Card turning may even deteriorate into spinning of the card. The response at 13 is also marked by a great deal of facial and general body overflow such as grimacing, frowning, sighing, raising eyebrows, drumming fingers on the table top, and tongue and lip overflow without verbalization.)

Second most prominent, and reaching their high point at this age, are those light-shade responses depicting reflection, water, wax, and the like. Twenty-two per cent of all shading responses are of this type. Again we see the individual searching, evaluating. His own sensuous reactions are engaging his thoughts and his reactions to a greater degree.

Diffusion responses—clouds, smoke—have dropped to 13 per cent. Interesting also in this regard, Clob, FC′, and C′F responses, never very high, reach their lowest point at 13, given only by seven children. And although there may be tendency toward dark shock, actual dark shock occurs only four times (two girls, two boys) in the entire group. Supplementing this is the fact that Dd, Hd, and Ad responses are not numerous. Thus, though the 13-year-old gives evidence of anxiety, he appears to be able to support it without having it dominate him. Such a tendency must, however, lend a minor, moody, and melancholy aspect to his behavior at times.

We have a pointed illustration in this regard in the experience of one of our own group who, after being given his annual follow-up test at the Institute, was invited to come in and take a second Rorschach as part of a demonstration of our procedures. He commented that he would this time give responses "with a lot of Freudian implications," since he had already taken his "real" test, and this didn't count. He then proceeded to give responses rife with blood, slime, accidents, torture. Commenting that up till now his real reactions had been "hidden in a shroud of moral restrictions and cultural inhibitions," he gave such responses as the following:

(X) "Mob scene. Beating each other over the head with frying pans full of green slime. Death and Destruction tearing apart a skull. They have a double spoon ready to goudge out two eyes at once. Person here squashed till he was only yellow. Crabs ripping out the insides of Death and Destruction and torn apart by Terror and Torture."

A 12-year-old girl on the same day under the same circumstances gave cheerful, light, ordinary responses, as on her original test. Here we see the possibilities of what Thirteen might project, but by admission, his restraint and inhibition are usually such as to withstand the tendency toward *laisser aller*.

Abstract responses, which are usually an elaboration of an affective state, a state dependent on the individual's own sensations, occur at 13 more than at any age to date, though still only a mean of .14. These responses are so few in number and so variable that they give only a clue as to possible implications for the age. They are more meaningful, however, at this age when we consider them in combination with the shading responses. The majority of the abstract responses given at 13 indicate some kind of conflict between two forces: "tug of war," "collision of two cars," "arguing after a grim and bloody fight." Other abstract responses, some with a morbid note, include "evil," "a fantasy," "somebody's thoughts."

In keeping with the generalized anxiety that shading responses seem to indicate, it is not surprising to discover that Thirteen is the second highest point in our entire age range for the giving of unpleasant, minor, unhappy adjectives. Though in keeping with Thirteen's general tendency toward a diminished response, fewer adjectives are used than at any age except 15; at no age except 15 is as high a proportion of these adjectives dysphoric. In both boys and girls there are four times as many unpleasant as pleasant adjectives (see Table 31). Both boys and girls give fewest pleasant adjectives of any age, 4 per cent each. Characteristic adjectives used by 13-year-olds are: queer, weird, torn, jagged, fantastic, evil, wild, bloody, dried up.

Nor is it surprising to find that Thirteen has a high number of "explosion" responses when compared with other ages. For in spite of his anxiety and worry and his willingness to regard a situation from many angles, he may not always resolve it satisfactorily. When restraint and inhibition have reached their limits, aggressive and chaotic behavior may ensue.

The mean experience balance shows our subjects, so far as group averages are concerned, to be introversive at every age in this range, the change from earlier predominant extratensivity to predominant introversivity taking place at 10 years of age. However, within this predominantly introversive period, subjects are obviously more outgoing at some ages than at others. By comparing the percentage of subjects who give any human movement responses with those who give any color, we find Thirteen to be the most introversive age in our range. The smallest percentage of any age (only 52 per cent) give some kind of color response, which means of course that half of the subjects at this age use no color at all. The percentage using any color is exceeded by the percentage who use any human movement (80 per cent), by a greater margin than elsewhere.

Mixed, conflicting movements occur here more than at any other age (19 per cent). They have increased at the expense of static movements that now constitute only 25 per cent of all movement responses. This leaves vigorous extensor movements (28 per cent) predominating. Dancing and swinging around as at most ages are the leading single kinds of human movement response, but simply "static postures" occur more here than at any preceding age.

In animal movement, as at other ages, vigorous extensor movements predominate, combative "running after, quarreling, fighting" movement occurring more than at any other age. In inanimate movement, tension movements definitely predominate, followed by explosion movements.

Thirteen's drives thus seem to be conflicting. He is prone to be aggressive and sees himself in an ambitious, active role. But his actual direction is less precise, varying between productive well-defined activity and more lethargic, static reactions. The mixed, conflicting movements are perhaps as characteristic as any of the reactions of Thirteen.

At 12 for the first time M responses clearly outweighed FM. At 13, this thrust toward maturity and independence seems not only stayed, but almost reversed. For, at least so far as medians are concerned, FM (median 1.8) slightly exceeds M (median 1.5).

As for color responses, as Table 7 shows, median ΣC is lower here than at any other age (.5). Mean ΣC (1.1) is lower than at surrounding ages. Of these responses, as at other ages, CF predominates. FC is lower than at any other age except 15.

As to type of perceptivity, percentage of whole responses has been decreasing steadily since 10 years, in a gradual approach toward what we presume is a more adult type of perception in which detail responses exceed whole. Though this trend will proceed even farther at 14, Thirteen marks a point where mean D% for the first time nearly equals W% (mean W% 46.2 per cent; mean D% 45.9 per cent). Dd% (mean 8 per cent) is about the same as at other ages in this range, except for 14 years when it is a great deal higher.

Use of white areas in the blot, as seen in WS responses, averages .8 such responses per child, about the same as in preceding years. S responses alone occur to the extent of .6 per child, slightly less than at surrounding ages.

However, the strong earlier tendency toward confabulatory DW is diminishing, there being fewer DW responses than at any age in this range to date. Nor do subjects seem to find it as necessary as formerly to mention parts that they cannot interpret. They may occasionally describe part of the blot and then say of the rest, "I don't know what that part is," but unidentified areas do not seem to disturb them as they did earlier.

Thus though in some areas Thirteen's progress toward maturity seems perhaps to be momentarily stayed or even perhaps reversed, in regard to his type of perception, Thirteen continues the trend toward maturity that was evidenced at 12. It is perhaps this concrete, realistic sense of the practical that is one of his most adequate reserves.

One of the greatest interests of Twelve was his interest in others and in the group. But just as Thirteen seems to have conceded some of the independence he felt at 12, he also appears to have relinquished some of his interest in others, even to possible withdrawal from other people. "Mask" emphasizes this withdrawal. And the mean H% (17 per cent) is lower here than at any other age in this range. (H) is only slightly less at this age than at surrounding ages.

The A% has diminished somewhat, beginning a trend that continues more or less until 16 years. Such a trend provides for less stereotypy and more individuality and is one we might expect in the individual's progress toward maturity.

The number of popular responses decreases very slightly. There is apparently at this age somewhat less conformity, somewhat less reaction to cultural pressures. Thirteen probably in general expresses a somewhat more original turn of mind than he did just earlier.

As to other content responses, the leading categories are object, anatomy, nature, and plant as at all the other ages in this range except 15. Anatomy responses which, among other interpretations, may indicate some concern about self, occur no more than at earlier ages (mean .6) and much less than at 14 years.

In supplement to our discussion of shading responses, we should mention here some of the details of content that seem related. Reflection responses, for example, are the highest here of any age to date (mean of .3), though less than at ages that follow. Analysis of the nature of the reflection responses indicates their somewhat immature character. In boys, all reflections are in water. Six are animals reflected, five are scenes, two are boats, and only two out of 15 are persons. Girls have four animals reflected in water and three scenes. Their two humans, however, are looking into mirrors—a small beginning of a trend that increases in later years.

Vista responses that seem characteristically indicative of the adolescent's search for himself in perspective make up only 8 per cent of the shading responses, as at 12. And texture responses, which are sometimes considered to be indicative of an effort or drive toward establishing or maintaining contact with others, constitute only 20 per cent of the shading response.

What, then, is the composite picture of Thirteen as represented by the Rorschach response for this age? Our first impression is that the developmental concept which holds that development does not continue in a steady upward progression but that periods of equilibrium are followed by periods of disequilibrium is illustrated in the Rorschach at this age. In the periods of disequilibrium, the individual contends with growth patterns that may be new and confusing to him and learns through them to consolidate his behavior, moving again toward a period of equilibrium. We have seen this tendency repeated as we followed the child's response on the

Rorschach from 2 years onward. But it has never been more forcefully illustrated than at 13.

Nor has it been possible for us until now fully to appreciate the Rorschach response at 7 years, which we reported earlier (1). Now at 13 years we see a reflection on a higher level of the kind of reactions that occurred at 7. At the earlier age, the child was not always able to inhibit his reactions and there were more frankly morbid and gruesome responses. By 13 years, the individual realizes the social implications of these reactions well enough to inhibit them, as one of our subjects (p. 174) illustrated markedly. At 7 years, also, shading responses are high, and only now in the light of our continued research can we fully appreciate the significance of this factor at 7 as at 13. Quite apart from the social, cultural, and intellectual pressures that may be operating, we must also consider the physiological and in turn the emotional changes that must be operating at these particular ages.

From 10 years onward, the individual seemed to move in a rather steady progression in all areas, until by 12 years he seemed to have reached a golden age of equilibrium. But at 13 we see a momentary halt, even in some cases what might be considered a reversal of pattern if we had no others means than the Rorschach for appraising 13-year-old behavior. For we see a reduction of response, a decreasing in both M and ΣC, an increase of refusals, FM again greater than M, fewer H responses, more "masks."

The 13-year-old appears to be contending with growth tensions that are at once exciting and disturbing to him. He is experimenting with the most effective ways of dealing with them, even though his techniques may be immature. The key to this particular phase of growth appears from the Rorschach to be in the shading responses. Thirteen appears to be more aware of his own sensations and of the reactions of others, though it is his own that concern him most. He scrutinizes, regards, searches, and worries about a situation as far as he dares. He uses restraint and inhibition insofar as he can, but when these have reached their limit, aggressive and chaotic behavior may ensue. He dallies and experiments with his own sensations, and although we seldom see him give way to morbid despair, his heightened sensitivity undoubtedly makes him appear moody, often irascible.

Although Thirteen's progress in some areas may seem to have halted momentarily, and his behavior is variable, wavering, often undirected, he still maintains his concrete, practical realism. Such reserves allow him to experiment. If a 13-year-old record were considered out of context, it might be said to be "disturbed," but when we view the total Rorschach picture of the age, we are able to see the emergence of a more sensitive and reactive individual who is learning to deal with new emotional and intellectual processes, thus providing the possibility of greater responsiveness to and more maturity in his relations with others.

Individual Determinants

Number: Mean R is 20, lower than at surrounding ages.

Area: W still predominates over D, but decreasingly. Mean W% now is 46.2; mean D%, 45.9. Mean Dd% remains about as earlier, 8 per cent. Again, however, median D% (49 per cent) surpasses median W% (42 per cent).

Form: This has increased very slightly to a mean of 63 per cent. F+% is 93 per cent.

M, FM, m: M and FM are both very slightly less than at surrounding ages. Mean M is now 2.1; mean FM, 2. This is, however, one of the high points for m, with a mean of 1.0.

At this age only, vigorous extensor M as a class predominate, static movements as a class coming second. The "vigorous extensor" movement of dancing, as at other ages, is the leading specific type of response. Among FM as at other ages, vigorous extensor movements as a class predominate, static movements come second. Tension movements lead among m.

Color: ΣC has changed very little from age to age since 10 years. Mean ΣC is now 1.1. As at other ages, CF responses predominate. Then come FC and C. Means are: CF, .7; FC, .3; C, .1.

Animal responses continue to predominate among FC responses; nature among CF; fire and explosion among C.

Shading: Shading responses continue to increase steadily in number. Mean F(C) is now 1.1. Differentiation of details within the blot is the leading F(C) response. Light-shade responses come second.

FC', C'F, FClob, Clob: Mean Clob is lowest here of any age (mean .07); and fewer subjects (only 7 per cent) use this determinant than at any other age.

Content: As at all ages, there are 20 different content categories in all used. The average number of different categories used per subject is 5.3. Mean A% is lower than at earlier ages, 46.8 per cent. Mean H% is also lower than previously, 17.8 per cent.

Animals is the leading category. Next come humans, objects, nature, anatomy, plant, in that order.

Characteristic Adjectives: queer, weird, torn, jagged, fantastic, evil, wild, bloody, dried up.

Length: For both boys and girls, records are longer than at 12 years; for girls, shorter than at 14.

Total Time: Mean time per subject for total response is now 12.9 minutes.

Semantics: Comparing blot to reality by use of the phrase "looks like" is the outstanding method of identification. Naming the blot comes second.

Best and Least Liked: Girls and boys both prefer Card X. Girls like least Card IV; boys like Card X least as well as best.

Refusals: Twenty-three per cent of subjects refuse at least one card, more than at surrounding ages. Card most refused is VI; next most, IX.

Popular Responses: Popular responses continue to be prominent. Mean at this age is 6.6; median 6.5.

Sex Differences

The Rorschach response of the 13-year-old is characteristically restricted as compared to that of the 12- and 14-year-old. There are fewer responses, fewer M, a lower ΣC, more refusals, but more shading.

Boys and girls both show changes in this direction, but for most determinants the change in the expected direction is expressed more conspicuously by boys.

Thus boys give fewer responses than do girls, and the change since 12 is greater in boys. Boys give fewer M responses than do girls, though the decrease from 12 is greater in girls. Boys give more refusals than do girls and the increase in refusal since 12 is greater in boys.

Color responses are approximately equal in the two sexes. Shading increases slightly more in boys. Reflection responses are most in boys. Abstract responses and "mixed-conflicting" M, both characteristic of this age, occur most in boys. H%, characteristically lower at this age, is lowest in boys. A%, too, is lower in boys.

As at 12 years, M now exceeds FM in girls, but FM still exceeds M in boys. Boys have a much higher W% (boys 56 per cent, girls 37 per cent), a much lower D% (boys 39 per cent, girls 52 per cent).

Comparison of Rorschach and Developmental Findings

DEVELOPMENTAL	RORSCHACH
Restricted response.	Fewer R than at 12 or 14; mean of 20.
Low energy output.	More refusals, and more subjects refuse cards, than at 12 or 14.
	Median F% is 66 per cent, highest of any age in this range.
Withdrawn, inwardized.	Mean experience balance reduced to
Unresponsive to environmental stimuli but also lack of inner drive.	2.1M:1.1ΣC (medians 1.5M:.5ΣC). Thirteen subjects give equation of 0M:0ΣC.
	Fewer subjects give color (only 52 per cent) than at any other age.
Introversive.	Experience balance shows introversivity.
	Percentage of cases using movement exceeds those using color, by a greater margin than elsewhere.
	Median ΣC lower than at any other age.
Unresponsive toward others, aloof.	Mean H% is lower than at any other age in this range.

Comparison of Rorschach and Developmental Findings

DEVELOPMENTAL	RORSCHACH
Less easygoing than at 12. Sensitive, aware, anxious, evaluative.	Mean F(C) of 1.1 higher than at any earlier age except 7. In seven cases the only determinant is F(C).
	Next to highest age for shock responses.
Brooding, morose, sullen, sulky, argumentative, rebellious.	High point to date for abstract responses, the majority of which indicate conflict between forces.
	Mixed conflicting M occur here more than at any other age.
	Among FM, more "running after, quarreling, fighting" movement than at any other age. Among m, tension movements predominate.
A minor, moody, melancholy affect.	High point in the entire age range for dysphoric adjectives. Typical adjectives: queer, weird, torn, jagged, fantastic, evil, wild.

Sample Record of 13-Year-Old-Boy T.W.

RESPONSE	INQUIRY		SCORING		
I. Well—uh—big bug.	(Entire center.) ? "Right there." Idea? "These—those are the feelers."	D	F+	A	
And two lions with wings—Egyptian or Babylonian.	(Side figures.) ? "These look like the wings—and Egyptian or Babylonian pictures." ? "I've seen pictures of them."	D	F+	(A)	
And crab. That's all.	(Top center only.) ? "Right here—claws."	D	F+	A	
II. Well, two bears sitting side by side.	(Whole.) ? "Not side by side, facing each other—the whole."	W	M	A	P
And butterfly.	(Lower red.) ? "Well, some of them have these things." (Indicates antenna.)	D	F+	A	
III. Well—monkeys.	(Is very careful to outline each monkey separately. They are in no way connected, thus usual M is withheld.) ? "Sort of look like monkeys—legs and arm and head."	D	F+	A	P
And this looks like the head of a beetle. (Else?) Don't believe so.	(Lower center black.) ? "The eyes and the mouth."	D	F+	A	
IV. (He opens his mouth as if to yawn, but doesn't. There has been a great deal of hand to mouth movement throughout.) Looks like a Scottie dog's head.	(Lower center head.) ? "Square nose and whiskers."	D	F+	Ad	

RESPONSE	INQUIRY		SCORING		
And a pair of big boots.	(Usual boots.)	D	F+	object	P
Head of a mountain goat.	(Upper part of blot, from center, above boots to top.) ? "See the horns." (Side proj.)	D	F+	Ad	
This here looks like a raccoon's head. That's all.	(Top center only.) ? "And the head that's been skinned." ? "Right there looks like the stripe."	D	F(C)	Ad	
V. Alligator's head.	(Side proj.) ? "Jaws."	D	F+	Ad	P
There's another butterfly. That's about all. (He pianos his fingers on table top.)	"The whole thing."	W	F+	A	
VI. A totem pole.	(Top D and center of lower D.) ? "This down the center from the top." Idea? "Well, the head, and this."	D	F+	object	
Bear rug. (Else?) No I don't believe so.	(Lower D.) "This whole thing."	D	F+	Aobject	P
VII. Looks like two rabbits. ∨ and ∧ (No further response. He pianos his fingers.)	(Top two tiers only.) ? "Ears."	D	F+	A	P
VIII. Well—um—(hand to face) this one looks like a hyena—both do.	(Usual animals. Form.)	D	F+	A	P
This back bone. (Else? He shakes his head no. Lowers and closes his jaw several times in a peculiar facial grimace.)	(Center of blue and gray.) ? "Just this." (Under further inquiry includes rib structure, but this was not spontaneous.)	Dd	F+	anatomy	
IX. (Mouth moving as he regards and frowns.) Lobster.	(Orange.) ? "I don't know—mostly the color."	D	CF	A	

Sample Record of 13-Year-Old-Boy T.W. (Continued)

RESPONSE	INQUIRY		SCORING		
A mummy. (Pianos table top.)	(Pink.) ? "Two of them—like the head of the mummy—and one there." (L fingers in mouth.)	D	F(C)		(Hd)
X. I don't know—emblem or something.	(Top gray.) ? "Just part of an emblem—like two lions looking at each other."	D	F+	⁄FM	object
Snowflake. (Head quite close to card. He regards and frowns.)	(Side blue.) ? "I don't know—oh I think the color—many pointed."	D	F+	⁄FC	nature
Something jumping—squirrel.	(Side brown.) ? "Right there—head—two front legs."	D	FM		A
Seed of a maple tree. (R thumb in mouth.)	(Center orange.) "Well, it looks like it."	D	F+		plant

Card most liked: (He chews on a piece of thread in his mouth.) "I'll take a bright one." He keeps looking at X, and finally chooses it. Ex. says she knew he'd like it, and he replies, "I *dislike* it."

Card least liked: "A very somber one." He regards all the cards. He chooses I. Why do you like it best? "It appeals to me." Why? But when questioned further says "No," and frowns. He has reversed the demand deliberately. Ex. now returns to X which he has said he "disliked." Why? "It's too mixed up—doesn't look like anything. Like a modern painting." Don't you like modern paintings? "No, I'm not a radical."

R:24

  2W = 8%W   19F = 79%F   11A

                 19F+ = 100%F+   3Ad

21D = 88%D   1Aobject

           1M, 1FM   1(A) = 67%A

1Dd = 4%Dd   1CF

          2 F(C)   1(Hd) = 4%H

           (→1FM, 1FC)   5 object (1Aobject)

                               1 anatomy

Succession: None   1M:12C   1 nature

Shock: None   1 plant

                                         7P

COMMENT   See page 186.

COMMENT This boy's record illustrates some of the age characteristics we have noted as typifying 13 years—a tendency to withdrawal, a wish to reveal as little as possible, an aggressive resistance. His manner is, however, highly individual and at 13, as at any age, there are as many ways of revealing age characteristics as there are individuals.

His choices of best and least liked cards reveal much about him. Asked to choose the one he likes best, he chooses the one he likes least, seeming delighted to confuse the examiner. He comments that it is too mixed up, like a modern painting, which he dislikes since he is "not a radical." Here he equates modernity with confusion and radicalism. (Is this a comment on the age Thirteen, on his personality, or on the culture?) For the card he likes best he chooses a "very somber one." While illustrating Thirteen's classic resistance and "minor key" moods, he seems to be enjoying his negativism.

Compared with other boys his age, however, he shows quite a number of scoring differences. He scores higher than usual (at or beyond the 75th percentile) in R, D%, F%, CF, F(C), and A%; lower than usual (at or below the 25th percentile) in W%, FM, m, and H%. His concepts are more concrete and matter-of-fact than those of most of his age group. He prefers facts and details to generalizations, and these facts are little embroidered. It is difficult for him to do more than name something. He even appears to begrudge an "a" as a descriptive article. His high F% and A%, his narrow experience balance, emphasize the withdrawal and minimal output typical of Thirteen, here in somewhat exaggerated fashion. This boy complies and follows the rules, but wants to reveal himself as little as possible. He shows Thirteen's "masking" response, but in a highly individual way, when animals become Egyptian and Babylonian symbols, lions become emblems, heads are those of a mummy or part of a totem pole. He shows his strong intellectual interests, as well as his distaste for personal engagement and responsibility in regard to it.

This boy's drive varies between active and passive, between introversivity and extratensivity. Such ambivalence can tend to diminish productivity and cause both inner and interpersonal conflict. This may be one of the keys to the aggressiveness and resistance of this boy. Pulled two ways at once, he finds it difficult to perform smoothly and without some disturbance. His image of self appears to be poorly defined. The bears at II are given human movement score, but actual identification does not appear strong. The only apparent human response is in "mummy's head," where identification is limited.

Age factors appear to be operating so strongly here that we might fail to identify this boy's real potentials if we did not recognize them. From his scoring profile, we must grant maturity in the perceptive processes, good intelligence, participation in social and cultural thinking, ability for social adaptation, even for empathy (though interest in others is restricted), and a broad intellectual horizon. And his "menagerie" is so extensive that if the animals ever come alive and begin to operate, one can look forward to more positive affirmation of self with a greater reserve of effective energy. At present this energy seems submerged in the developmental and personal ambivalence. He appears to enjoy resistance for resistance's sake and he places most of the responsibility on the environment for his direction and for the resolution of his difficulties.

Sample Record of 13-Year-Old Girl L.P.

RESPONSE	INQUIRY		SCORING		
I. Take as much time as you want to? Any angle? (Studies card for a long time.) Well, to me I think it probably might represent a bird. But sort of an abstract bird. No head, but wings. Might be an abstract eagle.	(Whole. Form.)	W	F+	A (abstract)	(P)
II. (Long regard). Laughs in an embarrassed way.) I—uh—this to me sort of—it looks like it might be a moth or butterfly except for the absence of the body. Feelers and wings but no body. Blank spot where body should be.	(Whole, including reds. Form.)	W	F+	Ad	
III. Well, I think these two figures represent two people. What they're doing, I'm not sure—not sure I can explain it.	(Usual figures.)	W	M	H	P
IV. Be different and turn it around. ∨ Could I tell just about the parts? ∧ Boots. I can't seem to figure this out. (Indicates lower center proj.)	(Usual boots.)	D	F+	object	P
V. Oh, this is about the closest I've seen to an insect. Body, wings,	(Whole. Form.)	W	F+	A	P

RESPONSE	INQUIRY		SCORING	
feelers. Closest to anything real I've seen.				
VI. This looks as if it might be the skin of an animal stretched out to dry, except no head. Legs.	(Whole.)	W	m	Aobject P
VII. (Long delay.) About the only thing I can think of—no—was thinking this might be parts of a cloud formation.	(Top two tiers only. Is conscious of shading.)	D	F(C)	nature
VIII. (Delay.) Looks to me as if it might be a horseshoe crab.	(Whole.) ? "More the shape. Difference in the colors only seem to confuse me. Can't see any reason for that."	W	F+	A
IX. (Delay.) This white in here to me represents body of a crab; outline, not the color.	(Center white.)	S	F+	A
This might represent a map of North American, except that it juts out too far and no Florida. Very irregular. Not the same on the other side.	(R green only.)	D	F−	map
X. Well! These blue spots seem to represent to me some animal that might live in the sea. Not octopus or crab.	(Side blue. She does not specify animal further. Shape, not color.)	D	F±	A (P)

Sample Record of 13-Year-Old Girl L.P. (Continued)

RESPONSE	INQUIRY		SCORING		
These look like two things that might come out of the sea, and appear to be fighting, facing each other.	(Top gray.)	D	FM	A	(P)
This looks like face of something with very long ears. Something on the eyes.	(Lower center green.)	D	F+	Ad	
These yellow spots look like two animals suspended from something. Facing each other and mouths open—may be talking or singing.	(Center yellow.)	D	FM ↗m	A	
These represent birds of some sort and they are suspended.	(Center blue.)	D	m	A	
Orange and green might be part of a cloud formation.	(Side orange and side green. Indicates nuances in shading.)	D	F(C)	nature	
Little brown spots remind me possibly of a pinchy crab.	(Side brown.)	D	FM	A	
These pink large blots look in some way or another like sea horses.	(Center pink. Form.)	D	F+	A	
This, if not so straight, could represent the leg of a horse or donkey.	(Center of top gray only.)	Dd	F+	Ad	

Card most liked: V. "Most real."
Card least liked: VII. "Most confusing."

R:19
6W = 31%W

11D = 58%D

1Dd
1S = 11%Dd

Succession: None
Shock: None (but II and VII are difficult for her)

COMMENT   See page 192.

Time:14 minutes
11F = 52%F
9F+, 1F±, 1F− = 86%F+

1M, 3FM, 2m
2F(C)

(→1m)

1M:0ΣC

10A
3Ad
1Aobject = 74%A

1H = 5%H

1 object (1 Aobject)
2 nature
1 map
    (1 abstract)

4P+3(P)

COMMENT An outstanding characteristic here is the feeling of incompleteness, the vagueness and lack of precision in response, all one version of the withdrawal and inhibition of Thirteen. This girl uses such expressions as "might be," or "represents" more than "looks like," and tends to qualify still further with "seems to represent to me," or "reminds me possibly." There is an absence of parts—"no head," "no body," even "no Florida." Expressions indicate what a detail is not, rather than what it is—"*not* octopus or crab." Indefiniteness is also marked in such expressions as, "what they're doing, I'm not sure"; "some animal that might live in the sea"; "face of something with very long ears."

Compared with median values for 13-year-old girls, this girl's scoring is "on the nose," as far as number of responses and area scores go. Her determinants and content tend to differ from the typical, however. Elevated (at or beyond the 75th percentile) are FM, m, F(C), and A%; depressed (at or below the 25th) are F+%, M, ΣC, H%. While she tries to think realistically and practically, one suspects her intellectual processes of being vague and imprecise.

There seems to be a desire to meet problems squarely, but there is a sense of frustration and inhibition that may be exercising too strong an influence at present. This may be a case where the age characteristics are exaggerated because of the personal tendencies sympathetic to such characteristics. Thus, as we have often seen in developmental studies, some individuals are characteristically more disturbed at certain stages than at others; and this may be because their own personal tendencies are reinforced by those of the particular stage of development.

The feeling of "suspension," of being immobilized against one's will, appears marked here, for example. This kind of interpretation appears so often in this range that we have already suggested that it is a mark of adaptability, an indication of ability to inhibit and restrain emotions and drives when necessary. But when such a tendency exercises too strong an influence, it can easily immobilize and sterilize the emotional and intellectual processes.

Such a tendency may also appear to be more of a handicap in the absence of any strong, clear-cut independent drives. The only H response here is two figures: "I think those represent two people. What they're doing, I'm not sure —not sure I can explain it." Her idea of self appears to be vague and diffuse, and she appears to be using emotional techniques characteristic of a much younger child. The only F(C) responses are "cloud formations" at VII and X indicating a diffuse, nonspecific emotional overflow in times of stress.

One wonders if some specific area of difficulty is not contributing to this girl's frustration and inhibition and to her emotional retardation. The greatest difficulty with the cards appears at II and VII. This suggests feelings of guilt, possibly relating to problems of sex, of birth or death, or of difficulty with maternal authority. One would like to know the status of this girl's sexual development. Is this the reason for her feeling of "suspension" and for her diffuse emotional overflow? This may represent an exaggeration of the awareness of physical sensation often seen at 13; it may be due to specific factors in her present situation or physical growth status; or it may be indicative of a basic personality pattern that tends to bring about diffuse, pervasive, and immature emotional reactions to internal or external stress.

This girl tends to quibble and worry, yet rather than coming to grips with problems, she removes herself from them ("seem to represent," "sort of an abstract eagle"). One has the impression that there is a somewhat impoverished intellectual horizon, which, combined with her diffuse anxiety and worrying tendencies, may point to rather obsessional, nonproductive activity at present. She probably finds it difficult and fatiguing to adapt to the personal and social demands of everyday living.

With some Thirteens involved in the difficulties of the age itself, one has the feeling that they will spontaneously evolve toward more mature levels. With this girl, one has the impression that her own personality characteristics may prolong this stage unless she can be helped, either through support and encouragement or through greater insight, to resolve her difficulties, both developmental and personal.

CHAPTER FOURTEEN

Fourteen Years

---

20 R	63%F	46%A
	93%F+	17%H
39%W		2.8 objects
50%D	2.4M, 2.3FM, .8m	1.0 anatomy
8%Dd	.3FC, .8CF, .2C	.8 nature
	1.2F(C)	.5 plant
		.3 reflection
	Mean 2.4M : 1.2ΣC	
	Median 1.9M : .9ΣC	7P

The typical 14-year-old has been described (11) as a youth coming into his own—happy, carefree, and self-reliant, the possessor of boundless exuberance and energy. He is reasonably firm in his emotional fiber, and stands ready to meet the demands made upon him. Hungry for experience, he shows himself increasingly capable of digesting the multiple experiences he demands.

Fourteen's Rorschach gives every evidence of his great amount of energy and his renewed appetite for experience. He appears to continue and enlarge many of the trends we saw earlier but that seemed in some instances to suffer a setback at 13.

The Rorschach response at 14 is not only more extensive than at any other age in this range, but also unusually enlivened. Most obviously, Fourteen gives more responses than does the subject of any other age—a median of 20 per subject. Girls especially give a considerably larger number of responses here than at any other age. Furthermore, fewer subjects (only 12 per cent) refuse any cards, and the mean number of cards refused (.2) is lower than at any age but 16, which it equals.

Not only are more responses given per subject at this age, but also more different content categories are used by any one child than at any other age except 16.

The typical 14-year-old in his Rorschach record not only expresses greater inner drives, but also responds more fully to environmental stimuli than at 13. Means for human as well as for animal movement are considerably higher than at surrounding ages, the mean of 2.4M being higher than at any other age except 12 years. Also, a larger percentage of subjects (88 per cent) give M responses than at any age except 16. The same is true for FM responses.

Color responses, too, are given more freely at this exuberant age. At only 10 and 16 years are more color responses given; and as with movement, the sum of color responses at 14 is higher than at surrounding ages. In fact, in most respects the vigor and fullness of the 14-year-old's response stand out sharply as contrasted with the comparative restriction of response at both 13 and 15 years.

The mean experience balance is $2.4M:1.2\Sigma C$. In contrast to the years that immediately precede and follow, only one girl and three boys have an experience balance of $0M:0\Sigma C$. On the other hand, this appears to be an age when individuality is making itself felt. For even though, judging from the totals, there is greater expression of both inner drive and reaction to environmental stimuli, we have 32 subjects at this age, or nearly one in three, who show ambiequal experience balance. This can indicate the tug of war going on within the individual. He has equally strong response to both inner and external stimuli. He finds it hard to choose, for both seem equally attractive. The environment and the strength of his own inner dynamic potential are vying for precedence, and we might expect that one or the other will establish its pre-eminence as the individuality asserts itself more definitely.

Though there are at this age fewer initial remarks than at 10 and 11, there are more than at any other ages in our range. Such initial comments as "Red one! Hm! Let me see!" "Oh well, this one is really something!" "Holy cow!" "Heavens, let me see now!" "Fancy!" "Wowie!" "That can drive anybody crazy. Gads!" "Oh brother!" seem not so much to represent a delaying action as to be expressive of the general vigor and enthusiasm with which Fourteen approaches a new situation.

Emotions are deepening at 14, deepening and to a large extent expressing themselves positively. We think of the 14-year-old boy or girl as being affable, buoyant, cheerful, positive. His use of adjectives in his Rorschach response gives evidence both of increased emotionality and of its positive nature. To begin with, for both boys and girls a larger percentage of adjectives are emotion-toned than at any other age to date. Twenty-two per cent of adjectives used by boys, 24 per cent of those used by girls are affective or emotion-toned. Though as at other ages there are definitely more unpleasant than pleasant adjectives used, both boys and girls use more pleasant and fewer unpleasant adjectives at this than at surrounding ages.

An initial clue as to Fourteen's feelings about and reactions to other people can be obtained from his reaction to the interpersonal situation involved in being given the Rorschach test. Fourteen-year-old boys in their total manner of responding achieve considerable rapport with the examiner. They also manage in a slightly condescending, almost patronizing manner to imply that they have the situation well in hand. Thus a good many of them begin their response with "Well," "Well now," or "Let's see!" Several comment on having taken the test before—giving the impression of "This same old thing," in a somewhat blasé fashion. Then nearly half tend to terminate their description with a self-satisfied "Guess that's about all," or "Well, I guess that takes care of that."

Girls show some of these same tendencies, but the total picture with girls is more one of wanting to get things right, to do well, to please the examiner, but of not being quite sure. Even more girls than boys comment about having seen the cards before and express their familiarity with them by such phrases as "My same old . . . ," "Still the same animals," etc. More characteristic, however, is such an approach as "Oh dear! Well! It could be . . . I guess. That's about all I can see."

Stating that the blot "could be" or "might be" the concept indicated is one of the chief means of identification. And for girls as well as boys, such expressions as "I guess, I think, I suppose," occur more than at any other age. Girls more than boys seem anxious to give a good, reasonable, and not foolish response. Thus one girl for Card VII protects herself to this extent: "Well it might be a rabbit. Just an imaginary one. Couldn't really turn around and look at each other like that. Like something you have on a greeting card."

Hence, in spite of his worldly manner, Fourteen shows a need to protect himself. This is also shown in a tendency to say "I don't know," or "It doesn't look like much of anything," "Kinda tricky," "I can't make anything out of this one," and then to go ahead and give a response. Conversely, subject may give his response first and then say, "I don't know," or "It doesn't look like anything." Or he may characteristically say "No" after giving his response, and then give a second response. Both responses may seem equally good to the examiner, and there is no actual denial of the first response. It just appears to be necessary for the subject to strengthen his position.

A similarly defensive kind of reaction appears in his criticism of the blots, reminiscent of his response at 8 years of age. Fourteen tends to complain about the inadequacy of the blot and makes suggestions as to how it might be changed to correspond to his concept more adequately: "It would be more lifelike if these parts were cut in," "Cutting off these parts here," "If you take the black spot off on top," "If it weren't for these red spots." This reflects the concern with detail evidenced at this age, but it also shows a tendency to blame the environment for difficulties. There is seldom the dogmatic "should be" in his complaint, however, as appeared at some earlier ages.

Thus we see that for all his outward appearance of assurance and his man-of-the-world attitude, the 14-year-old shows some feelings of insecurity and a self-protective need. (In supplement, we also note that the F% remains relatively high at this age as it does throughout our range.) But even though he must protect himself at times, Fourteen is also capable of self-criticism. Boys, for instance, remark, after giving a response: "That's stupid, of course," "You could make this into a witch from a childish point of view," "Kinda far-fetched." Or, "O.K., I'm nuts! I know!"

Girls express an even more direct and personal concern about their own individualities. "Guess I don't have such a wild imagination as I thought," "Am I abnormal?" "That connects me with reality? I suppose I'm normal because I'm asking if I'm normal. Do all teen-agers?"

This concern with himself and his own personality continues the trend seen clearly at 13. Thus shading responses, which were notable at 13 because of their sudden prominence in relation to other responses, continue to increase in the slight but steady manner that has been manifest since 10 years. Mean F(C) realizes its high point of 1.2 at this age.

In analysis of the shading responses, however, we can see the changes that have taken place as the individual continues to mature. The most conspicuous age factor here is the increase in the number of vista responses. An average of 18 per cent of all F(C) responses are now vista responses, more than twice the number given at 13. This high point for vista suggests the 14-year-old's earnest search for self, his effort to see himself and his behavior in perspective. Both diffusion and texture responses occur somewhat less than at surrounding ages.

Reflection responses, too, are increased in number. This self-study and self-interest is especially strong in girls. One fourth of girl's reflection responses depict persons looking at themselves in mirrors, as "Goofy character reflected in a mirror," or "A girl looking at the back of her dress in a mirror." One girl who gives more reflection responses than anyone else comments, "Disgusting, these reflections!" In these instances we can also see the self-criticism (even to the point of self-depreciation at times) which we feel is a characteristic of Fourteen. The majority of reflection responses given by girls, as well as nearly all of the boys' reflection responses, which are in general less personal, depict scenes, especially trees, reflected in water. Anatomy responses are also higher here than at any other age, which indicates not only the possibility of concern with self but also the intellectual vanity and aspiration of the age.

The empathy characteristic of this age, the concern about one's own feelings as well as those of others, the search for self, often brings with it feelings of anxiety, perhaps overconcern. This is first observed in the amount of generalized bodily overflow, which was also noted at 13, and which continues here in laughing, sighing, raising of eyebrows, frowning, grimacing. At 14, however, there is more evidence of contemplation and of search for perspective, in the characteristic gesture of holding the card at arm's length and studying it from all angles. Card turning is prominent and many ask if the card may be turned, or comment on the fact that they are turning it. Such gestures are more measured and studied than they were at 13, and card turning seldom degenerates into card spinning as it sometimes did earlier.

Fourteen is trying to refine and to specify his thinking, as evidenced in the sudden rise of Dd% at this age. The median Dd% at 14 is double that of any other age in our present range. (There is also an increase of Hd in comparison to whole H responses.) Too great concern with detail can, of course, be a reflection of anxiety, but Fourteen appears to have achieved the closest ratio to the expected adult type of perception of any age in our range. Only at 9 years were these ratios approximated previously. The median D% has reached its peak here, surpassing the W% more than at any other age. At 15 and 16 years, the ratio of D:W is again reversed and W% again exceeds D%. Thus Fourteen appears to have achieved a balance between practical, realistic considerations and more abstract, generalized concepts, while at the same time not neglecting the more precise, detailed aspects of a situation. Supplementing this we have more objects given at this age than at any other (mean of 2.8) and fewer abstract responses (mean .1) than at surrounding ages.

This interest in precision is also communicated to the environment in the interest the boy or girl of this age evidences in making himself clear to the examiner. There is a considerable amount of comment to the effect, "This here," or "Just this part." Unlike Fifteen, who often seems not to care whether the examiner can follow his responses or not, Fourteen seems to want to make perfectly clear just exactly what he sees and how he sees it.

Analysis of movement and color responses gives us further clues as to Fourteen's feelings about himself as well as indications concerning his interpersonal relations. The outstanding single type of human movement is dancing or swinging around, as it is throughout this range. The drives toward independence and toward heterosexual adjustment, which are often considered the keynotes of adolescence, may perhaps achieve their greatest impetus in this socially acceptable activity. At 14, the next most prominent type of human movement is "lifting, holding, and carrying." These are active and productive reactions as well as socially effective. Fighting responses are least for any age. As at other ages, the predominant class of movements is extensor.

In animal movement the vigorous extensor movements lead, predominating over any others slightly more than at any other age. The vigorous action of climbing is the leading single type of movement. Fighting and quarreling animal movements appear much less than at the preceding age.

So far as inanimate movement is concerned, tension responses are definitely predominant. Explosions are second in number.

One special kind of movement response may be particularly noted. On Card I, two side persons or animals acting on a center person or animal, and on Card V two side persons or animals meeting actively in the center (both unusual and infrequently given responses at most ages), occur conspicuously.

A review of the movement responses plus the fact that many Fourteens show ambiequal experience balance indicate the possibility that Fourteen is fighting a battle with himself. What he wants to do and what he does are not always perfectly reconciled. But at the same time we see better definition of direction and stronger self-identification, less interpersonal difficulty than earlier. The aggressivity shown by Fourteen (corroborated by the number of S responses, which reach their high point of mean .9 at this age) may be taken out more on himself than on others.

As to the color responses, CF still predominates. Increased interest in others and a slightly increased adaptability to the demands of the world about him, are suggested by a slight increase in the mean FC response. The only especially conspicuous changes in content of color response are the decrease in CF food responses and the increase in painting responses. Flower responses also reach their high point here. Among pure C, fire and explosion responses are now in marked decline. Blood responses are high in comparison with other ages, exceeded only at 16 years.

Thus, to judge from the color responses, though Fourteen appears to be still egocentric, with emotional reactions that may not be too well modulated and are at times immature, there is also evidence of a more objective attitude in emotional reactions than earlier.

Fourteen's interest may still center mainly in himself, but we have seen the changes that have occurred in the structuring of this interest. His interest in others, which is also high, reflects some of these same changes. In his Rorschach response, Fourteen gives more human responses (though not a greater percentage of human responses) than does any other age. Mean H is 4.8. Table 19 shows that the mean for boys (3.3) is higher than at surrounding ages and the mean for girls, (6.3) far exceeds *any* other age. However, the relatively high (H) and (Hd) responses found at this age may indicate feelings of a somewhat belittling or derogatory nature, or feelings of fear or superstition in regard to others. Analysis of these responses at 14 shows that almost half of the 14-year-old girls' (H) responses are witches. A quarter more are monsters, dwarfs, devils, clowns, or comic-book characters. In contrast, only about one in seven is an attractive or friendly creature such as a pixie, elf, or angel. In boys' (H) responses, only a quarter are witches, one fifth are devils. Approximately one in five is a friendly creature—mermaid, brownie. Fourteen's reaction to others, as his reaction to his own personality, shows wider intellectual and emotional range than at surrounding ages, an attempt to study more carefully, even to be more objective. There is certainly great interest in others, but there may also be some mistrust and lack of confidence in his relations with them and in himself.

The fact also, mentioned earlier, that the Hd response increases markedly here may indicate some feeling of anxiety in interpersonal relations. Girls give more Hd responses at 14 years than at any other age and show a higher Hd:H ratio. For boys, this is one of the strongest ages for Hd. Since, however, mean Hd never surpasses mean H, we presume that this is also a reflection of the increased ability in intellectual functioning, that of being able to refine his concepts and to make them more precise, to be more objective.

There are no particularly remarkable changes in content other than those we have already mentioned. The number of categories has increased slightly, indicating an enlargement of intellectual horizon. The number of anatomy responses suggests intellectual ambition, even intellectual pretensions, which may sometimes surpass actual intellectual achievements.

Fourteen gives evidence of greater complexity, greater individuality, of being an individual seeking greater perspective both for himself and in his relations with others. But with enlargement of horizon in both the intellectual and emotional spheres, it is not unusual to find that some Fourteens may also elaborate on the moody, melancholy note felt at 13. For although the total Rorschach records show few "trouble indicators," some individuals of course show more than do others. In the m responses, for example, things smashed or broken occur conspicuously, though the total mean m response is only 0.8, and tension and explosion responses take precedence. And among the C responses, blood responses, which increase here, are presumably a less agreeable and less mature type of response. Fourteen is also the high point for FC′, C′F, and Clob responses, though since only 12 per cent give any such responses, these cannot be considered as outstanding characteristics of the age. And actual Clob shock plus any tendency to Clob shock occurs here less than at any other age. In fact, at 14 the number of subjects giving no evidence of shock or tendency to shock in *any* area is greater than at any other age.

How, then, can we characterize Fourteen from the composite Rorschach results as shown for the age?

First of all we feel the increasing complexity of the individual personality at this age. We have evidence of his exuberance, his vigor and enthusiasm, his seeking of new experiences, and his ability to handle new situations with increasing maturity. He is interested in himself, but he now tries to be more objective in his view of himself and in his relation to others. He is seeking a more adequate perspective both emotionally and intellectually. He is capable of self-criticism, and he appears less pedantic, less rigid in his attitudes. He is even willing to be wrong occasionally.

Fourteen appears blasé and man-of-the-world, but this is sometimes belied in his occasional need for self-protection and a tendency to blame the environment for difficulty. Lack of confidence in interpersonal relations, some mistrust of himself and others, are at times apparent.

His direction seems better defined than earlier, his self-identification stronger, though what he does and what he would like to do are not always well reconciled or integrated. There may be a tug of war within him as his individuality strives to make itself felt. Aggressivity at 14 is probably directed as much toward the self as toward others.

The intellectual horizon is widened and intellectual functioning is enhanced over earlier years. The 14-year-old is intellectually ambitious, perhaps even pretentious at times. He appears to have achieved a balance between practical, realistic consideration and more abstract generalized concepts while at the same time not neglecting the more precise detailed aspects of a situation.

Thus, although 14 appears to be an age where there are few signs of difficulty, feelings of anxiety and insecurity are not entirely lacking. For where both emotional and intellectual activity are widened, possible areas of difficulty likewise increase. But so too, in the normally developing individual, does the amount of reserve to meet the difficulties.

Fourteen is resolving some of the difficulties we saw at 13, and although there is vigor and enthusiasm, there is not the frankness and whole-heartedness of 12. The subject is now more conscious of his own personality and its demands as well as of the demands of the environment. A critical regard for himself and others is perhaps one of his greatest steps toward maturity.

Individual Determinants

Number: Mean R of 23.4 is highest for any age in this range.

Area: D% for the first time in this range definitely exceeds W. Mean W% is 43 per cent; mean D% is 47 per cent.*

Form: This age is one of the high points for number of responses determined by form alone—mean F% is 63 per cent. This is also one of the high points for good form—mean F+% is 93 per cent.

M, FM, m: This high point for M(2.4), is exceeded only at 12 years. FM is approximately the same, 2.3. Mean m is .8.

---

* Median D% is 50 per cent, median W% 39 per cent. This is the high point for median D% in the entire age range. At Fifteen, both median and mean W% will again exceed the D%.

Extensor M predominate as a class. Dancing, swinging around is still the leading single type of M. Among FM, vigorous extensor movements predominate; static and moderate extensor movements come second. Among m, tension movements predominate.

Color: Mean ΣC, 1.2, is about the same as at surrounding ages, and as at other ages CF, FC, C occur in that order of frequency.

Among FC responses, animal responses lead as usual, but now "objects" comes a very close second, and nature a close third. Among CF responses, nature continues to lead. Among C, blood-anatomy and paint-stain tie for first place.

Shading: Shading continues to increase, mean F(C) being 1.2. Differentiation of details continues to be the leading types; light-shade and vista come next.

FC', C'F, FClob, Clob: This is the highest point for these responses, but even here only 12 per cent of subjects give such responses (mean of .13).

Content: Total number of different categories used remains 20. Mean number used by individual subjects is 5.6, more than at any other age except sixteen. Mean A% is 46 per cent, lower than at any age but 16. Mean H% is 19 per cent, one of its highest points. Animal responses are the leading content category, followed by humans, objects, anatomy, nature, and plant in that order.

Characteristic Adjectives: modern, nice, fancy, comical, dancing.

Length: Records are longest of any age for girls. Among the longest for boys.

Timing: Mean time is now 13.7 minutes, equaled only at 10 years.

Semantics: Blots are chiefly identified by comparing them to reality through the use of the phrase "looks like." The second leading method is simply naming the blot.

Best and Least Liked: Girls and boys both like Card X best. As at most ages, girls like IV least; boys like X least.

Refusals: This is the low point for refusals. Only 12 per cent refuse any cards. Cards most refused are IX and VI.

Populars: Popular responses continue to occur conspicuously. Mean for P is 6.6 per child; median, 6.5.

Sex Differences

Fourteen is again, like 12, an expansive age so far as the Rorschach response is concerned. With only minor exceptions, this expansiveness is expressed more fully in girls' responses than in boys'. Thus girls give many more responses than do boys. They also give more M responses, more F(C), and a higher ΣC. Other characteristics of the age—reflection responses, a high D%, and a high H%—are higher in girls than in boys. Boys' responses are much more global than are those of girls. (Boys, 49%W, 43%D; girls, 36%W, 52%D).

Boys give fewer refusals than do girls, and more vista responses. As earlier, mean M exceeds FM in girls, but not in boys.

Girls show the greater change in the direction of increased expansiveness in R, M, FM, ΣC, F(C).

Comparison of Developmental and Rorschach Findings

DEVELOPMENTAL	RORSCHACH
Seemingly boundless energy, tremendous appetite for experience, strong drives.	Highest mean R of any age. Fewer refusals than at any age but 16. More different content categories than at any age but 16. More M than at 13; higher D% and Dd% than at any other age.
Responds fully to environmental stimuli.	ΣC higher than at surrounding ages.
Emotions deepening and subjects express selves positively.	Largest number of emotion-toned adjectives to date. More pleasant adjectives than at surrounding ages.
Greatly concerned about self.	Higher Hd (girls) than at any other age. Most F(C) of any age to date—sharp increase in vista responses. Largest number of reflection responses, especially looking at self in the mirror, of any age; highest anatomy of any age.
Great interest in other people.	H% higher than at other ages.
Thinking is practical and detailed, more than general, theoretical or abstract.	D% and Dd% highest of any age; global responses fewest. Fewer abstract responses than at surrounding ages.
Relatively egocentric and unmodulated.	High point for C responses.
Critical of others.	Relatively high (H).

Sample Record of 14-Year-Old-Boy W.G.

RESPONSE	INQUIRY		SCORING		P
I. (Pause) Well, this part right out here looks like two dogs of some kind—maybe collies or German shepherds.	(Wing proj. to top, each side.) ? "Nose (side wing) ear, neck. That niche destroys the neck or part of it. The eye is the indentation there" (just above wing).	D	F+	Ad	
Kinda hard to guess what the inside is. As a matter of fact, it looks like a woman standing—standing there with her arms stretched up like that. But of course, there's no head. That's about all I can get.	(Center figure.) ? "Well, her figure here and her skirt here—you can see it's a very light skirt—you can see through it. Hands up with elbows bent. She has no head."	D	M ⟋F(C)	H	
II. Well, when I first looked at it, I thought it was two forms, but after that I thought two bulls or cows, standing up on their hind legs, snubbing their noses or balancing something.	(Black only. See spontaneous elaboration on next response. Is conscious of shading when he delineates eye. Also see inclusion of blood in last response for card.)	⟋DW D	FM ⟋F(C)	A	P
The red spots don't mean anything much, I guess. The red spot might be geese up in the air, except that they're sort of connected to the cows. I've changed my mind about cows—I think they're cows' heads are longer.	(Top red.) ? "Geese are up here—wings, head—stretched out in flight. They're just about to come in to land with the wings back acting as brakes. Feet way down. These two dashes in here might indicate that they're smoking cigarettes or spitting at each other."	D	FM	A	(elaboration of first response)

RESPONSE	INQUIRY	SCORING			
					P
Balancing that in the center on their nose. See eyes—little dark spot in here.	Really they're not connected with the rest of the picture.				
This red at the bottom might be blood or something. Seems like it because it's sort of connected up with the cows themselves.	(Bottom red.) ? "Seems sort of connected with the body of the calf, and if he were to have a bloody spot there, that's what it would be. Except that it's sort of sudden there. The thing that sort of spoiled the picture is the sort of suggestion of an ear here (dark red spot inside black at position of ear). The ear is really at the back here. (Indicates proj. on black which is ear.) Guess that's about all."	D	CF	blood	
III. At first I took it for two men, arms out here, legs here.	(Usual figures.) ? "They turned out to be women anyway. Holding a couple of balls down here. Feet sort of unnatural, like fish. I can't figure out what this lump here would be—might be a knee." ? "This jutting out here."	DW (Confabulation)	M	H	
But if you look at it, it might be a face of some sort. Yes, matter of fact, I think it's more like a face.	(Whole, including white spaces and reds.) ? "If it was a face, borders would come down here (indicates outside top reds and outside of blacks), the chin here. This red is the cheek (top red), eyes here (head of usual	WS	╱F(C) F±	Hd	

Sample Record of 14-Year-Old-Boy W.G. (Continued)

RESPONSE	INQUIRY	SCORING
Then these look like blood splotches where the blood hit here, then ran down an inclined plane slightly, here. It could only splash like that if you dropped it, then put paper or something over it, and then hit it hard with your fist (demonstrates). Then it would all spatter out like that. I can't tell what that is (center red). Let me see—might be—no, I can't tell.	figures), mouth (bottom center black), sort of teeth inside (light center gray). The black sort of destroys the impression that it's a mouth—but it still looks like one. Oh, this is the nose (center red) but it's too far down on the face. The other black splotch here (body and arm of men) is just sort of lines in the face." (Side red.)	CF blood m D m
IV. (Pause, frowning.) God, I haven't said anything yet (as he notes Ex.'s notation). Looks most like the large and tanned carcass of	(Whole.) Ex. asks which side of skin this is. "That (top center) looks like the under part 'cause you can see the fine wrinkled part of the skin. But down	W m F(C) Aobject P

RESPONSE   INQUIRY   SCORING

some animal such as a moose or a deer which has been slightly mutilated. Forelegs or skin of forelegs coming out here. Seems the legs haven't been skinned— the bones left on the pelt. Or been badly mutilated so only part was left. This is the neck up here, the nape of the neck, and here's the backbone going down the middle. This is the side going down here, and here's part of the hind leg—the rest has been cut off somewhere. This is—I *guess* —the tail, but actually it would be more lifelike if these two light parts weren't cut in here. Actually it's too thick for the tail. Guess that's about all.

here there's no indication. But right here (shadings in top and side) you can see the light shining on the fur. But the nap distinctly seems to be the inside."

V. Well, that's either a butterfly or a bat. It seems more like a bat to me—wings are very irregular and it has an antenna on the front and a double tail in back. Bat ordinarily has a little tiny, tiny tail on the back. I'm not sure. Head here, wings here. Two humps here (on wings) don't es-

(This long spontaneous verbalization leads to confabulatory combination of bat with snail's head. In order to clarify, Ex. asks where he would see a bat like this.) "In a picture. Most definitely it's not the real thing. Wouldn't see it except in a picture. Most likely in a comic or something, where not very much care is taken to

DW   F+   ↗Aobject
A   P

Sample Record of 14-Year-Old-Boy W.G. (Continued)

RESPONSE	INQUIRY		SCORING	

pecially suggest a bat—usually skin is stretched tight on the wing bones, but here it's not stretched tight at all. Not graceful curves and lines which a bat usually has. Head—well wait—two tails are down here. On second thought, the head looks exactly like a snail's head. But that's about all I can handle.

INQUIRY: make it look lifelike."

I don't know what the two sort of legs are doing out here. Might be the calves of a human—sounds sort of strange, but that's all I can visualize.

INQUIRY: (Side proj.) Connected with bat? "Oh no. Not possibly. OK, I'm nuts, I know it."

D   F+   Hd

VI. Whew! (softly. Pause.) Well, the very top part there (covers all lower part of card with palm) looks like a two-winged owl.

INQUIRY: (Top D.) ? "Head, wings, lower wings just part of the large wings—all one wing really. Where the tail broadens out, there it stops. Can't see feet—more of a silhouette. See eyes as black hollow spaces."

D   F(C)   A

The rest looks like very soft skin, sort of like chamois on the inside.

INQUIRY: (Lower D.) ? "Very soft and fine—not a bad pelt at all. The inside—or if it's the outside, little or no hair on it, but very short and fine and soft." ? "No, just the texture of it. Could be

D   F(C)   Aobject P

RESPONSE	INQUIRY	SCORING
		P A FM W

RESPONSE	INQUIRY			SCORING	
				P	A
				FM	
	an animal's skin—chamois deer. Legs here—shouldn't be out like that—in a real pelt they should be out diagonally. Little round dots in here (light center shading) must indicate boils in the skin—sort of like knots in wood or something." ? "Some disturbance in the skin—might be wounds, anything."		W		
VII. (Sighs, grimaces, scratches head. Pause.) Well, I guess it is—two —um—lady goats, I guess, such as you see them in cartoons, rushing away from each other. Horns, head, shoulders—wearing short monkey jackets, petticoat of some kind.	(Whole.) ? "If you read the comics the way I have you would see the faces are turned backward saying a few last words. Here's the back coming down, rump here, noses here. This is the eye. That's all."		W	FM	
VIII. Oh, getting fancy here. Four colors. Well, at first seemed to me some kind of a—funny—looks like some child had spilled its paints, except it doesn't look like spilled paints. Just a mixture of colors—form doesn't look like paint or anything. (Pause.) One thing just a formless mixture of colors —I really can't—(sucks teeth).	(Whole. This is perhaps more color comment, but since there is content indicated, it can be scored.)		W	C↗ m	paint

Sample Record of 14-Year-Old-Boy W.G. (Continued)

RESPONSE	INQUIRY		SCORING	
Well, the part right in back there might be part of the human spine and ribs.	(Center detail. Form)	D	F+	anatomy
If you took it bit by bit, this could be a lioness climbing upon some rocks. Lioness, not lion. Head is much smaller. Almost no neck. The inside portion has no particular form at all I can think of. Lioness is only thing I can think of besides the ribs. Darn, I was gonna make you do a page on each one, but it didn't work out. Guess that's about all I can think of.	(Usual animal.)	D	FM	A P
IX. Oh nuts—one of these colored things again. Well, the orange are two sea horses—	(Orange. Form.)	D	F+	A
or on second thought, might be two pot-bellied gremlins of some kind.	(Orange.) Gremlins? "Tremendous ears, animal's ears, eyes, nose is a long, horny, spiny kind of thing. Sort of a baboon's chin or jowls. Sort of like an English airedale. See the indentation where the neck is. Here's the pot-belly down here. That's all you can say for them."	D	F+	(H)

RESPONSE	INQUIRY	SCORING		
The green down here—of course no connection with those two—looks like a walrus with a tremendous mustache. Just the head. The legs of the gremlins are cut off by the head of the walrus.	(Green with white space as eye.) ? "Eye, ear, snout. Nose is slightly disconnected by the white spot here. Tremendous mustache here—the neck is cut off here." Cut off? "Blocked from view."	D	F+	Ad
The pink has no meaning at all. And I can see where the ear (of the walrus) when they made it, green ink blurred with the orange, produced a light khaki there of some kind.		Color description		
This might be an animal with a large round head. Eyebrows, nose, eyes, ears. Can't tell what the black spot is. Might be a mouth, but if it is a mouth, it would be in a completely ruined spot. The indentation in there looks like the head was chopped off clean, ready for mounting on the wall or something like that. 'Sabout all.	(Pink. He sees the light shading that halves the pink, each side, as the place where it is "chopped off clean." He also sees an infinitesimal shading in lower R pink only, which he terms "black spot.")	D	↗F(C) / F+	Ad
X. Oh boy (disgustedly). Gee whillikers. (He puts card down, turns head so he can't see it). Shucks.				

Sample Record of 14-Year-Old-Boy W.G. (Continued)

RESPONSE	INQUIRY		SCORING	
God, have I said that much already? (Looks at Ex.'s notes. Pause.) Well, 'bout the only thing I see right here is two dogs. Uh—got large neck made large by thick, luxuriant fur coming out, doing some trick by standing on a barrel. Dark yellow spots in the center ought not to be there. Ears are like a cocker's—something—but large yellow spots ought not to be there.	(Center yellow.)	D	↗F(C) FM	A
The buttercup grows on the branch of the tree. I don't know where the main tree is. Blocked from view.	(Side yellow, attached to brown. Form and color.)	D	FC	flower
This part right there looks like a human head sucking on a bottle or something.	(Pink profile attached to center blue.) ? "I don't know. Nose, eye, mouth and chin goes down to a blue bottle." ? "Just looks like sucking on something. I don't know what. Guy that made the bottle wanted it to be blue."	D	↗FC M	Hd
This gray up here is two octopi having a fight—look very angry at each other, mainly because of the mouth snarling. These things	(Top gray.)	D	FM	A · P

RESPONSE	INQUIRY	SCORING		
sticking up are some kind of sharp sticker sort of spines. Fighting around a pole, both hanging on to it or standing on either side.				
The blue looks like someone dropped a bottle of blue ink. Spread out from a main—well, not exactly like it. Well, if you drop some ink and put paper over it, and bang it real hard with your fist—(demonstrates).	(Side blue.)	D	⟋CF m	paint
Head of a goat right in there with horns. Just his head. That's all on that.	(Center green. Form.)	D	F+	Ad P

Card most liked: "Most realistic or what? Well, disregard that, and that (he eliminates X, IX, VII, II, VIII)—process of elimination—this (discards I). I guess that one's best." Chooses III. ? "Well in form of a face, sort of realistic. It's a smiling face. I don't know why it sort of appeals to me—most realistic thing there."

Card least liked: "I'll show you." Chooses X. "Too complex. Color combination not a particularly striking one. Too many small—um—disconnected forms and—um—I guess that's about all."

Sample Record of 14-Year-Old-Boy W.G. (Continued)

R:27

5W
1WS = 22%W

21D = 78%D

Succession: None-orderly

Shock: None

10F = 37%F
9F+, 1F± = 95%F+

3M, 6FM, 2m,
1FC, 1CF, 1C
3F(C)

(→1m, 1FC, 2CF, 5F(C))

3M:3ΣC

9A
4Ad
2Aobject = 55%A

2H
1(H)
3Hd = 22%H

1 anatomy
1 flower
2 blood
2 paint

9P

COMMENT   This record characterizes the marked contrast between Thirteen and Fourteen (as well, of course, as representing an individual of rather striking personality structure). The length of the protocol alone indicates the release of verbalization that occurs at this age. Fourteen is ready for many experiences, and this boy apparently does not want to neglect any of them. His range of intellectual and emotional activity is widespread and his reactions are mercurial. This boy is not only eager for new experiences, but he appears quite willing to try all of them at once. If some slight emotional indigestion ensues, owing to his impulsiveness, his shifting of responsibility to others, his ambivalence and indecision, he still has reserves of realism and practicality, a consciousness of and ability to adapt to social demands, a good intelligence, and apparently indefatigable energy.

Along with his elevated responsiveness (his R is closer to the girls' mean than the boys'), we are not surprised to find an elevation in many other scores. At or beyond the 75th percentile are D%, M, FM, m, FC, C, ΣC, F(C), H%, and P. Only W% and F% fall below the 25th percentile. Thus we see an outpouring of responses, emotionally enriched but only loosely organized and controlled.

We see the beginnings of a development in his emotional and intellectual processes that should eventually provide him with greater discrimination and precision. It now appears difficult for him to give just one response to a given area or to let a response stand once it is given. All the possibilities seem to present themselves to him simultaneously. If we look at the progression of response on Cards II, III, and IX, we find that at times multiple concepts seem hopelessly entangled, with sensual and emotional considerations taking precedence in influencing his concepts. Then his process may be that of blocking out one concept in favor of another with the progression sometimes ending in a less mature though a well-defined response. Finally he is able to handle two concepts serially and clearly without difficulty.

The amount of verbalization alone may be a great factor in his apparent inability to establish limits for himself and to organize his thinking in a well-defined and orderly fashion. For even his best defined concepts begin to deteriorate if his verbal flow is activated. His work habits must be fatiguing, for his intellectual and emotional processes are far from efficient. The fact that he himself is beginning to recognize this is indicated at Card V, when after adding "snail's head" to the "bat," he says, "But that's about all I can handle."

From the character of the M, there appears to be some sense of incompleteness and some ambivalence in his drive toward independence. Perhaps there is also some ambivalence in his feelings of sex identification. The human head "sucking on a bottle" may indicate an impetus toward oral activities. But when we set this response beside the "cigarette-smoking geese," we see that it has projections forward as well as backward in time, in that drinking and smoking are symbols of adult privilege to which many teen-agers aspire.

The animal movement indicates ambition, aggressivity, a desire to excel, to be grown up, and to have a supply of strength that he has not yet acquired. Though his idea of self may not be too well integrated and his self-assertion is far from complete, he appears to have a great reserve of energy that when organized will undoubtedly provide him with more productive potential. The nature of the m response supplements this possibility. Both responses are strongly colored, demonstrably splattered ("blood" and "ink"). This potential of unemployed energy, which contains a restrained destuctive tendency, may emerge forcibly when he feels too frustrated or inhibited. Such energy adequately employed should provide him with a powerful dynamic for productivity.

This boy has an unusually high number of shading responses (3F(C) plus five tendencies), all characterized by texture or differentiation of shading within the blot. There is little if any interpretation involving vista or perspective. This seems to indicate a marked sensual and sensitive reaction to his own physical and emotional sensations. He is probably highly sensitive to sensory stimulations in many modalities, coming from without as well as from within. The soft "chamois skin" has "wounds" and the "deer skin" is "mutilated." Such responses appear indicative of concern with problems of sex development, particularly with masturbation anxiety.

Color tends to disturb this boy, and he appears to handle it, in general, with techniques that we may consider typical of a younger stage. However, "blood" and "paint" as such do appear at this age, and so we cannot consider them atypical. At Fourteen, many young people appear mature in many things, but one complaint of parents is that they still do many "childish" things. Development cannot always proceed in a perfectly harmonious and integrated way and this boy gives ample evidence of it.

General impression is of a boy who shows exuberance, vigor, enthusiasm, ability of self-criticism, desire and ability to accept new experiences, all typical of Fourteen. His own personality characteristics would seem to be basically active and ambitious, but his drive toward independence and his self-identification are still in a somewhat ambivalent state. He undoubtedly attempts to be grown up by imitation; he is dissatisfied with himself; things that are too complex disturb him and yet he himself makes things difficult. He can become so involved in his own intellectual and emotional processes that the simplest concept seems to have multiple facets not easily untangled. His concern over problems of sex and sex development may be giving him the most trouble at present.

His emotional reactions are not always mature, perhaps, but they are certainly direct. When the personal or developmental manifestations and concerns have been resolved, it might be expected that this boy's wide intellectual and emotional range will emerge into a more clear-cut, independent, self-assured, better organized, more efficient productivity. At present this boy appears to be motivated by many strong drives, many of which he appears to enjoy, but which are pulling him in many directions at once.

Sample Record of 14-Year-Old-Girl L.F.

RESPONSE	INQUIRY	SCORING
I. Looks like the gargoyle of Notre Dame looking in a mirror—a reflection.	(Two side figures, meeting in center.) ? "Well, it's kind of hanging on to something. This is his fingers—and head broken off—and that's one leg, and one hand and tail. I don't know if they have tails or not."	DW M object (reflection) P
Looks like a kind of a funny mask—something you tie on. I don't know how to account for four eyes, but . . . > Oh, it looks like a pig—reflection in the water. (Else?) No.	(Whole, including white spaces as eyes.) (Whole.)	WS F+ object P DW F+ A (reflection)
II. People jitterbugging.	(Whole.)	W M ↗CF H P
Looks like some giant dinosaur eating something—another dinosaur. He's bleeding—just got into a fight.	(Black with red as blood.)	DW FM A (blood)
Two gorillas—these are shadows on a red linoleum floor and up here indicates noise, or they've run into each other or something.	(Black are gorillas. Bottom red with "shadows" is "red linoleum floor." Top red indicates "noise" or movement.)	DW M ↗CF, C_{symb} ↗m ↗F(C) abstract ↗O A

Sample Record of 14-Year-Old-Girl L.F. (Continued)

RESPONSE	INQUIRY		SCORING	
III. Looks like a couple of waiters—head waiters in a restaurant carrying a basket of dirty dishes out. That's the back of the cook, with a red apron, and the red things hanging down are frying pans like in a Colonial kitchen.	(Usual figures. She incorporates both reds into the scene, but form of cook is somewhat neglected.)	DW	↗m ↗CF M	H ↗scene	P (0)
> Looks like somebody coming off a diving board and the reflection. All these things are reflections. Doing a jackknife.	(Whole, including side red.) ? "This is where his bathing cap came off."	DW	↗m M	H (reflection)	0
V This man has a face like those in the funny books—nose, earrings, eyes. That's just overweight or fat here.	(Whole, including white spaces; side red as earrings; center black as eyes, center red as nose.)	WS	F ±	Hd	
IV. Looks like a bear rug. I remember this, too.	(Whole.) ? "They took the head off and it's hanging up on the wall. It's not skinned very well because it's messy."	W	↗F(C) m	Aobject	P
< Trees on the shore of a lake—no, a river. That's a dead tree and that's a live tree.	(River is mid-line, from center to top. Trees are shading around the mid-line.)	Dd	F(C)	scene ↗M?	

RESPONSE	INQUIRY	SCORING		
V That's the bat man—bat not fat.	(Whole. Points out wings and mask. Inquiry indicates no movement, though position implies it.)	W	F+	(H)
V. Bat!	(Whole. Form.)	W	F+	A
V Funny looking butterfly.	(Whole. Form.)	W	F+	A
< Forest fire reflected in the water.	(Whole.) ? "Well, that's the light down there and these are the flames and that's the smoke going up." (Is conscious of shading in center as "water." Center proj, top and bottom are "flames," as well as side proj.; darker portions of wings as "smoke going up.")	DW	↗m F(C)	0 ↗scene nature (reflection)
VI. Icky poo! Reminds me of a cat that got stepped on—absolutely flat —that's his nose and these are his whiskers and here's his front legs and back legs.	(Whole.)	W	m	A
< Still looks like trees reflected in water—I'm in a rut!	(Whole with water at mid-line.)	DW	F(C)	↗scene nature (reflection)
VII. Two brownies.	(Top two tiers only.)	D	F+	(H)
V Girl looking in mirror at back of her dress—that's her body, and that's her nose, and she's looking around—and that's the front of her dress—that's the rear end.	(Whole.) ? "That's a new hair-do. And this is the other one—pulling up a slip strap or something."	W	M	H (reflection)

Sample Record of 14-Year-Old-Girl L.F. (Continued)

RESPONSE	INQUIRY		SCORING	
VIII. Oh this was the other forest fire— I can't explain it, but there's smoke and flames and mist.	(Whole. Color is most important determinant, but indication of "smoke" and "mist" also implies F(C))	W	⟋F(C) CF	fire
That looks like a face with eyes and nose coming down there and teeth.	(Center white.)	S	F+	Hd
< These are cliffs with a funny kind of red clay. This is a dead tree and a granite rock and a cat crossing over from end to end.	(Usual animal; center blue is cliff; top gray is dead tree; lower center red as clay.) ? "Like a reflection. Disgusting these reflections. That's all."	DW	⟋scene ⟋CF FM	A P (reflection)
IX. Dragon preening in the mirror.	(Orange. Points out nose, scales, and toes to Ex.) ? "Well, he just looks like a dragon."	D	FM	(A) (reflection)
∨ Clouds	(Pink.) ? "Well, they're just puffy."	D	F(C)	nature
∨ Looks like more water—reflected in water—looks like ocean and marshes and the green looks like a tree and the red is sunset.	(Pink and green. The shadings impress her first, thus inducing idea of "water" and "reflection," but the color originates the content.)	D	⟋F(C) CF	nature
X. (Makes face as she regards.) It doesn't look like anything but what it is—just dropped a whole lot of colored ink and folded the paper on it.	(No further elaboration on inquiry.)			Refusal with color description.

Card most liked: Picks up VII and turns it V. "I like this one best." Why? I don't know—it's cute—a little girl looking in a mirror."

Card least liked: X. "Too mumbly-jumbly. There's no point to it."

R:25 (1 refusal)   Time: 13 minutes

8W   8F = 32%F   8A
9DW   7F+, 1F± = 94%F+   1(A) = 36%A
2WS = 76%W

4D = 16%D   6M, 3FM, 2m   4H
                                    2CF   2 (H)
                                    4 F(C)   2Hd = 32%H

1Dd   (→1M, 3m, 3CF, 4F(C))   3 object (1Aobject)
1S = 8%Dd   1 scene (+→4)
                                                                 4 nature
                                                                 1 fire
                                    6M:2½C
                                                                    (1 blood)
                                                                    (1 abstract)
                                                                    (8 reflection)
                                                                 8P, 3 0

Succession: Loose-none
Shock: None (difficulty with X)

COMMENT   See page 222.

COMMENT While the 14-year-old boy in the preceding protocol appeared to be more or less equally torn between the environmental stimulation and his own introversive drives, this girl is definitely more oriented toward her own interests. The boy was more involved in doing things; the girl is more interested in thinking about things, in studying them. The boy escaped into realism and practical direct action; the girl escapes into daydreaming and flights of fancy. The boy was perfectly capable of accepting illogical combinations of well-defined perceptions such as "bats" with "snail heads" or "geese flying" attached to a "calf's nose," but the girl is willing to integrate a poorly defined concept into a beautiful scene or idea that is pleasant to her and agreeable to others, even though some of the details may be neglected (see the "cook" interpretation at III).

This girl shows the characteristic vigor of Fourteen in the number of responses, in the widespread color, movement, and shading responses, as well as in the concern with herself. She appears, however, to be moving toward 15 in her unusual refusal at X and in her restraint during inquiry.

Statistically, her scores on W%, M, FM, m, CF, F(C), and H% are high for a 14-year-old girl (at or above the 75th percentile), while D% and F% are low (below the 25th). Her most outstanding characteristic is one that is increasingly common throughout the adolescent range but is greatly emphasized here: the reflection responses and the tendency to abstraction. The perspective of scene and the consciousness of doubling of the blot as "reflection" is mentioned on almost every card. Such responses are seen so frequently in this age range, especially in girls, that they seem a sign of maturity at this stage, even though later an overemphasis on them would have different implications. At present it appears to be evidence of attempts by the developing individual to understand himself and others. The characteristic is exaggerated with this girl, however, and is combined with possible feelings of disillusion, frustration, and depression ("bear rug hanging on the wall . . . messy," "Cat that got stepped on," "dead tree"), suggesting that her search for self-understanding is a troubled one.

She may have at times a rather aggressive idea of role and she is probably not modest in her idea of herself, though there is perhaps no particular reason why she should be. She shows a confident and well-considered survey of problems in any given task, combined with an equally confident completion of a task once it is understood. One cannot help but contrast this intellectual and emotional efficiency with that of the boy preceding and yet this response lacks none of the vigor and exuberance of the age.

Her introversive drives are so strong that she tends to withdraw from and to resist environmental demand. She says of X, which she refuses, "It's too mumbly-jumbly. No point to it." She finds it more difficult than do some of her contemporaries to conform. The need for confirmation of her own personality seems so strong that it obviates all other considerations for the moment.

Only once does she make an unpleasant remark about the "reflections" and this occurs at Card VIII, when she says during inquiry, "Like a reflection. Disgusting, these reflections." Is this a reaction to the color? Since she refuses Card X entirely, one suspects that she resents the intrusion of environmental demands on her own interests. She attempts to deny, at least for the benefit of others, her own strong introversive tendencies. If this were an adult protocol, it might be suspect as one showing inadequate ability to handle realistic environmental problems. However, we might presume from the indications that this girl has given us that, once her own self-affirmation is satisfactory to her, she will be more willing to compromise with the environment.

This girl's possibilities seem great. She has creative imagination, a good deal of originality, empathy, patience, confidence, energy; she is thoughtful, serious, sometimes arrogant. She is independent, but probably strongly suggestible to her own emotions. Though she can be very social, she really prefers her own company. She is warm and sympathetic to others, but indifferent as to her adaptation to them. And if the environment demands too much of her, she is capable of withdrawing entirely. This tendency plus some feelings of frustration and anxiety perhaps brought about by her sharp awareness of her own emotions are probably the areas that give her most difficulty at present.

CHAPTER FIFTEEN

Fifteen Years

15 R	64%F	44%A
	94%F+	16%H
51%W		
43%D	1.8M, 1.6FM, .5m,	2.0 objects
0%Dd	.3FC, .7CF, .1C,	.7 anatomy
	1.3F(C)	.6 nature
		.4 scene
	Mean 1.8M : 1.0ΣC	
	Median 1.4M : .6ΣC	6P

Unlike his buoyant, expansive, energetic earlier self, the typical 15-year-old boy or girl often shows himself as indifferent, apathetic, lazy. He displays new sensitivities, resistances, and suspicions that frequently make him in his relations with others not only argumentative, but even hostile and belligerent. In his temporary restriction of activity and his withdrawal and turning away from his parents, teachers, and even at times from his own friends, he shows a listlessness and lack of energy. Mature enough to be aware of his problems and to recognize that at least to some extent it is up to him to solve them, he has not yet worked through to a solution, and thus may appear moody and self-critical as well as hostile to others (11).

Many of these characteristics are reflected in the Rorschach response at 15 years. When an examiner finishes a 15-year-old examination, he often feels either that he has failed or that the subject has. For the response tends to be terse, monosyllabic, and painfully sparse. In addition, it may he whispered or muttered so that one is never quite sure of its exactness. The card is often held so that it is very difficult for the examiner to see it. There is much less pointing out of the selected areas in an effort to make things clear to the examiner than at other ages. Inquiry is difficult. There is considerable manipulation of the cards. Subjects turn them, twirl them, or even turn them over. They hold them at arm's length and tip them flat at eye level. Fourteen often manipulated the card, holding it at arm's length, but the result was usually a thoughtful and studied response. With Fifteen it may be the prelude to no response at all. Some laugh in a deprecating manner, or sigh in a disgusted or resigned fashion as they view the cards. The stereotyped disdain with which they may preface their response to each card sometimes seems alarming. Thus one subject may make the response, "a folded piece of paper," or "cut on a fold," or "ink blot" to every card before giving a more significant response. And when he has finished, the result often seems to be completely inadequate. One feels as though an absolute nadir of intellectual and emotional expression has been reached.

Now what has brought about these signs of "blocking"? (The results at 15 leave us little leeway to use another expression, though since it is also typical of Fifteen, it cannot have quite the suspect meaning that it might have at other ages, especially in the adult.) A look at the tables giving mean and median scores for both boys and girls at each age reveals at least one aspect of the responses at 15 at once explanatory and encouraging—the matter of sex differences. For boys, many determinants reach their low point for the entire age. It is this factor that in many instances depresses the totals. Corollary to this is the fact that this is not a sudden, unexplained drop in boys' scores, but the low point of a gradual trend that began around 12 years with boys, especially in the movement and color responses. (The girls' totals appear to be more stable throughout.) At 16, we see an upward trend for the boys in almost every area.

Chapter 18 will treat sex differences more in detail, but we must here comment that there is a marked differential between the sexes in their reactions to factors of growth and development, as well as to environmental factors, which is made increasingly clear at this age.

Now let us proceed to a consideration of the actual scores. That Fifteen is a restricted and less productive age is most apparent for both boys and girls in the sudden drop in total response as compared to Fourteen and Sixteen. The median number of responses is the smallest of any age in this range—only 15. Median for boys alone is even lower than this, 14. Not only are fewer responses given, but the total record for both boys and girls is shorter than at any other age in this range.

This is complemented by the high number of refusals. Thirty-two per cent of the boys at this age refuse at least one card, a higher percentage than at any other age; and 26 per cent of the total group refuse at least one card. Mean number of refusals (.4) is also higher than at any age but 10 and 11.

There are fewer movement responses here than at any of the other ages —not only human movement, but animal and inanimate movement as well. Mean M is only 1.8; mean FM, 1.6; mean m, .5. Not only are the means low, but also fewer subjects give such responses than at most other ages. Only at 11 years do as few subjects give M responses. Only at 13 do as few give FM. At no other age do so few give m.

Color is similarly diminished. Mean ΣC of 1.0 is lower than at any other age in this range except 11; and pure C of .1 is lower than at any other age to date. Only 58 per cent of subjects give any color responses at all, fewer than at any age except 13. FC is given by fewer subjects than at any other age, though more give CF than at the preceding age.

In fact, expression of both movement and color is so low at this age that 12 girls and 23 boys give only 1M:1ΣC or less; of these one girl and seven boys have an equation of 0M:0ΣC. (Here again we see the marked sex difference.)

Fifteen is not only less expressive in both the introversive and the extratensive spheres, but the median M:ΣC ratio of 1.4M:.6ΣC shows him to be relatively more introversive than either Fourteen or Sixteen. With both M and C responses lowered, the mean F% is higher than at surrounding ages, presumably another sign of "restriction" (although the F% is higher than the adult expectancy throughout our entire age range).

Along with fewer responses than at other ages, it is not surprising that there are fewer different content categories (mean of 5.2) than at surrounding ages. Median of 44% A is lower than at any age in the present range. Mean of 18% H is lower than at any age except 13 years, and the median drops to 16% H. However, throughout our range, H% varies only within two points for both median and mean. (H) and (Hd) responses occur less frequently here than at any other age.

Within the Content classification, Fifteen is the only age that changes the order of relative prominence for categories other than A and H. For all other ages, the four next leading categories are object, anatomy, nature, and plant. With Fifteen, the category of scene takes precedence over plant, with map and flowers closely following. Mask responses, which again indicate the withdrawn and restrictive attitude of Fifteen, are as prominent as at 10 and 13. Reflection responses are almost as high as at 13, and abstract responses increase markedly over 14, being higher than at any age but 16. Blood and explosion responses occur least here of any age, and fire less than at any age but 16. The number of popular responses, both median and mean, decreases from 14.

It would appear from the characteristics of the content of response that the intellectual horizon of Fifteen is somewhat restricted even though he may be concerned with problems that are more profound. The use of map and scene indicates the possibility of intellectual and emotional reactions that appear to be more vague and diffuse than at some other ages. And the use of reflection and abstract responses indicates a more introversive, contemplative, though not always resolved or satisfactory, emotional and intellectual reaction.

Here we should mention the reversal in trend that occurs in the type of perception at 15. The medians of 43% D and 0% Dd are the lowest in the entire age range; conversely, 51%W response is the highest in the range. Thus the ascendancy of D% over W% that began at 11 years and reached a high point at 14 years is reversed at 15. Although the F% does not diminish appreciably, Fifteen appears willing to neglect the more detailed, practical, and realistic concepts in favor of more generalized abstract thinking. The drive to refine and specify thinking seems to be less in the ascendant.

It may well be the kinds of problems with which Fifteen is concerned that have brought about this characteristic change in his thinking. Whatever the reason, it is interesting here to survey the nature of the abstract responses that occur at 15. For although they occur much less than at 16 years, they have more than doubled in frequency since 14. Such responses are considered by some to come from deeper levels than other responses, and to indicate strong emotional states that have not been resolved. They will be indicative of some of the problems with which Fifteen is concerned.

With the exception of the responses of one boy and one girl, the abstract responses at 15 appear to be of a troubled or unpleasant nature. The largest proportion of abstract responses given at this age represent some kind of conflict between forces: "Two unicorns fighting to death in combat" (II); or more grandiosely, "Conflict between mankind . . . opposite forces" (III). Next in number come concepts of evil: "Witches casting evil spells across the 38th parallel at each other" (IX); "Bad, poisonous spiders. Orange and yellow shows the poison and the bad these animals are doing. Snake's head and awful, hypnotic, evil vision" (X). Religious concepts, too, are occasionally given as abstract responses: "Symbol of God—the whole Universe revolving around that" (X); or "Holy Ghost coming down in the form of tongues of fire or flames of fire" (VI).

Certainly such responses, when they are given, may be indicative of deep-seated, personal, emotional conflicts, but they may also represent a stage in an individual's development when he is suddenly a more conscious social being. He is coming to grips with social and religious, even mystic and cosmic problems and his intellectual and emotional reactions reflect the concern he feels in trying to evolve his own answers.

Such concern may well tend to create a minor strain, a moody, easily discouraged reaction. This is also evident at 15 in the adjectives used in describing the Rorschach blots. In keeping with the typically sparse response of the individual at this age, fewer adjectives are given altogether by the group than at any other age. However, a larger percentage of these adjectives are "affect" as opposed to "neutral" adjectives in the case of both boys and girls. Characteristically unpleasant adjectives given at 15 include: strange, weird, dead, evil, deformed, eerie, odd, distorted, and dried up.

In view of the problems with which Fifteen appears to be concerned and the characteristics we have thus far described, the nature of movement and of color responses will be of interest.

Among the movement responses, extensor human movements predominate over other kinds of movement by the smallest margin of any age, virtually tied by static movements. Furthermore, at only one other age, 13, are there as many "mixed conflicting" human movement responses.

As to single kinds of movement rather than classes of movement response, the leading response is "lifting, holding, or carrying." Next comes "static posture." At every age except 15, the leading single type of movement is "dancing or swinging around," but at this age such activity appears to have given way to more socially useful and at the same time less joyful, exuberant expressions of inner drive.

Animal movement at all ages tends to be of a more vigorous nature than does human movement. However, though those movements classed as "vigorous extensor" do predominate, at 15 static animal movements occur to a larger extent than at any other age. Here is perhaps one of Fifteen's greatest sources of stabilization. For the nature of human and animal response appears to be more parallel than at many other ages. What he wants to do and what he does are perhaps more reconciled here than we might imagine. Fifteen may appear to have less energy than earlier, but his own basic inner drives may be more harmonious. And athough production is down, Fifteen has not relinquished his drive for independence and greater self-identification, for the M response still remains higher than FM.

Of inanimate movements, the leading type is tension movement, which occurs here more than at any other age. This again portrays the "inhibited" characteristic of the age.

Among the color responses, we find that blood and explosion responses are decreased and fire is on the decline. Flower, on the other hand, is as high as at 14. Flower responses may well indicate Fifteen's interest in and desire for satisfactory heterosexual relationships. And from the decrease of blood, explosion, and fire, it may be indicated that conflicts provoked by the environment occur less than earlier.

Difficulty with the environment may thus occur more frequently because of the preoccupations of Fifteen rather than because of actual interpersonal embroilment. Parents, siblings, or friends may be perplexed, even angry or hurt at Fifteen's withdrawal. And unless they can accept that this is his way of working out some of the problems that even he may not be able to explain, it may be one of the causes of greatest difficulty.

In keeping with the more introspective, contemplative attitude of Fifteen, one area that does not indicate either a diminution of response or a reversal of trend is the F(C) or shading response. The increase of response in this area, begun at 12 years of age, continues here as it will through 16.

Analysis of the shading responses reveals that there is less response based upon fine differentiation of shading within the blot and an increase of diffusion and texture, particularly of the latter. X-ray responses, too, increase in number. There are more vista responses than at any other age except 14.

Thus we see that concern with himself, with his own emotional reactions, even his own physical sensations as at 13 occupy a good deal of the energy of Fifteen. But his search for perspective about himself as well as perspective about his relations to others continues, in fact greatly increases over 13 and 14, and there is or appears to be a strong desire to make satisfactory interpersonal contacts.

However, the increase of diffusion responses (supplemented by map, scene, and abstract responses, plus the reversal of W:D ratio) indicates the vague, somewhat nonspecific reactions that seem characteristic. And with the increase of X-ray responses, we might surmise that Fifteen sometimes assumes an emotional and intellectual sophistication that he does not feel.

The shading responses themselves give evidence of his own sensitivity as well as his increased ability to empathize with others. It is because of this very sensitivity, plus a consciousness of problems both personal and social that might seem formidable to anyone (and for which his experience, both emotionally and intellectually, may not as yet adequately equip him), that the environment may have the impression that he will "go all to pieces" in too difficult situations. Such an impression may be heightened by the fact that he does not always give the expected response (popular response is slightly diminished); that he may like to make up his own mind about rules and regulations (A% is down slightly); and may even appear to be less interested in people than earlier (H% is decreased).

But although the environment may judge him somewhat harshly, we feel that evaluation of the total picture reveals the characteristics of 15 as a logical and integrated pattern of the maturing individual in a period of necessary retreat. It is a period where the subject is evolving answers for himself about the problems that concern him most especially in his relation to society.

We should perhaps conclude our analysis of the age on the same note with which we began. For this may be a more critical age for boys than for girls. We mention in conclusion that 60 per cent of the boys but only 34 per cent of the girls at this age give evidence of shock or tendency to shock in some area. (Girls appeared the more vulnerable to shock at 13 years—see Table 30.) Thus although boys and girls share some similar characteristics of Rorschach responses at 15, the sex differences at this age cannot be overlooked.

We must preface any characterization of Fifteen with the indication that this may be a more critical age for boys than for girls, and that the sex differences at this age are conspicuous.

However, the general picture according to the Rorschach response presents Fifteen as an age of retreat, withdrawal, and restriction. The totals are lowered in many areas and this apparent restraint is enhanced by refusals, by mask responses, and by a terse, monosyllabic production of speech. Stereotyped remarks and vulnerability to shock, especially among boys, lead one to suspect more "blocking" at this age than at many others. But since characteristic of the age, these tendencies cannot be thought to be as suspect as they would be in the adult protocol.

Fifteen is extremely sensitive in his own emotional reactions and sensitive to the personal reactions of others. There is a minor, moody, sometimes a morbid tinge to his reactions. He appears less energetic, more passive and quiescent than at 14 and his thinking sometimes appears vague, confused, and unrealistic. The environment may judge his response as inadequate under emotional or intellectual challenge. Certainly he does not always appear to conform to social pressures. Rather than hurt or be hurt, however, it would appear that Fifteen's most characteristic reaction is one of withdrawal, retreat, or inhibition.

But though apparently more passive than formerly, Fifteen has not relinquished his drive toward independence and self-identification. What he does and what he wants to do may be more in accord than before. And although he may appear less social, there is evidence that the desire for satisfactory interpersonal relationships and heterosexual adjustment is even stronger than earlier.

Fifteen appears to be giving a good deal of his energy to evolving his own personal and social concepts. In trying to work out answers for himself to problems of such gravity, he may not be able to give the effort necessary to maintaining satisfactory interpersonal relationships, even though his social consciousness has increased. It is perhaps here that Fifteen may well be a "misunderstood" age. For in view of the problems that seem to concern him most his restriction, restraint, and withdrawal seem a necessary retreat and a rightful necessity in allowing him to mature his concepts, his thinking, and the emotional equipment necessary to make the next step toward maturity.

Individual Determinants

Number: Mean R is the lowest here for any age in this range, 18.3.

Area: Once again whole responses predominate—mean W% being 50.5 per cent; mean D% being 43.5 per cent; mean Dd%, 6 per cent. Ratio for medians is about the same as for means at this age.

Form: Sixty-three per cent of responses are determined by form alone. Mean F+% is 92 per cent.

M, FM, m: Mean M, mean FM, and mean m are lower here than at any other age in this range. Mean M is 1.8; mean FM, 1.6; mean m, .5.

Static M is close to extensor M in frequency. Among FM, vigorous extensor movements lead; static movements come second. Among m, tension responses lead.

Color: Though ΣC varies very little from age to age, this is one of its two low points, mean ΣC being 1.0. As at other ages, CF responses predominate, followed by FC and C in that order.

Among FC responses, animal responses and object responses lead, occurring about equally. Among CF, nature responses lead. Among C, blood-anatomy responses lead, but food responses are prominent.

Shading: Mean F(C) is the highest to date, 1.3. Texture responses are now the leading type.

FC', C'F, FClob, Clob: These responses have declined very slightly, the mean now being .09.

Content: Total number of different categories used at this age is 20. Average number per child is slightly lower than at surrounding ages, 5.2. Mean A% is 47 per cent. Mean H% is 18 per cent. Leading categories are animals, humans, objects, anatomy, nature, and scene in that order.

Characteristic Adjectives: strange, weird, dead, evil, broken-off, deformed, eerie, odd, distorted, sad, dried up.

Length: Records are shorter here than at any other age for both boys and girls.

Time: Mean number of minutes per record is lowest here of any age, 11.8 minutes per child.

Semantics: The leading type of identification is comparing the blot to reality by means of the phrase "looks like." Naming the blot comes second. This is the low point for qualifying identifications.

Best and Least Liked: Both girls and boys like Card X best, though Card V is also frequently chosen by boys. Girls like Card IV least. Boys like I least, with both Cards IV and IX close runners-up.

Refusals: More cards are refused at this age than at any age but 10 and 11, mean number of cards refused being .41. More subjects refuse cards here than at any other age but 10 and 11, 26 per cent here. More boys refuse cards than at any other age, 32 per cent. The card most refused is Card IX; next most, IV.

Populars: There are fewer popular responses here than at any other age; mean number of populars is 5.8; median, 6.

Sex Differences

At Fifteen, both boys and girls give fewer responses than they did at Fourteen, but boys give fewer than do girls. M, FM, and m responses are fewer, in both sexes, than at Fourteen, and boys give fewer of each than do girls. ΣC is smaller than at Fourteen, and here again, boys give fewer responses than do girls.

Shading responses have increased slightly. They are higher in girls than in boys. There are a great many refusals at this age, boys refusing many more cards than do girls.

Both abstract and map responses are conspicuous, occurring more in boys than in girls. H% is low for both sexes, but lower in boys than in girls.

There are fewer popular responses here than at any other age in this range, and boys have fewer than do girls. Responses are more global than at any other age in this range except Ten, boys having a higher W% than girls.

Therefore it will be seen that, in nearly every respect, the behavior characteristics of this age—that is, the giving of a limited, restricted, global response, less enlivened than at surrounding ages—are expressed more clearly by boys than by girls.

Girls give not only a more enlivened response than do boys (even though more restricted than at surrounding ages), but also their responses are more variable than those of boys.

Comparison of Rorschach and Developmental Findings

DEVELOPMENTAL	RORSCHACH
Restriction of energy output, minimal response. Limited intellectual and emotional expression.	Lowest mean R of any age in this range. Shorter total record. Fewer M, FM, m of any age. Fewer subjects give M, FM, m than at most ages. Static M as common as extensor M. Mean ΣC lower than at any age except 11. Fewer adjectives used than at any other age. Fewer content categories per child than at surrounding ages. Less turning of card than at any age except 16.

Comparison of Rorschach and Developmental Findings

DEVELOPMENTAL	RORSCHACH
Social and emotional withdrawal from others; shuts people out.	Lower H% than at any age but 13.
	High number of refusals, especially among boys.
	Delays before responding, manipulates cards, whispers response, does not indicate area selected.
	Relatively many map and mask responses.
	Lack of elaboration of response seen in lack of detail responses. Dd% lower than at any other age.
	ΣC lower than at surrounding ages.
	Lowered M and FM in comparison with surrounding ages.
Thoughtful and reflective rather than expansive or expressive; seems to pull together and organize thoughts and perceptions.	Response is characteristically introversive.
	Most abstract responses to date.
	Marked increase in W%.
Tries to evaluate and to see self in perspective.	Most shading responses to date; high number of vista responses.
Individualized and somewhat unpredictable responses.	Lowest mean P of any age.
Considerable rebellion and conflict with authority; unadaptable.	Of m, tension movements lead. More tension m here than at any other age.
	Popular response lower than at any other age.
	More initial shock or tendency to initial shock than at any other age.
Unhappy, negative emotions conspicuous.	Abstract responses primarily represent conflict between forces, or depict some form of evil.
	Higher tendency to dark shock, especially among boys, than at any other age.

Sample Record of 15-Year-Old-Boy B.B.

				SCORING	
RESPONSE	INQUIRY				
I. Face of an animal—a wolf.	(Whole plus white spaces.) ? "Eyes and ears."	WS	F+	Ad	P
(Else?) A map. ∨ ∧ All.	(Whole. No further elaboration.)	W	F+	map	
II. ∨ (Scratches head. Slight delay.) ∧ Bearskin rug. (Else?) No.	(Whole.) ? "Shape of the outside of it."	W	F±	Aobject	
III. Looks like a crab or a spider.	(Black, including some space.) ? "The claws." ? "The arms and the face." (Claws are legs of usual figures, face of spider is lower black center plus white.)	WS	F+	A	P
IV. Looks like two feet. >∨∧ (Else?) No, that's all.	(Usual feet. No further elaboration.)	D	F+	Hd	
V. ∨ Bird or butterfly. (Discards at once.)	(Whole. Form.)	W	F+	A	P
VI. (Turns head rather than card. Some delay.) This one looks like a skin of some kind.	(Whole.) ? "The shape of it."	W	F+	Aobject	P
VII. Couple of islands surrounded by water.	(Blot is "islands." White surrounding blot is "water." Map form.)	WS	F+	map	
VIII. Top part of this would probably be a hat.	(Top blue. Form.)	D	F+	object	
And the whole thing in general would be a skull of some kind.	(Whole plus white spaces.) ? "Just a human skull."	WS	F±	anatomy	

RESPONSE	INQUIRY		SCORING		
					object
IX. ∨ (Long regard.) ∧ Couldn't say what this one was. (Ex. encourages him.) This reminds me of Hallowe'en. Witches' costume.	(Orange. Sees only costume.)	D	F+		object
(Else?) This would remind me of an Indian chasing the buffalo.	(Sees Indian in green, points out head, tomahawk. Buffalo is pink. However, Indian is going in wrong direction to chase buffalo; it would really be vice versa.)	D	M ↗FM	H	
X. ∨∧ Looks like a—spiders and insects.	(When asked to define area, he indicates "the whole thing.")	W	F+	A	(P)

Card most liked: X because of the color.
Card least liked: IV because it looks like a nightmare or something.

R:13   Time: 10 minutes

5W	12F = 92%F	3A
4WS = 69%W	10F+, 2F± = 93%F+	1Ad
		2 Aobject = 46%A
4D = 31%D	1M	
	(→1FM)	1H
		1Hd = 15%H

Succession: None
Shock: ? Red, ? Movement   1M:O∑C   2 map
      ? Color   2 objects(2Aobjects)
                                       1 anatomy

                                       4-5P

COMMENT   See page 236.

COMMENT Here we see the type of Rorschach responses that at first gave us great concern, but which we now consider an almost classic example of a protocol at Fifteen. It appears impoverished, restrained, and the subject appears withdrawn, reluctant, and somewhat less than enthusiastic. We can suspect red shock, movement shock, dark shock, even possibly color shock though his response on the color cards is enlarged in comparison to that on many of the other cards. But it is difficult to presume any or all of this "shock" when the total response is so restricted.

In most scoring values this boy is close to the median for boys of his age. The low R and narrow experience balance are characteristic. He tends to exceed most 15-year-old boys only in W% and F% (scores beyond the 75th percentile) and is exceeded by them in D%, FM, and P (scores below the 25th percentile). In his use of global, unenlivened forms, he highlights the general trend of development at 15. His reticence in inquiry and his "map" responses reveal his vagueness and evasiveness, both characteristic of many boys' records at this age. His avoidance of the obvious, popular responses seems unusual even for Fifteen.

But even though he may attempt to resist the more usual and acceptable modes of behavior, there is a strong sense of what is expected, just the same. He is even willing to force his perceptions toward a complete reversal of facts resulting from automatic response. At IX, he sees an "Indian" in an attitude of chase and he sees a "buffalo." Since Indians are normally presumed to chase buffalos, he makes the combination regardless of the fact that the Indian is preceding the buffalo. Is this indicative of the unimaginative response of Fifteen in general, or of this boy in particular? Is this type of response the basis of the complaint of teachers and parents, "He just doesn't think"? Does it indicate that there is a certain amount of vegetation necessary at this point of development and that many responses become automatic rather than go through the higher centers of cerebration?

He remarks of IV that it "looks like a nightmare or something," and yet he gives a popular response here, indicating that conformity is possible even in the face of disagreeable reactions. Or perhaps it is conformity that relieves the general malaise whenever or wherever it tends to appear.

If this protocol appeared at any other age we might be tempted to say, because of the strong inhibition, evasiveness, lack of self-assurance, apparently low energy, the low participation in social and cultural thinking and the apparent low conformity, that this individual was possibly subject to various neurotic and unhealthy reactions. Nor can we deny that the implications of such an interpretation are present here. But many of the traits that seemed to be developing throughout the age range seem suddenly to disappear at 15, or to go in reverse. There is little evidence of intellectual or emotional range, little reflectiveness, lessened regard for others. Energy seems lacking and independent drives seem to have come to a stand-still or to be confused. This boy seems to incorporate all these traits.

Since this kind of protocol seems to appear with depressing regularity at 15, we must admit that it is typical, and much as we have to learn about the reasons for such a response, the fact that it is typical seems somewhat reassuring.

Sample Record of 15-Year-Old-Girl. P.O.

RESPONSE	INQUIRY		SCORING		
			$\nearrow$F(C) M	H	
I. I feel so terrible 'cause every year it looks like the same thing. Female figure inside a coat with hands raised over neck. And you have —(holds card at arm's length) hm! (laughs)—you have blurs, but I don't think you want to call them shadows.	(Center figure as woman. Sees shading around figure as "coat," and rest of blot as "blurs" or "shadows" made by the woman.)	DW	M	H	P
II. Now here we have two animals jitterbugging. That's all.	(Whole including reds.)	W	FM	A	P
III. And here you have the conflict between mankind. You just have the opposite forces represented. Whole blot.	(Makes no further personification during inquiry. Each side as a "force" opposing the other.)	W	m	abstract	O
IV. That still looks like the same thing. (Pause) Some kind of a rug made out of an animal. A little strange because feet here, but head and fur.	(Whole.)	W	F(C)	A object	P
V. (Some delay.) Some kind of flying animal.	(Whole.) ? "Head up here." ("Flying animal."="animal that flies," not FM)	W	F+	A	P
VI. It looks like some kind of a design, an—I don't know—Indian rug.	(Whole.) ? "Not the rug, just the design." (Sees the entire blot as an element of Indian design.)	W	F+	design	O

Sample Record of 15-Year-Old-Girl P.O. (Continued)

RESPONSE	INQUIRY		SCORING		
This, too, looks like the hide of an animal.	(Whole.) ? "Animal—looks as though you represent the whole thing."	W	F+	Aobject	P
VII. Nice one! Still reminds me of two bunny rabbits.	(Whole. No further elaboration.)	W	F+	A	P
VIII. I hate this one! Mm—(Delay) I don't like the colors together. Here you have the mountain, and up here you have some kind of flags—two—and here are some animals and they're tearing down the flags. Mountain part of it. I don't like those colors (indicates bottom pink and orange).	(Usual animals; pink and orange lower center is mountain; center blue is flags.)	DW	FM	↗scene A	P
IX. Doesn't look like anything. Perhaps the whole thing could be a flame, different types—yellow, blue, etc., in a flame—way it comes up at the top.	(Whole.)	DW	↗m CF	fire	
X. It looks like something from the seashore. All very disorganized. (Delay.) In it you can see all your little different types of sea animals. (Else?) No.	(Whole.) ? Names "sea horses, little crabs," but sees all other parts included as sea animals.	DW	F+	↗?scene A	P

Card most liked: III, "except if it weren't for the little red things on it which give the same impression as this (X)—scatter and disorganization."

Card least liked: X.

R:11   Time: 9 minutes

7W   5F $=45\%$F   5A
4DW $=100\%$W   5F$+$ $=100\%$F$+$ 2A obj $=64\%$ A

                                                                   1H $=9\%$H

                                        1M, 2FM, 1m   1 abstract
                                        1CF, 1F(C)   1 design
                                                                   1 fire
                                        ($\rightarrow$1m, 1F(C))   ($\rightarrow$2 scene)
                                                                   7P
                                        1M:1ΣC   2 O

Succession: None
Shock: None (though expresses "hate" for VIII and feeling of "disorganization" for X).

COMMENT   See page 240.

COMMENT There is again certainly no great exuberance or elaboration here, as shown in the reduced number of responses and the difficulty of eliciting response during inquiry. But this girl maintains the trends we have seen as important characteristics throughout the age range in her use of abstraction, scene, and shading response.

Her scoring values are high (at or beyond the 75th percentile) for W%, FM, m, and A%; low (at or below the 25th percentile) for R, D%, F%, M, and H%. While she has not by any means the confidence and self-assurance she will probably have later (low H% and M, female figure in protective or protected attitude), she is not at all quiescent or passive in her search for self. She is undoubtedly more introversive than extratensive, though the scoring indicates ambiequality at present. She is seeking answers through as much intellectual, emotional, and physical activity as she is capable of at present.

She has social and adaptable inclinations but she sees herself as a destroyer of symbols and has a desire for power that she has not yet acquired. Response to Card III is "conflict between mankind." This may indicate a strong intellectualization of self, an attempt to identify self in society. This is almost a negation of human contact; intellectualization appears important to her.

In fact, her initial response at VIII is "I hate this one." This dislike of the color, together with her objection to III because of the red, indicates the possibility of color shock. She calls X "disorganized." This indicates a resistance to and dislike of environmental demand. And yet with her energy and intellect, she is able to give a very perceptive though aggressive response at VIII and an acceptable response at X. She attempts to refuse IX, but her "flame of all colors" indicates a warm though impulsive and egocentric emotional reaction in spite of herself.

Thus she appears to have many personal problems to solve, and she is undoubtedly in conflict with the environment. Such tendencies in an adult protocol would be termed neurotic, and we cannot deny that they may also have such a connotation wherever they are found. With Fifteen, however, such distrust and withdrawal seem typical. It seems a very critical age and one may ask if so-called suspect protocols from subjects at later ages may not be given by those individuals who have not surmounted the developmental problems of this period.

One presumes, however, that with this girl's warm emotional response, her sensitive perception and empathy, her energy and intellect, her contacts will become more personal and productive once her intellectual and emotional independence is established.

CHAPTER SIXTEEN

Sixteen Years

19 R	59%F	45%A
	93%F+	16%H
50%W		2.6 objects
44%D	2.3M, 2.4FM, 1.0m	.8 anatomy
4%Dd	.5FC, 1.2CF, .1C	.8 nature
	1.6F(C)	.5 plant
		.4 flowers
	Mean: 2.3M:1.7ΣC	.4 abstract
	Median: 1.9M:1.2ΣC	
		6P

Sixteen is characteristically a happy age. Happy but not overexuberant, the 16-year-old gets on well both with himself and with the world. "The best age yet," say not only 16-year-old boys and girls, but their parents as well. "Well-adjusted, well-balanced, smooth, easy to get along with, perfectly content," are among the phrases that people use to describe Sixteen. He tends to like other people and to get on well with them, but he is also independent. This is not so much a matter of striving for independence and demanding it as was the case of Fifteen. Sixteen really *is* more independent. Life in the present seems good to him, and his plans and daydreams lead him to look forward with optimism to the future. The need either to rebel against the outside world or to restrict his experience and to shut himself off from the world is now less intense (11).

When we compare the Rorschach response at 16 with that at 15, for example, we see at once the increase in totals that indicates the emergence from the restriction of Fifteen, and we are permitted at the same time some insight into the evolution of intellectual and emotional reactions to problems that concerned the individual at the earlier age. For though Sixteen appears to be concerned with many of the same problems, he has developed more energy and greater expansiveness both intellectually and emotionally and thus is better able to cope with them.

The 16-year-old record is in almost every respect longer and much more enlivened than that of the 15-year-old. To begin with, there are many more responses at this age. The median number of responses increases

241

between 15 and 16 years from 15 to 19. There are more different content categories used at this age per individual than at any age but 14. Furthermore, not only are records markedly longer, but single responses are elaborated in much more detail than at 15.

There is much greater response to both environmental and inner stimuli. Sum C, with a mean of 1.7 is higher, and more subjects (74 per cent) give some color than at any other age in this range. Mean M of 2.3 as well as mean FM of 2.4 is considerably increased over 15 years, and more subjects give M responses (88 per cent in all) than at any age but 14. At this age only 11 boys and 7 girls, as compared with 23 boys and 12 girls at 15, have an experience balance of only $1M:1\Sigma C$ or less. Only three 16-year-olds have an experience balance of $0m:0\Sigma C$.

Conversely, F% is by far the lowest of any age in this range and the mean of 56%F is lower than any previous age except 7 years.

There is a marked increase in FC responses at Sixteen. The mean FC is now .5, highest of any age in this range and twice as high as at 15 years. As at all ages, however, CF is the predominating color response. If CF is considered to be indicative of less well modulated reaction and less adaptable response to environmental stimuli, then none of the ages in our range is as adaptable as might be expected. (We must pause here to ask ourselves whether or not we should re-evaluate the meaning of the CF response, and whether it is "normal" or even desirable for CF to be subordinate to FC. CF may well be indicative of the emotional vigor and productivity of the individual. FC may be indicative of the subordination of his reactions to social pressure, but FC responses may be less individually productive.) Pure C responses at 16 are infrequent, lower than at any other age in this range, with a mean of .1. This category, which is often characterized as indicative of nonadaptable or more asocial reactions, thus seems here to conform to presumed expectancies.

As to the nature of movement responses, as at all other ages in this range, extensor human movements are the predominant type of response, these having increased in proportional use since 15 years. Also, as at all other ages, the more active "vigorous extensor" movements lead among animal movements. In human movement, the four main single kinds of movement are "dancing, swinging around," "sitting, resting, lying, leaning," static postures such as "head up," and "fighting, quarreling, arguing, battling." In animal movement, the leading items are "running and jumping," leg actions and clapping, and "fighting, quarreling, attacking."

If we compare the most prominent human or animal movements, we see that at least the two leading movements appear to be in opposition. However, *variety* is the outstanding characteristic here and Sixteen appears to enjoy swings from extremely active to more passive reactions and back again. What he does and what he wants to do may not always be reconciled, but he appears to have a good deal more enthusiasm than earlier for both.

The 16-year-old's entire response to the cards seem to be much more open, easy, and pleasurable than it was a year earlier. Actual refusals (both the percentage of subjects refusing and the mean number of refusals) are much fewer than at the age preceding. There is less muttering, less card turning. Sixteen seems to have a much easier rapport with people and with situations.

The nature of the content of responses, too, seems more positive, less concealing. Mask responses are sharply reduced, map responses slightly so. Both the median A% and H% have increased slightly over 15. Popular responses remain about the same as at 15. Plant and flower responses occur conspicuously here, this being next to the highest age for plant responses (mean number .5) and the highest age for flower responses (mean .4). Food responses take a slight upward swing and may indicate an interest as well as a need in relation to the energy exhibited. Anatomy responses are exceeded only at 14 years. Although boys give more anatomy responses than girls, an average of almost one for each subject, the responses of the girls tend to show more concern, by such expressions as "horrible, bloody, biological pictures." With boys, such responses appear to indicate intellectual ambitions more than emotional concern. Abstract responses are given more than twice as frequently at 16 as at any earlier age.

As at 15, the greatest number of abstract responses deal with some kind of conflict between two forces: "War of the worlds" (III); or more specifically, "French Revolution in the streets. Black and red mixed together for blood and thunder. Kind of wild looking" (II); or more elaborately, more philosophically, "The road from good to bad. Blue is good. Pink and orange are trouble. Pink is trying to climb upward; gray is pushing it back" (VIII); more intellectually: "This is a war going on here. Green is the aggressor country. Perhaps an attack on the pink. See advance guards going out here. Right here the war is not going so well for them as the line is clear-cut, which means that the orange is holding its own and just below filtering in here into this place that was the green's country" (IX); or tolerantly, "Two forces fighting playfully, not really serious" (II).

A second theme, more indicative perhaps of the feeling of being at the mercy of an unfriendly environment, or of identification with faintly understood but powerful forces: "Sorcerer weaving wierd spells" (I) or "An eerie person standing over a castle going to end their fate" (I).

Indicative also of the strong potential and inner dynamism of Sixteen is the abstract response: "Fantastic picture of the inside of an engine. Piston, cylinders, spark plugs" (X).

Since more girls than boys at this age give abstract responses, it may be interesting also to indicate the general tenor of the girls' responses. We have some idea of the hopes, the dreams, the fantasies of Sixteen in "Somebody's daydream. Blue is the sky. Gray is the castle above the sky. Daydream (the pink animal) is aspiring to the castle in the sky. You can't see the dreamer" (VIII). Even sadness or sorrow has its hopeful side and is not necessarily connected with evil: "This is an old statue of the God of Sorrow. Little white hopes going up. Cloudy black which the head of the statue is blowing down. Part of the statue droops to symbolize sorrow, the sad way it droops" (IV).

But though such free association and confabulation may seem unrealistic, it can at times be humorously specific and very much related to reality. Thus to Blot IX one girl responds,

A candle through the center. Wax dripping down. On our altar at church. We have a maroon cloth that color on the altar. That's Uncle Williams, our minister, peering out with the eyes. He's looking at Judy and me in the choir because we're talking. One deer must be Hortense, one Mrs. Harrington, only they're not speaking to each other. Judy and me talking; our eyes are here, blurred because we're talking so fast.

Thus, if abstract responses may be considered to give us a clue as to some of the problems that concern Sixteen, we see "conflict" with its social implications as we did at fifteen. But reactions seem less anxious than at 15, and those things which concern him are much more varied than earlier. There are "more strings to his bow," so to speak; the affect is in general more hopeful, less acute.

A sign of the evolution at 16 is in the type of perception. At 15, we saw a reversal of trend in the W:D ratio, with whole responses again predominant. Fifteen's thinking seemed more oriented toward abstract, synthetic perception, and his ability to refine his thinking and to specify fine details seemed minimal. At 16, although whole responses still predominate, there is a slight decrease of W% (median 50 per cent) and a slight increase of D% (median 44 per cent). And the Dd% (median 4 per cent) is increased over 15. Thus, although Sixteen still perceives more easily in the global and inclusive manner, he appears to be slightly more realistic and practical, and able to refine his thinking more readily than a year earlier.

That 16-year-olds, especially girls, can be fanciful and daydreaming, however, is suggested by the characteristics of the (H) and (Hd) responses given at this age. Such responses are slightly higher than at any other age, but the characteristics of such responses picture supernatural beings as being less menacing than at some other ages: "The whites could be side view of a fairy symbolizing that she was a good queen" (IV). "Looks like a witch because here's her pigtail and her back and this is her witchcraft" (IX). "Mermaids (the pink) shaking out little blue baby sweaters. They have crowns and long flowing hair" (X). Thus such symbols of power, even evil, appear to have more benign human qualities; they are those with whom it is perhaps even desirable to identify. Such responses would indicate an increased confidence in self, as well as in interpersonal relationships, which we have not always seen earlier.

The generally pleasant affect that prevails at this age is suggested by the fact that 16, for girls, is the high point for the use of pleasant, the low point for the use of unpleasant adjectives. For boys, this is a low point since 12 for unpleasant adjectives, one of the high points for pleasant, though as at every age, there are more unpleasant than pleasant adjectives used. At 16 only do girls give almost as many pleasant as unpleasant ones (12 per cent pleasant, 13 per cent unpleasant). Furthermore, in keeping with the general expansiveness of 16, girls use more adjectives at this age than at any age preceding. Among the more characteristic positive adjectives are: fluffy, good, beautiful, nice, artistic, colorful, dignified.

Vulnerability to shock appears less at 16 than at 15; 56 per cent of the boys and 72 per cent of the girls give no sign of shock or vulnerability to shock in any area. The greatest vulnerability appears to be on the color cards, but this is not as high as at some other ages.

A trend that has continued throughout this age range and reflects the ever-increasing sensitivity, empathy, and awareness of the maturing adolescent is the small but constant increase in shading response. It has increased from a mean of .7 at 10 years (with a slight dip to .6 at 11 years) to 1.6 at 16 years. If we include the secondary as well as primary shading scores, this mean is considerably higher. Also, the highest number of subjects (58 per cent) of any age use at least one shading response.

The most prominent of these responses are texture responses, especially soft and furry textures. Then come such responses as reflection, water, wax. Reflection responses, both as shading and simply as form responses, increase in general throughout the age range, though the pattern is not consistent. Sixteen is one of the high points of reflection response. Third comes shading used to define fine differentiation within the blot. Sixteen is also a high point for vista response, which constitutes 14 per cent of all shading response. X-ray as a class of shading response is also given more at 16 than at any other age.

Such responses indicate the awareness of Sixteen of his own sensuous and emotional reactions as well as his frank pleasure in them. Such reactions also suggest greater perceptiveness of the reactions of others, and texture responses possibly indicate a search for more satisfactory interpersonal relationships. Reflection responses are sometimes interpreted as narcissistic attitudes, which they may well be, but we also feel that combined with the vista responses they indicate a desire to obtain greater perspective of self, of role, of relations with others. Flower response might also

be considered here since it may indicate the desire to make more satisfactory heterosexual adjustment.

The use of painting and X-rays suggests that Sixteen tends to assume
a more intellectual sophistication when he feels insecure or disturbed. Supplementing this is the use of anatomy responses, and the fact that perceptions tend to be more global, all of which testify to intellectual ambition.
Such responses, although they may be defensive, are admirably so, and
help to sustain the subject, who at this age does not give the impression
of "going all to pieces" as he may have done earlier.

As Sixteen indicates a great deal more vigor and enthusiasm, he also
seems to have a greater potential of unemployed or inadequately employed
energy than at any other age except 13. Mean m at 16 is 1.0. Among these
responses explosion is most prominent, with tension movements (things
hanging or stretched out) next, and finally things "smashed, broken, split,
or squashed." And although pure C responses are negligible at this age,
there is in this category an increase in blood, fire, and explosion. Such responses may well combine with the nature of the m responses to indicate
that although Sixteen may inhibit under emotional or intellectual challenge,
he is also capable of explosion or of rather heated interpersonal clashes.
One of the rarer minor notes at sixteen is in the feeling of things "smashed"
or "broken." This may express the subject's own feelings under frustration.
Again it may be owing to his having much more energy than is productively
employed and for which he has not found the proper outlets; or it may be
that society has not responded to the active needs of the age, thus giving
him more violent feelings of frustration and futility.

The behavioral summary given at the beginning of this chapter, as
in many chapters, seems also to summarize rather well the Rorschach
responses of the age.

Sixteen, as reflected in his Rorschach responses, is certainly more
energetic, more expansive, and undoubtedly finds life more exciting than
he did at 15. He is both intellectually and emotionally more productive
than he was earlier. Though he is concerned with many of the same problems as at 15, he seems to have many more possibilities in his approach
to them, and they thus seem less anxiety-charged, less acute.

His direction may not always be too well defined, but his energy
drives him to seeking and finding satisfactory new directions. He continues
his search for greater perspective in regard to himself and to his relations
with others. He is reaching out for new ways and means of greater self-
identification as well as improved interpersonal relations. As at 15, he may
not always give the expected response, but he now conforms to rules and
regulations with less resentment or overconcern.

His attitudes in general seem much more open, easy, and pleasurable than earlier, and although his own increased emotional sensitivity gives him difficulty at times, he mobilizes his intellectual defenses more readily, and he seldom gives the impression of "going all to pieces" as he may have done at 15. If there are warm interpersonal clashes, it may be because his greater expansiveness and his greater amount of energy allow him the luxury of such involvements. The amount of intellectual and emotional expansion that occurs at this age, though it provides greater possibility for difficulty, also gives him greater reserve to solve difficulties when they do occur.

Because of the amount of energy available, Sixteen may tend to react explosively to frustration, though he has not discarded inhibitive reactions that undoubtedly serve him in good stead. One of the few minor notes appears to be the number of things "smashed" or "broken." Society might do well to note the amount of productive energy, both intellectual and emotional, available at this age. In integrating such potential into more purposeful social outlets, reactions of futility might be avoided and energy more adequately employed.

Individual Determinants

Number: Mean R of 22.5 is larger than at any other age except 14.

Area: Responses continue to be primarily global. Mean W% is 50 per cent, mean D%, 43 per cent; mean Dd, 7 per cent.

Form: Mean F% is 56 per cent, lowest of any age to date except 7 years. Mean F+% is 93 per cent.

M, FM, m: All three of these factors have increased over the preceding age. Mean M is now 2.3; mean FM, 2.4; mean m, 1.0.

Among M and FM, extensor movement responses as a class predominate, vigorous extensor movements standing out. Among m, explosion responses occur most, tension responses second.

Color: ΣC is highest here for any age in this range, mean ΣC being 1.7. Mean CF is especially high, 1.2. Mean FC is .5; mean C, .1.

Among FC responses, animal responses lead; among CF, nature responses; among C, blood-anatomy.

Shading: There are more shading responses here than at any age to date, a mean of 1.6. As at Fifteen, texture responses are the outstanding type.

FC', C'F, FClob, Clob: The mean for all of these responses combined is .10.

Content: As at other ages, there are 20 different content categories used in all. The mean number per child, 5.6, is higher than at any other age except 14. Mean A% is 46 per cent; mean H%, 18 per cent.

Leading content categories are: animals, humans, objects, anatomy, nature, and plant, in that order. Abstract responses also occur conspicuously.

Characteristic Adjectives: fluffy, good, beautiful, nice, artistic, colorful, dignified, magic.

Length: Boys' records are longer and girls' appreciably longer than at Fifteen.

Timing: Mean time in minutes for the total response is 13.5, exceeded only slightly at 10 and 14 years.

Semantics: For the first time in this age range, simply naming the blot is the leading type of identification. Comparing the blot to reality by use of the phrase "looks like" comes a very close second. There are fewer qualifying expressions of identification than at any other age except 15.

Best and Least Liked Cards: Girls and boys both like Card X best. Girls like IX and VI least. Boys like least II, IX, X.

Refusals: Sixteen is one of the three lowest ages for card refusals, mean number refused being only .16. Card most refused is IX; next most refused is VII.

Populars: This is one of the two lowest ages, along with Fifteen, for the use of popular responses. Both mean and median are only 6.

Sex Differences

Sixteen is, again, an expansive age and here as at the just earlier expansive age of 14, we find signs of expansiveness in the responses of girls more fully than in those of boys.

Thus there are more responses per subject at this age than at 15, more in girls than in boys. All kinds of movement responses—M, FM, and m—increase at this age and are higher in girls than in boys. ΣC is higher than at 15, as is the mean number of shading responses. Both are higher in girls than in boys.

W% exceeds D% in both sexes, but girls give a higher W% than do boys. There are fewer refusals than at 15, and girls have fewer than do boys. The giving of both abstract and confabulatory responses, characteristic of this age, also occurs most in girls.

Girls not only express the characteristics of this age more fully than do boys, but also for most determinants the change in the expected direction, between 15 and 16, is greater in girls than in boys.

Comparison of Rorschach and Developmental Findings

DEVELOPMENTAL	RORSCHACH
Expansive, outgoing. Emerges from the restriction and withdrawal characteristic of 15. Emotions deepened; inner drive stronger than at 15.	Larger number of responses and more different content categories per child than at any age except 14.
	ΣC larger than at any other age; M and FM increased over 15.
	More subjects give M than at any age except 14.
	Fewer refusals than at any other age but 14.
	F% lowest of any age in this range.
More open, less concealing.	Mask responses sharply reduced here.
	Lower mean number of refusals than at any age but 14.
Conforming, adjusts well to others. Generally pleasant, "on an even keel."	Mean FC highest in this age range, almost twice that of 15.
	High point for pleasant, low point for unpleasant adjectives.
	Fewest turn cards of any age.
Warmly interested in and responsive to other people.	A high point for human responses.
Increased sensitivity to and awareness of others, as well as concern about self, own role, and relations to others; self-evaluation.	High point for F(C) responses, especially texture, reflection, vista, and X-ray responses.
Fanciful daydreaming, at least in girls, especially before going to sleep.	Considerable confabulation. Largest number of (H) and (Hd).
More straightforward and surer of self.	For the first age, naming the blot without any qualification predominates.
	Fewer refusals than at most other ages.
	Less evidence of shock or tendency to shock than at 15.
General lack of inner turmoil and tension.	Relatively few disturbance indicators.
	Next to lowest point for shock responses.

Sample Record of 16-Year-Old-Boy P.T.

RESPONSE	INQUIRY		SCORING		P
I. Animal flying like a bat. At first glance it looks like people dancing, leaning back, and holding hands.	(Whole.) (Two side figures, hands meeting in center.)	W W	FM M	A H	P
II. ∧>∨ Two men having a fight—one foot only on each—but each other's blood spattering from where they hit each other. Man or animals. Gorilla. Man not that shape. Gorilla is heavy—heavy fur.	(Whole, with black as gorillas and red as blood.)	W	↗m ↗F(C) ↗CF M	A	
III. ∧∨ Looks like a—you see it in the movies—space men from Mars. War of the Worlds. Heads, big eyes, hands. ∧<∧ Looks like two girls bending over a table. Picking up a basket or something.	(Sees two figures.) (Usual figures.)	W W	M M	(H) H	P
IV. ∧>∨ Mm! ∧ (Long regard) Looks like a clown to me, from bottom up. Big feet, ruffle on neck, can't see his head. Didn't look like anything at first.	(Whole. Seen in perspective; shading in "ruffle.")	W	F(C)	(H)	P

RESPONSE	INQUIRY		SCORING		
V. ∨ ∧ ∨ (Long regard—laughs) ∨ Water line. Girl with fur coat jumped into water—arms extended and reflection. ∧ Bat.	(Mid-line is water line. Girl's arms are one proj.: top and bottom center; legs are side proj. Head not visible. Black and shading give idea of fur coat.) (Whole. Form.)	DW	M ↗F(C)	H (reflection)	0
		W	F+	A	P
VI. ∧ > ∨ < ∧ Water line and ducks, shot down, and fell into water. Neck, rest of body, and reflection.	(Mid-line is water line. Top D is duck.)	DW	m ↗F(C)	A (reflection)	0
VII. ∧ ∨ < ∧ Looks like two rabbits facing each other or at least turned around backward facing each other.	(Whole.)	W	FM	A	
VIII. ∨ ∧ < ∨ Some weird thing from another planet and two animals trying to kill it, and it is pushing them away. Human thing. Don't know much about things from another planet.	(Center is "weird thing from another planet." Usual animals.)	DW	M ↗FM	↗A ↗scene (H)	P 0
IX. ∧ ∨ < ∧ Can't see anything on this one. (Try again, Ex. encourages.) Doesn't seem to make any sense. (He asks Ex. if she is from Massachusetts.)	(No further response on inquiry.)	Refusal			

Sample Record of 16-Year-Old-Boy P.T. (Continued)

RESPONSE	INQUIRY	SCORING
X. ∧ V ∧ V > V < ∧ Looks like some picture—tricky—that Walt Disney might put out. Whole bunch of animals in color under water. Fish, eels, or sea lions.	(Includes all parts. Top gray are fish, lower center green are eels or sea lions.)	DW FC $\nearrow$scene A

Card most liked: X. "I like color contrasts."
Card least liked: IX. No reason given. Ex. thanks him, and he replies, "Thank you, I enjoyed it."

R:12 (1 refusal)   Time: 14 minutes

8W=100%W   1F=8%F   6A=50%A
4DW   1F+=100%F+

    6M, 2FM, 1m   3H=50%H
    1FC, 1F(C)   3(H)

Succession: None   (→1FM, 1m, 1CF, 3F(C))   (→2 scene)
Shock: None   2 reflection

    6M:½ΣC   5P, 3 O

COMMENT This boy seems to recapitulate and combine many of the characteristics of the entire age period that we have seen gradually emerge in the progression from 10 to 16 years. At the same time he indicates the kind of maturity that we presume is expected as the youth becomes the adult.

Statistically, his response may be characterized as high (at or beyond the 75th percentile) in W%, M, FC, and H%; low (at or below the 25th percentile) in R, D%, F%, and P. The low number of responses, plus one refusal (at IX) and the lack of elaboration in inquiry reminds us of Fifteen. Although he appears a good deal more mature than many, he is still uncertain enough not to want to reveal himself to others more than is necessary.

The tendency to reflection, abstraction, and scene as well as the number of shading responses illustrates clearly the characteristics we have seen gradually increase as our population aged.

He, like the girl at Fifteen, has also only W responses, indicating a very personal difference in type of intelligence and in intellectual processes. He prefers synthesis and organized total concepts rather than detailed analysis.

Just as there are only W responses, though these contain a great deal of variety and many different qualities, the content is restricted to A and H responses only. The quality and expanse of his response within these two categories cannot be indicated as stereotyped or banal, but one suspects that this is not a boy to disperse his interest and attention.

His restraint in verbalization, including a refusal, may seem more like Fifteen, even though there is certainly little restraint in his turning of the cards as they are presented to him. Thus restraint may well be an individual rather than an age characteristic with him and may imply concentration rather than inhibition. He may not ever be highly verbal, but he is active, thoughtful, and full of ingenuity and independence. Too much turning of the card may well indicate indecision, insecurity; but any such interpretation here is belied by his manner of contemplative thoroughness and by his responses which seem clear and direct.

This boy's assertion of self and his independence seem quite positive. He is aggressive, ambitious, jealous of, and capable of defending, his interests. He appears confident in himself, though there is still an active search for greater self-identification and perspective. With the "space men from Mars," the "weird thing from another planet," and the "gorilla" one might even ask if he has overshot the margin of confidence. Does he tend to identify with the superhuman and the brutally strong? A more realistic conception should be attained as he continues to mature.

This boy certainly appears to be trying to consolidate his introversive drives more at present than his extratensive ones. Movement responses far outweigh color responses. But his interest in the color cards is evident in spite of his refusal at IX and his indication that he likes it least. For he still chooses X as the card he likes best because "I like color contrasts." Thus there is an attraction for environmental stimuli. The high H% also seems indicative of this. But his interest at present is in control of the environment by intellectual means and failing this, by withdrawal. It would be very interesting to see whether, once satisfied and secure in his introversive reactions, more color will appear in this boy's response.

The general impression, then, is that of a boy whose intellectual and emotional processes are efficient, orderly, and productive. Any emotional immaturity is probably disguised by rationalization. He is not highly verbal but he has a good deal of originality, which differentiates his thinking from that of others. He may well feel "different," and his withdrawal and restraint may be protective for him. He is self-critical, observant, emphatic, patient, tolerant, confident, self-assured, ambitious, aggressive, and energetic, and can be occasionally moody though well within limits.

Greatest difficulty for him may stem from feelings of frustrated power, from a possible latent destructive tendency, and from the resentment he must incur when he refuses the importunate demands of the environment.

Thus we see that even though we can identify some of the common age characteristics in this boy's protocol, by sixteen we are compelled to consider the strongly individual constellation. Earlier we often felt that we could study individuality through development. Perhaps from this period on it will be possible to study development only through individuality.

Sample Record of 16-Year-Old-Girl C.B.

RESPONSE	INQUIRY		SCORING	
I. This looks like two witches standing with their cloaks streaming out.	(Two side figures.) ? "This is the head and this is the cloak streaming down."	D	↗m M	(H)
And two Eskimos waving good-bye.	(Center. No connection between Eskimos and witches.) ? "Two heads and the mittens—just this upper portion."	D	M	H
As a whole, it looks like a butterfly.	(Whole. Form.)	W	F+	A
II. This looks like a ritual dance. Maybe one of those French provinces, with their funny hats. (Else?) No.	(Whole. Two figures.)	W	M	H
III. Looks like a tug of war, and modern dancers facing a pedestal or something.	(This seemed at first two concepts, one abstract and one with figures. But in inquiry, it emerges as one concept.) ? "The idea of them both wanting the middle part." Who? "These two people—sorta like woodpeckers." Modern dancers? "The modern dancers have black tights on." ? "Female—same two figures" (as the two woodpecker people).	W	↗FC' M	↗abstract H	P

Sample Record of 16-Year-Old-Girl C.B. (Continued)

RESPONSE	INQUIRY		SCORING		P
IV. A bear rug. That's all.	(Whole.) ? "Looking at the perspective, feet are large, head here."	W	F+	Aobject	P
V. Sorta like a scared rabbit.	(Center detail.) ? "These are his ears and the feet out back here." ? Legs straight out—wind blowing ears."	D	↗m / FM	A	
(Else?) Some kind of a fly—a butterfly or—let's see— (Anything else?) No.	(Whole.) ? "It's in flight."	W	FM	A	P
(Pause) A totem pole.	(Top D.) Idea? "This object—points—sorta arms."	D	F+	object	
And well, resembles a map—a peninsula—a body of water and an island, and this is a reef.	(Whole. Form.)	W	F+	map	
(Else?) Just an idea—this is a lighthouse up from the ground. Here's a cloud. (Else?) Guess that's all.	(Top D. Center is lighthouse and proj. as cloud.)	D	F(C)	object	
VII. Two little elves.	(Whole.) ? "Their faces, two little hats. I guess they're sitting on one of those watching each other—on the tops of the cliffs."	DW	M	↗scene (H)	P
And this looks like those houses built in the cliffs and, mm . . . that's all.	(Third tier as cliff, with center light detail as house.) ? "Well this is the cliff and this object is the opening."	D	F(C)	architecture	

RESPONSE	INQUIRY		SCORING		
				A	P
VIII. These two look like two boars.	(Usual animals.)	D	F+	A	
This looks like a mountain—a natural formation eaten away by the erosion.	(Center blue. Indicates shading as "erosion.")	D	F(C)	nature	
(Anything else?) Tree roots under the ground—the way they're spread out here.	(Top gray.)	D	F+	plant	
IX. (Pause) Seems like a table top. A floral decoration—maybe not flowers, but a table decoration. The bowl is on a stand—fall leaves—two sprigs. Can I look at it upside down?	(Pink is table top. Orange and green are fall leaves spreading from bowl which is center white.) Idea? "Well, the bowl here—the sprigs—the shape gave me the idea."	DW or WS	FC	object	
V Well, this way it looks like two eyes peering through.	(Center white slits.)	S	↗M F+	Hd	
And this is something like a mushroom effect from an atomic bomb. That's all.	(Pink. Form only.)	D	↗m F+	explosion	
X. A naturalist's box with all collection of bugs.	(All parts combined. Form of bugs.)	DW	F+	A	
And this general motion is two deer leaping outward.	(Side brown.)	D	FM	A	
(Anything else?) Um . . . two strange type of bugs with their antennas. They look quite angry at each other.	(Top gray.)	D	FM	A	

Sample Record of 16-Year-Old-Girl C.B. (Continued)

RESPONSE	INQUIRY		SCORING	A	P
(Anything else?) This looks like some type of marine life—jellied middles—legs and feelers.	(Side blue. Sees shading.)	D	F(C)	A	
This looks like the cement decorations—lions or those sides in sorta classical decoration used to adorn the outside of temples. (Else?) No, guess that's all.	(Center yellow.)	D	F+	Aobject	P

Card most liked: II. "It shows sorta the happy side of life."
Card least liked: VIII. "Has no real—doesn't strike your eye or make you feel interested."

Time: 20 minutes

R:24

6W	$10F = 42\%F$	$5M, 4FM$	8A
$3DW = 37\%W$	$10F+ = 100\%F+$	1FC	$2Aobject = 42\%A$
$14D = 58\%D$		4F(C)	2H
$1S = 5\%Dd$			3(H)
		$(\rightarrow 1M, 3m, 1FC')$	$1Hd = 25\%H$

5M:½2C

3 object
1 map
1 architecture
1 nature
1 plant
1 explosion
   (1 scene)
   (1 abstract)
8P

Succession: None-orderly
Shock: None

COMMENT Here we have a protocol that seems somewhat more typical of Sixteen than did that of the boy just preceding, even though the individuality is marked. Number of responses, area balance, F%, and H% all approximate more closely the average response at 16 than did those of the boy. Still, the girl has greater than average emphasis (scores at or beyond the 75th percentile) on M, FM, FC, F(C), H%, and P; less than average (scores at the 25th percentile) on CF and ΣC.

Shading responses are especially emphasized, with a perspective quality to many of them. This girl's self-identification and independence seem well on their way to a more mature level, and there is an active searching for perspective and self-evaluation. It is interesting to compare the abstract responses given in this and the two preceding records. The girl at 15 gave "conflict of mankind," the boy at 16, "war of the worlds," and this girl uses "tug of war." The first is depersonalized and generalized, identifying personal with social conflicts, the second shows conflict between superhuman beings, but in "tug of war" there is a more personal identification. This more personally conscious, realistic treatment appears to offer better possibility of resolution.

The acceptance of responsibility that increasing independence brings with it seems affirmed by this girl in the card liked best (II), where she sees a ritual dance of another culture and says, "It shows sorta the happy side of life." This would seem to be an assertion of self-confidence and to show a dynamic adaptability and a happy merging of intellectual, social, and emotional components that will probably serve her well. Her process of spontaneous intellectual and emotional adaptation may be seen in her responses at I and III. At I we have an initial response of "witches" and then "two Eskimos waving good-bye." Thus, although there may be an initial suspicion and mistrust of herself or others in a new situation, she overcomes this immediately in the warm, personal-social response that follows. Again, at III, we see the abstract "tug of war" merge immediately into "modern dancers facing a pedestal or something." In inquiry she indicates the intermediary step in her thinking when she personalizes the tug of war by "the idea of them wanting this middle part." She may attempt detachment when she does not want to accept responsibility (people given caricature aspects) but a personal identification comes through, and her realism and practicality will not allow her to retreat.

Only when fears overtake her may she tend to retreat to reverie with a watchful, perhaps even humorous regard of the situation (see evolution of responses at V, VI, and VII). One might question whether these fears are concerned with problems of sex, birth, and/or death. But at no point does she give any indication of not having adequate reserves to handle them.

The "erosion" response at VIII is the type of response sometimes felt to be indicative of masturbation. Since it is a shading response on a color card, we should be inclined to credit a perceptive, searching approach to environmental situations. This is supplemented by the consciousness of shading in the popular response at X.

This girl's emotions are usually well controlled by her strong intellectualization, though she may have occasional sentiments of being supervised too closely. She probably looks first to herself for fault whenever there is difficulty, though it is possible that she is also capable of being somewhat haughty and arrogant with others.

Her strong intellectualization is a reserve for her and yet may tend to hold her up too rigidly at times. But one would predict that this is a basically introversive type of personality that will modify but will probably not change fundamentally. In the 16-year-old boy, for example, one could ask whether or not the extratensive might not come in more strongly once he was satisfied with the organization of his introversive drives. It does not seem as likely with the girl. She says of Card VIII, which she likes least: "Has no real—doesn't strike your eye or make you feel interested." Reality for her comes from within.

Thus, this final protocol at Sixteen continues to be more characteristic of the individual than of the age. Even though one can identify traits that seem typical of the age or of the age range, one finds the personality compelling more and more consideration.

How close is this girl to adult expectancies and how much more evolution can we expect in her basic characteristics? The D : W ratio approaches 2 : 1; F% is well below 50 per cent; F+% is high (toward rigidity); M is higher than FM; there is 1FC and no CF. There are 42% A, 25% H, 7P, and 8 content categories, all indicative of normal expectancies in the adult. Only the shading response is higher than we expect in the adult, and it is perhaps here and in the color response that the maturing youth must have more time and experience in order to resolve the problems of development with which we have seen him to be seriously concerned.

Part Three

CHAPTER SEVENTEEN

Longitudinal Survey of Individual Subjects

We have, throughout this volume, been primarily concerned with differences that appear *on the average* between successive age groups, and with differences in *average* scores for the major variables. However, in actual practice, whether the Rorschach is used for clinical or for research purposes, such age differences as we may define are of practical value only if they represent changes that actually take place—more or less as we describe them—in individual children. As in measuring any individual child against any norm, we would not expect in the present instance that he would follow precisely the route that we have charted, giving a fuller response, for instance, exactly at 12 years, a more restricted one at 13, again more expansive at 14.

Though the present study does not attempt to follow longitudinally the progress of individual children, we shall present findings on one pair of fraternal twins seen by us at yearly intervals from 10 to 16 years, as an illustration of the extent to which individual subjects might be expected to conform to the averages pictured in this volume. These findings are not given as much to provide a personality picture of these two subjects as to show that individual subjects may to a rather striking extent follow the variations in response that we have found to be characteristic of our group as a whole.

For the twins in question, Girl A and Boy B, we have yearly Rorschach records for the ages from 10 through 16.

Table 32 gives M:ΣC ratios for each at each of the ages in question. It gives also the number of content categories used, and the total number of responses.

It will be seen clearly that for each of these three major variables, both Girl A and Boy B follow almost without exception the pattern that group averages have established: a fuller response at 10, 12, 14, and 16 years; a more restricted response at 13 and 15.

263

It is this *direction* of change and the order in which expansive and more restricted stages alternate, that are of primary interest to us in evaluating the individual applicability of the group averages. In the case of these two subjects, however, not only is the sequence of changes the same as that set up by group averages, but the actual timing is identical, both expansive and more restricted stages coming at the same time as do the group changes.

We are more interested in the present chapter in the direction of change than in the amount of change. However, we present Table 33,

TABLE 32. COMPARISON OF SCORES FOR GIRL A AND BOY B
AT SUCCESSIVE AGES

	$M:\Sigma C$		Number of content categories		R	
Age	*Girl A*	*Boy B*	*Girl A*	*Boy B*	*Girl A*	*Boy B*
10	5M:3ΣC	4M:0ΣC	8	5	33	22
11	0M:1ΣC	1M:0ΣC	2	5	27	16
12	5M:1½ΣC	3M:0ΣC	7	5	26	17
13	0M:0ΣC	1M:1½ΣC	6	4	19	16
14	3M:1½ΣC	3M:0ΣC	4	2	17	15
15	2M:0ΣC	1M:½ΣC	5	3	19	10
16	3M:1ΣC	1M:1ΣC	7	5	21	17

TABLE 33. RANGE OF RESPONSES, 10 TO 16 YEARS,
FOR GIRL A AND BOY B

Variable	*Girl A*	*Boy B*
R	17–33	10–22
M	0–5 M	1–4 M
FM	0–3 FM	4–9 FM
m	0–2 m	0–3 m
ΣC	0–3 ΣC	0–1 ΣC
Shading	0–2 F(C)	0–1 F(C)
Content	2–8 categories	2–5 categories

which indicates the *range* of responses for a number of variables for both these subjects for the entire age period.

This table suggests that the changes in fullness of response from age to age are wide, particularly in Girl A. Except for FM and m, Boy B shows greater restriction (that is, less change with age) for each of the variables considered here.

Though space prevents reproduction of the entire protocol at each age for these two subjects, we shall present the age changes in response to two selected cards, Cards III and IX. These will allow the reader to compare for himself both age changes in each subject and differences between the two. We shall comment briefly on both topics.

Girl A

CARD III

10 Years:

WS	F±	Ad		This looks like a cat. Nose, ears, ribbon on the cat.
same				>∨ This way it looks very much like a cat upside down. (Same cat?)
WS	F+	architecture	O	Also a cave—cave and outside.
D	F±	A		∨ Hens or something (top reds).

11 Years:

D	F+	A	P	(Much wiggling and jiggling and turning cards and self.) Well this here looks like a butterfly.
D	F+	anatomy		∨∧ This here (center black) looks like top part of a skeleton.
Dd	F−	Ad		Ears of fox. (Usual men's heads.) (Else?) No.

12 Years:

WS	F±	Ad		A cat's face.
D	F+	object	P	(Turns card >∨<∧.) I don't see anything else except the bow.

13 Years:

WS	F±	Ad		Cat. (Shows eyes, ears, nose.)
D	F+	object	P	Ribbon—or bow. (Idea?) Just looks like ribbon.

14 Years:

↗M,FC′

W	FM	A	P	Oh, two ducks or something, trying to pull a round thing out of the water. (?) Well, there are the men—legs, arms, things they're pulling out (dark part of lower center), water (lower lighter part). (?) Because it was lighter. (Later—two things?) Ducks. (Did you say men?) OK, one's a duck, other's a man.
D	FC′	Ad	P	Also, well, a cat's nose (lower center dark). (?) Looks like it. (?) It looks like our cat's nose—shape and the coloring.
D	F+	object	P	(Else?) Ribbon.

15 Years:

W	M	H		Oh, two boys trying to pull up a stone.
D	F+	object	P	Ribbon in the middle.
WS	F±	Ad		And then the whole thing except those (top red), a cat, nose, etc.
				∨ Nothing else.

16 Years:

WS	F±	A		Oh well whole idea could be the head of a cat. Nose (center black).
W	M	H	P	Two men trying to lift up something.
D	F+	object	P	A bow.

∨ < (Holds at eye level.)

CARD IX

10 Years:

DW	M	(H)	O	∧∨∧< Water (pink) and here is an elf (green) climbing out onto sand (orange). Same upside down.

↗F(C)

DW	M	(H)	∧ Two witches (orange). Noses here, grinning at each other; came out of a great cloud of mist (all rest of blot).

11 Years:

D	F+	object	∧∨ Oh a blouse right up there (pink). ∧∨<∨ (Long regard) ∧ I can't think of any more. (After long regard.)

12 Years:

W	CF	flower	Well in there (between orange) flower and leaves (green), and that's the ground (pink). (Top orange part of flower too.) (Idea?) Flower without color but green gave idea of leaves.
D	FC	food	Oh I see something else. Here are two carrots, and the tops, and nothing there (pink off). That's all.

13 Years:

DW	m	explosion	Could be a volcano with molten lava and the top of the mountain with heavy erupting. (Idea of lava?) Well, that's what it is!

14 Years:

DW	m	explosion	∨ > (Pause) Oh, I don't know. ∧ Well, um—a volcano, I'd say—lava and stuff down there, erupting up the top of the mountain. (Lava?) I guess this part coming out. (About it?) I don't know.
D	F(C)	object	This could be a candle holder and a candle —leaving everything else out (mid-line and pink only)—just looks like a candle and the light about it (upper shading).

15 Years:

D	F+	plant	(Some turning) Well, just this and the pink could be ∨ some kind of a tree. Trunk and top. Nothing more.

16 Years:

D	m	explosion		Um! ∨ ∧ Some sort of a volcano exploding from under the earth. (Idea?) Just the way it sort of comes up.
D	CF	nature		Green, could be grass.
D	M	(H)		(Else?) These might be some sort of silhouettes of witches, pointed hats, leaning back.

Boy B

CARD III

10 Years:

W	M	H	P	Looks like two crazy people fighting over something. (Turns upside down.)
DW	m	scene		Looks kind of like a river going in and coming out at the end . . . the end of a river. (Twirls card around.)

Doesn't look like anything too much.

(People?) Points out. (What made you think crazy?) They look kind of crazy . . . their legs are separated from the rest of them.

(River?) Something like this . . . Here's the sides and the river's coming down here and something inside of it.

11 Years:

W	M	H	P	This looks like two people. (Tell about?) They're sort of bowing. Have boxing gloves (black center) on.

(Else?) ∨ No.

12 Years:

W	M	H	P	Two people boxing. ∨ > ∨

13 Years:

W	M	H	P	Two boxers—two men bowing to each other.

14 Years:

W	M	H	P	Well, looks like two people, sort of ending a dance or something facing each other. (Ending?) Bowing to each other.

Guess that's all for this one.

15 Years:

W	M	H	P	This could be two characters standing next to each other, reaching their hands together.

16 Years:

W	M	H	P	This could be two creatures facing each other. (Idea?) Couldn't say. (Human or animal?) More like human.
D	F+	object	P	This looks like a bow tie.

CARD IX

10 Years:

D	FM	A	Looks like two creatures on top of a tree . . . or some kind of thing howling at each other and making faces at each other. What are they doing with their hands? They're sticking them out in front of them.
D	FM	A	This way it looks like two things with bears in the middle of them looking out . . . looking in the opposite way. (Bears looking out?) Yes, in the opposite way.
D	m	object	This way it looks like something with an arrow ready to shoot out of it.

11 Years:

D	F+	Ad	Two heads. (Green) Animal's heads. (Else?) No.

12 Years:

DW	FM ↗CF A		∨ > ∧ ∨ This could be some kind of flying animal (pink). An imaginary animal on top of some rocks. (? Green and orange, both form and color. Eyes of animal in center.)

13 Years:

D	FC	food	Could be carrots and stems.
D	F+	(Hd)	Could be a horned person—no such thing. (Idea of carrots?) Orange and green and the shape.

14 Years:

D	FC	food	∨ This way could be two carrots with stems (orange and green). Shape of carrots.
DW	m	object	∧ Or could be a heavy implement used to grind things and these are the things being pushed up. Handle (mid-line), crusher on the bottom (pink), and that's splashed up around the edges, or forced up (rest of blot).

15 Years:

D	FC	food	∨ From the other side, could be carrots in the ground, with their stems (orange and green). (In ground?) Not in the ground.

16 Years:

D	FC	food	∨ Well these look like carrots—these being the green stem (orange and green).

Age Changes in Card III

GIRL A　There is a rather consistent individual response at all ages except 11 and 14 years, that of the WS "cat" response. This breaks up at 11 into mere D's, and at 14 to "two ducks" plus separate D's.

This girl follows the age changes in her own individual way, but there are nonetheless very definite changes with age. At 10 years, she is more expansive than the characteristics of the age seem to imply, with generalized whole responses and one detail response. By 11 years of age, there are only detail or small detail responses. At 12 and 13 years, we see greater restriction in response. At 14 years, she responds for the first time with the two usual figures, introduced first as animals, then gradually metamorphosed into men. At this age, her usual "cat" response is reduced to "cat's nose." But the expansiveness at this age is evident in the number of responses and in the fact that movement appears here for the first time. These characteristics continue in this subject at 15 and 16 years.

BOY B   Unlike his sister, this boy gives no WS at any age. He is most expansive at 10 years and again at 16 years, when he has one additional response besides the two usual figures which appear at every age. It is in the quality of the activity that we see the age changes in this subject. At 10 years, the two "crazy people" are "fighting over something." By 11 years, they are "bowing" but they have "boxing gloves." At 12 years, there is no restriction or politeness in his expression, and the men are frankly "boxing." At 13, they are still "boxers," but again they are bowing to each other. At 14 years, the expression is much more social in "dancing and bowing." By 15, there is must less activity in "reaching their hands together," and at 16 years it is almost static in just "facing each other." This boy, then, appears to be more expansive at 10, 12, and 14 years; more cautious at 11, 13, 15, and 16 years.

COMPARISON OF GIRL A AND BOY B   In their reactions to Card III, both subjects show their individuality as well as the age changes that occur. For the girl, the most expansive ages are 10, 14, 15, and 16 years, while the boy indicates a more expansive attitude at 10, 12, and 14 years. Thus, for this particular card, the girl has a longer period of restriction, followed by a longer period of expansion. The boy tends to follow the in-and-out pattern of the age group trends more closely.

If this were the only card available for analysis, we might indicate that the boy appears much more consistent, more focal (average of 1.1 responses, as compared to the girl's average of 2.7), more global, more active and mature, more willing to accept responsibility than does the girl, as well as being more susceptible to group pressures than his twin.

Age Changes in Card IX

GIRL A   Here the age changes are much more obvious than on Card III. The increase of response as well as the use of a greater variety of determinants is marked at 10, 12, 14, and 16 years. At 11, 13, and 15 years, there is only one response and F is the only determinant, except at 13 years, when there is an additional m response. The use of movement, color, and shading responses at the more expansive ages and their absence at the more restricted ages lend support to our feeling that not only are individuality factors operating, but that lawful developmental characteristics must also be considered as the subject matures.

BOY B   On this card, this subject seems most restricted at 11, 15, and 16 years, when only one response is given. In this, as in the fact that the carrot stem response is repeated at 13, 14, 15, and 16 years, he appears to be rather consistent with his own pattern on Card III. His response follows in general the characteristic age changes of the group.

COMPARISON OF GIRL A AND BOY B   On Card IX, both subjects tend to reflect the age changes of the group more readily than on Card III. If we judged only by the response to Card IX, we might say that the girl appears to have a much wider emotional spread than the boy, and greater maturity. The boy appears to be socially more adaptable, more restricted, less complex than his sister, who tends to a more personal, individual emotional expression than he does. His aggressive attitudes probably exhibit themselves in defensive and strongly resistant characteristics, while hers tend to be more explosive and pervasive. There are conspicuous similarities in that both give the response "carrots," and have either witches grinning at each other or creatures howling at each other, at 10 years.

GENERAL COMPARISON OF GIRL A AND BOY B   (See Table 33 showing comparison of determinants and content.) Girl A, in general, shows greater variation of response. She has a greater number of responses, greater range of M, color, content, and shading. Boy B has wider range in FM and m only.

Girl A is introversive at every age but 11 and 13 years. Boy B is introversive at every age but 13 and 16 years. Girl A is extratensive only at 11 years, Boy B only at 13 years, and both of these by a very narrow margin.

For both Cards III and IX compared above, Boy B is more consistent and focalized in his response, more restricted and less variable from age to age. Girl A has a wider variety of response. The girl on Card III appears to follow a more individual pattern from age to age, while on Card IX she follows the age group changes more closely. The boy on both Card III and Card IX indicates both his individuality of response and at the same time conforms to the age changes of the group.

A further study now in progress follows the changing Rorschach response of 30 individual boys and 35 girls for whom we have yearly records for the age period from 10 to 16 years. Preliminary analysis of these records suggests that, of the girls studied, at least two thirds do follow the main trends described in the present study. That is, they give a relatively restricted response at 13 years of age, a fuller response at 14, again restriction at 15, and again expansion at 16. Restriction is seen in a reduced experience balance, fewer responses, increased F%, and increased A%.

Boys, too, show these trends, though less uniformly than do the girls in our population. Thus, of the boys whose records were available at yearly intervals for all or most of the age period in question, nearly half show the age changes described in this volume. Most of the others do show alternate periods of expansion and restriction, but unlike the girls they show some tendency to linger for two years, rather than for one only, at any given stage. Thus a period of restriction or of expansion may continue for two successive ages.

Perhaps as important as the exact nature of the changes that occur from age to age is the fact that any individual subject appears normally, in the teens, to show very marked age variations in his Rorschach response. Equally important is the fact that most major changes do not occur in a straight-line direction.

CHAPTER EIGHTEEN

Sex Differences

Sex differences in Rorschach responses in the years from 10 to 16 are, in our population at least, conspicuous, relatively consistent, and for the most part, statistically reliable. In fact, one of the outstanding characteristics of the response in this range is the often striking difference between performances of boys and girls. For every determinant it seemed necessary, in presenting our data, to give figures separately for boys and girls, a procedure for the most part deemed unnecessary for the first 10 years of life.

With certain minor exceptions, boys present a consistent picture of a more global, more restricted and thus less enlivened, less precise, less full, and less variable response. Girls' responses are, conversely, more detailed, more enlivened, longer, more precise, and more variable.

For the major scoring variables, we find the following specific sex differences for this age period as a whole:

Area:

Boys give definitely more whole responses than do girls except at 16 years. Mean W% for boys is 51.5; for girls, 44.3.

Boys exceed girls in DW at 11, 12, 13, and 14, though only slightly. Boys give more WS at all ages except 10.

Girls give a higher D% at every age but sixteen. Mean D% for boys is 41.9; for girls, 46.6. Girls give more Dd than boys except at 10 and 16 when they are equal.

Thus girls are more interested in the details, both D and Dd. Boys quite consistently respond more to the whole blot. These differences are least at 10 and 16.

The Median test shows these differences to be statistically significant—the differences in D% at the .05 level, differences in W% and Dd% at the .01 level.

Form:

F—Differences are variable. Girls appear the more restricted at 10 and 13 years; less restricted at 12, 14, 15, and 16. (Means and medians agree except at 11.)

F+—At every age but 12 the mean and median F+% for girls is higher than for boys.

Differences in F% are not statistically significant. Differences in F+% are significant at the .05 level.

Movement:

M—At every age but 11, girls give more M than do boys. Also except at 11, more girls give M than boys. Girls exceed in static, extensor, and flexor-passive movements. Boys exceed in mixed or conflicted responses only.

FM—Boys exceed girls in mean FM at 12, 13, and 14. Girls exceed at 15 and 16. Means are nearly equal for the two sexes at 10 and 11 years. Girls give more static; but boys give more extensor, flexor-passive, and mixed or conflicted movements.

m—Almost an equal number at almost every age.

Differences in M are significant at the .05 level. Differences in FM and m, however, are not statistically significant.

Color:

FC—More girls than boys give FC at every age but 13. Also girls give more FC than boys at every age but 13, when they are nearly equal.

CF—More variable. An equal number give CF at 10 and 11. More boys than girls at 12; more girls at 13, 14, 15, and 16. But girls give slightly more CF than do boys at every age except 12 years.

C—Equal numbers give C at 10 and 16. More boys give C at 11, 13, and 15; more girls at 12 and 14. Differences in means are small except at 14, when girls exceed slightly.

ΣC—Though differences are slight, ΣC is higher in girls at every age.

Sex differences, except those for C, are significant at the .05 level.

Shading:

Sex differences are marked. At every age except 11, definitely more girls than boys give shading. These differences are especially marked from 14 years on. Also, the mean number of such responses is definitely higher in girls than in boys except at 11. The sex difference is significant at the .01 level.

At five of the seven ages, boys give more differentiation responses than do girls. At five ages, girls give more light-shade. Vista occurs sooner and more extensively in girls.

Content:

For most content categories, girls give more responses at each age than do boys. They give more animal and human responses except at 12 years, when boys give a higher animal response and at 10 years, when boys exceed in human response. Girls have a higher A%, however, only for 10, 11, and 13 years. Boys have a higher A% at 12, 14, 15, and 16. Girls have a higher H% at 11 through 16 years. The only age at which boys exceed is 10 years when percentages are fairly close—boys 19.5 per cent, girls 18.2 per cent. Differences in H% are statistically significant at the .01 level.

Girls give more object, nature, fire, food than do boys at every age but 11. They give more scenes at every age but 11 and 13; more architecture at every age; more reflection at every age except 11 and 13, when they give the same number as do boys.

Boys exceed girls for anatomy at 11, 14, and 16. They give more blood at every age except 14 and 16. More explosion from 10 to 13. More mask except at 15.

Number:

Girls give more responses, usually considerably more, at every age except 11, when means are equal. These differences are significant at the .01 level.

Popular Responses:

Girls except at 11 give either the same number or more populars than do boys, so far as the means are concerned. Medians are more variable: girls higher at 10 and 13; boys at 11 and 14; equal at 12, 15, and 16.

Timing:

Girls' records are of longer duration at every age.

Thus far we have considered sex differences for the total age period. A detailed summary of sex differences for each separate age will be found in each of the age chapters. Here we shall consider sex differences for each age more from the point of view of the total age picture than for the specific scores.

By Age

10 years: Girls at this age give more D responses than do boys, more M, slightly more shading. They are more precise than are boys, and give more popular responses. Boys give more global responses than do girls.

The 10-year-old response has two rather paradoxical characteristics. It appears to be rooted in clarity and banality and yet at the same time it shows confusion, uncertainty and some unreality. The girls' responses particularly emphasize the banal side of the age; the boys' responses, the confused side.

Girls give more WS responses, fewer unpleasant adjectives, than do boys. As to content, girls have a higher A%, more architecture, fire, reflection, and abstract responses. Boys have a higher H% (unlike other ages), more explosion, blood, and mask responses.

11 years: Though at this age the records of boys and girls seem more different from each other than at most other ages, so far as scores for the main determinants are concerned the two sexes are actually more alike than at most ages. Girls' responses tend to be longer and more detailed than those of boys, to express much interpersonal engagement with the examiner, and to contain a good deal of more or less "stream of consciousness" material. Fewer boys have this kind of response. Also boys more than girls make qualifying remarks, give vigorous M and FM responses, fire responses, WS responses, and have the two sides acting on the center of Card I.

However, in spite of these conspicuous qualitative differences, we find that, while *at every age but 11* girls give more M than boys, more shading, more responses, more populars, at 11 scores for the two sexes for these items are almost equal. Thus boys and girls appear more alike at this age than at other ages in this range. The only conspicuous scoring differences are that girls give more D and Dd responses than do boys, and have higher F+, A%, and H%.

12 years: Sex differences, both qualitative and quantitative, are actually much greater here than at 11. Girls' records are, on the average, more expansive than those of boys. Thus, girls give more responses than do boys, and more detail responses; have a lower F%, more movement, and slightly more color responses, more shading responses. H% is higher in girls but A% is higher in boys. An increased expansiveness is one of the most outstanding characteristics of Twelve, and thus in this respect girls more than boys express the age. Girls more than boys use the predominantly unpleasant adjectives characteristic of the age. Girls and boys give about equal numbers of the popular responses characteristic of the age.

In many respects, however, boys give more fully than do girls the kinds of responses that appear characteristic of Twelve. Thus refusals are fewer in boys, DW responses increase more in boys than in girls from 11 to 12, and more are given by boys. Boys give more of the typically vigorous M responses than do girls and also have a higher percentage of quarreling and fighting responses. Boys give more qualifying responses than do girls, and also more WS responses.

Thus some of the kinds of responses most characteristic of this age are given most by girls; others by boys.

An interesting sex difference that occurs for the first time at this age is that here girls give considerably more M than FM, whereas in boys, mean FM still exceeds mean M.

13 years: The Rorschach response of the 13-year-old is characteristically extremely restricted as compared to that of the 12- and 14-year-old. There are fewer responses, fewer M, a lower ΣC, more refusals, fewer Dd responses, though more shading.

Boys and girls both show changes in this direction, but for most determinants the change in the expected direction is expressed more conspicuously by boys.

Thus boys give fewer responses than do girls, and the change since 12 is greater in boys. Boys give fewer M responses than do girls, though the decrease from 12 is greater in girls. Boys give more refusals than do girls and the increase in refusal since 12 is greater in boys.

Color responses are approximately equal in the two sexes. Shading increases slightly more in boys. Reflection responses are most in boys. Abstract responses, and "mixed-conflicting" M, both characteristic of this age, occur most in boys. H%, characteristically lower at this age, is lower in boys. A%, too, is lower in boys.

As at 12 years, M now exceeds FM in girls, but FM still exceeds in boys.

Boys have a much higher W% (boys 56 per cent, girls 37 per cent), a much lower D% (boys 39 per cent, girls 52 per cent).

14 years: Fourteen is again, like Twelve, an expansive age so far as the Rorschach response is concerned. With only minor exceptions, this expansiveness is expressed more fully in girls' responses than in boys. Thus girls give many more responses than do boys. They also give more M responses, more F(C), and a higher ΣC. Other characteristics of the age, reflection responses, a high D%, and a high H%, are higher in girls than in boys. Boy's responses are much more global than are those of girls (boys, 49%W, 43%D; girls, 43%W, 52%D).

Boys give fewer refusals than do girls, and more vista responses. As earlier, mean M exceeds FM in girls, but not in boys.

Girls show the greater change in the direction of increased expansiveness in R, M, FM, ΣC, F(C).

15 years: At 15, both boys and girls give fewer responses than they did at 14, but boys give fewer than do girls. M, FM, and m responses are fewer in both sexes than at 14, and boys give fewer of each than do girls. ΣC is smaller than at 14, and here again boys give fewer responses than do girls.

Shading responses have increased slightly. They are higher in girls than in boys. There are a great many refusals at this age, boys refusing many more cards than do girls.

Both abstract and map responses are conspicuous, occurring more in boys than in girls. H% is low for both sexes, but lower in boys than in girls.

There are fewer popular responses here than at any other age in this range, and boys have fewer than do girls. Responses are more global than at any other age in this range except ten, boys having a higher W% than girls.

In nearly every respect, the behavior characteristics of this age—that is, the giving of a limited, restricted global response, less enlivened than at surrounding ages—are expressed more clearly by boys than by girls.

16 years: Sixteen is, again, an expansive age and here as at the just earlier expansive age of Fourteen we find signs of expansiveness in the responses of girls more fully than in those of boys.

Thus, there are more responses per subject at this age than at 15, but more in girls than in boys. All kinds of movement response, M, FM, and m, increase at this age and are higher in girls than in boys. ΣC is higher than at 15, as is the mean number of shading responses. Both are higher in girls than in boys.

W% exceeds D% in both sexes, but girls have a higher W% than do boys. There are fewer refusals than at 15, and girls have fewer than boys. The giving of both abstract and confabulatory responses, characteristic of the age, also occurs most in girls.

Girls not only express the characteristics of this age more fully than do boys, but also for most determinants the change in the expected direction, between fifteen and sixteen, is greater in girls than in boys.

By Cards

Card I: Boys give relatively more whole figure responses than do girls; girls have more separate side figures than do boys from 12 years following. The

WS face response falls off earlier in girls than in boys, for whom it remains a leading type of response throughout the age range. Girls give more ghost, devil, witch responses than do boys except at 14 years. Boys have twice as many emblem responses as do girls; girls through 13 years have more headless middle responses than do boys and in general there is more emphasis on the central part of the blot in girls.

There is more M in girls; more FM in boys; more shading in boys.

Card II: Girls give twice as many "two persons" responses for the total age period as do boys, and about the same number of "two animals." There are more WS responses in boys than in girls and they continue longer in boys. Use of the white space alone is slightly more common in girls than in boys. Boys give more airplane, explosion, anatomy responses. Girls have more M, about the same number of FM, fewer m. Girls give somewhat more color responses of every type.

Card III: Sex differences are very slight for this card, two men being the leading response in both at all ages. There is a steady increase in this response with age, greater in girls than the boys. Boys do give slightly more WS for the total age range, WS falling off in girls but not in boys at the later ages.

Card IV: Sex differences here are marked at every age. Girls place a much greater emphasis than do boys on a large, threatening figure. Thus girls give more giant, monster, and dragon responses. Girls also place a greater emphasis on figures sitting on a stump; and on tails, snakes, pockets, than do boys.

They also give more flower responses; more birds, bats, butterflies; more bearskin rugs. Boys give more M, slightly more FM. Girls give more m. The concept of large person or animal decreases, then increases in girls with age. In boys it decreases steadily, with no later increase. The basic form is seen as old, ragged, torn, decayed by many boys from 10 to 13; by many girls from 12 to 14.

Card V: Sex differences here are slight, though girls do appear to be more advanced in the shift from a predominance of bat to a predominance of butterfly, and in the dropping out of a rabbit response. Boys put more emphasis on the wings of flying creatures than do girls, but girls give more scenes, more reflection responses, more profile faces, more scissors and tweezers, more bugs, more M and m, more shading. The response of the girls is more varied.

Card VI: Boys exceed girls in the use of the W "animal skin" response, but girls exceed in the use of W "animal." Boys also exceed girls in the use of lower D for animal skin or rug except at 12 and 14 years; but girls exceed in the use of the top D interpreted as animal, insect, bird except at 12 and 15 years. "Totem pole" is given slightly more by boys than by girls.

Card VII: Sex differences on this card appear to be rather small and variable. For the total age range, boys definitely exceed girls in the number of W or DW animals given; girls exceed boys in the number of persons. Girls also exceed in the number of responses to the center details of tier 3, details which frequently appear to have a strong sexual implication.

Card VIII: There is quite a strong similarity in responses of the two sexes on this card. However, boys do give more global responses than do girls. Girls give more color and more shading responses and there is some difference in content. Girls give more nature and more clothing responses than do boys and give a different kind of animals. Girls give more of the larger animals (bears), boys more of the smaller ones (mice, rats).

Card IX: There is considerable difference in the area of this card stressed by girls and by boys. Global and Dd responses occur more in girls; D more in boys. Changes in area from age to age are less in boys than in girls. Also the responses of girls are more enlivened than are those of boys, girls giving more movement, more color, and more shading. Content, too, differs considerably. Both sexes are extremely variable but boys more so than girls. Girls give more witches, lobster, person, geyser-waterfall, clouds or smoke, fire, clothes, eyes, mid-line rodlike objects, pink fuzz or cotton, reflection, scene, painting. Boys exceed in dragon-monster, explosion-eruption, paint. Boys give more refusals than do girls. Girls' m tends to occur in water forms; boys' m is more related to explosion and eruption.

Card X: Boys give somewhat more global responses than do girls to this card. Girls give many more separate D lists of animals. And, though leading content categories are similar, girls do have considerably more flowers, snake-worm-caterpillar, sea horses, dogs, bones, people, and butterflies. Girls give slightly more M and FM than do boys; boys exceed in m. Girls also give more FC and CF responses than do boys.

To summarize these sex differences briefly, we may say that at Ten, girls emphasize the banal side of the age; boys the confused, uncertain aspects. At Eleven, the actual scores of the two sexes are much alike. Girls' responses, however, seem to be somewhat more mature; there is more interpersonal engagement with the examiner; responses are more "stream of consciousness" in girls. Records of the more mature boys resemble those of the girls.

At Twelve, the response is characteristically detailed and expansive. Girls show this in most respects more than do boys, though the characteristically vigorous M, the many DW, the fewer refusals, do show up more clearly in boys' records than in girls'.

The restriction of Thirteen is shown most clearly by boys; the expansiveness of Fourteen, by girls. The restriction of Fifteen is, again, expressed most fully by boys; the expansiveness of Sixteen by girls.

The changes presented here as characteristic of the different ages do occur in both sexes. However, with minor exceptions, in this total age period girls give longer records made up of more responses, more M, more shading, more popular responses, slightly fewer refusals, a higher D% than do boys. Thus, it is not surprising that girls show most clearly the behavior characteristic of the more expansive, boys the behavior characteristic of the more restricted ages.

CHAPTER NINETEEN

Discussion

Rate of Development

As the human organism develops, its rate of change tends generally to become less and less rapid. In our publications describing behavior in the earliest period of life, for example, we found it necessary to consider ever-increasing intervals: before birth, weekly intervals; in the first year of life, monthly intervals; from 18 months to 5½ years, six-monthly intervals; thereafter intervals of one year.

Through the present age range, yearly intervals seem to continue to suffice. However, though we continue to describe behavior changes from 10 to 16 in yearly intervals, as we did for the preceding five-year span, the amount of change from year to year appears to slow down. Growth changes are still great enough and rapid enough for us to be able to describe characteristic 10-year-old, 11-year-old, 12-year-old, etc., records as differing conspicuously from one another. But age changes in mean values for the major scoring variables during this entire period are relatively small.

TABLE 34. SPREAD OF MEAN SCORES IN TWO AGE PERIODS:
MAXIMUM AND MINIMUM FOR EACH VARIABLE

Variable	Between 5 and 10 years	Between 10 and 16 years
R	14–19	19–23
W%	42%–58%	43%–51%
D%	33%–48%	41%–51%
F%	52%–70%	56%–63%
F+%	78%–89%	90%–93%
M	0.4–1.7	1.8–2.6
FM	1.1–1.9	1.6–2.5
m	0.2–0.8	0.5–1.0
FC	0.2–0.7	0.3–0.5
CF	0.7–1.5	0.7–1.2
C	0.2–0.8	0.1–0.2
ΣC	1.5–2.9	1.0–1.7
F(C)	0.4–1.1	0.6–1.6
A%	41%–49%	46%–50%
H%	9%–17%	18%–19%

Table 34 compares the spread of means for the major scores during the years from 5 to 10 with the spread during the years from 10 to 16. Such scores as R, D%, F+%, M, FM, m, F(C), and H% tend to increase from the earlier period to the later one, while W%, F%, and the color responses tend to decrease. But with one main and one minor exception, the *range* of mean scores is greater in the earlier period.

The exceptions are the slight increase in spread of means in FM and the somewhat greater increase in spread of F(C) means. The remaining differences in spread are all greater for the earlier period, and range from small differences, as in R (a spread of five points in the 5-to-10-year period, four points in the 10-to-16-year period), to relatively large ones, as in H% (a spread of eight points in the earlier period, only one point in the later one). This decreasing variability indicates the slowing of the growth process, and also suggests a greater stabilization as individuals progress toward maturity.

There is indication that F%, F+%, H%, and to some extent A% undergo relatively great stabilization between the two age periods, with a restricted range in the later as compared with the earlier years. This may imply that some intellectual factors, and perhaps some forms of personal-social reactions, stabilize earlier than do other characteristics of development. Area, movement, and color scores, although reduced in range at the later ages, still show more characteristic developmental fluctuations, implying a longer continuing exploration of types of intellectual activity and shifting patterns of extratensive and introversive personality reactions.

The increasing changes in F(C) appear to relate to the increasing importance of reactions implied by this score in the personality of the adolescent. As he becomes an increasingly self-conscious being, he shows changing sensitivities to his own moods and physical sensations, to subtleties of others' behavior, as well as changing inclinations to adapt tactfully to others. The continuing shifting of FM trends in relation to the stabilizing M suggests the immaturities, "regressions," and spontaneous breaking through of childish impulses that accompany progression toward maturity, stable self-concepts, and independence.

Thus, in general, the course of development reflected in Rorschach variables is slowing down, but the curves are flattening more rapidly in some areas than in others.

Comparison With Adult Expectancies

It is to be expected that as the child grows older, his Rorschach response will tend increasingly to resemble the response expected of the normal adult. This we found to be true in our earlier study of child Rorschach responses (1), and we anticipated that continued progress toward adult expectancies would be shown by our adolescent subjects.

TABLE 35. RORSCHACH SCORES AT SUCCESSIVE DEVELOPMENTAL LEVELS: MEAN RORSCHACH SCORES AT 5, 10, AND 16 YEARS, AND IN PRESENILE AND SENILE OLDER SUBJECTS, COMPARED WITH "NORMAL ADULT EXPECTANCIES"

	Age in years			Adult expectancy	Presenile	Senile
Variable	*5*	*10*	*16*			
R	14	19	23	20–40	16	14
W%	56%	51%	50%	20–30%	43%	46%
D%	34%	41%	43%	50–70%	47%	45%
F%	70%	62%	56%	under 50%	64%	92%
F+%	78%	91%	93%	over 80%	81%	50%
M	0.6	2.0	2.3	2–4	1.6	0.2
FM	1.1	2.4	2.4	1–3	2.0	0.3
m	0.2	0.6	1.0	0–1	0.3	0.0
FC	0.2	0.3	0.5	3	0.3	0.0
CF	1.2	0.7	1.2	1	0.5	0.2
C	0.2	0.1	0.1	0	0.1	0.1
ΣC	1.6	1.3	1.7	2.5	0.7	0.2
F(C)	0.4	0.7	1.6	2–3	0.9	0.4
A%	44%	49%	46%	35–50%	55%	40%
H%	9%	19%	18%	10–15%	17%	5%
W:D	2:1	1:1	1:1	1:3	3:4	5:7
W:M	13:1	4:1	4:1	2:1	4:1	10:1
FC:CF	1:6	1:3	2:5	3:1	2:3	—
M:FM	1:2	5:6	1:1	2:1	3:4	2:3

Table 35 compares mean scores on a number of Rorschach variables at a succession of developmental levels. The 5-year-old means are taken from our earlier study (1), the 10- and 16-year-old means are from the present study. The adult data are a rough summary of "average expectancies" reported by a number of investigators. Finally, from our study of older adults, aged 70 to 100 years (2), we present mean scores for those subjects classified as "presenile" and as "senile." It will be seen that for nearly all variables the 16-year-old record is closer to the expected adult performance than is the 5- or the 10-year-old record. However, on a number of variables, notably area and color scores, the 16-year-old is still far from the adult values, and the change from 10 to 16 years is relatively small. That is, in many ways Sixteen seems considerably more like Ten than like our expectation of the normal adult.

This finding may point to the relative immaturity of this sample of 16-year-olds, or it may instead indicate the inadequacy of present adult "norms." For example, the 3FC:1CF:0C color ratio proposed by Rorschach as the most common normal values seems to typify a more controlled, less spontaneous social response than is characteristically found in adult American records. Further normative studies of normal young adults would be of value for refining our expectancies.

Maturity and Individuality Factors

In our earlier study (1) we discussed in some detail the relative strengths of maturational and individuality factors in shaping the Rorschach response in the first 10 years of life. We concluded that during this early period developmental factors appear to be so strong and so rapidly changing that children between the ages of 2 and 10 years may well express more strongly the characteristics of age than of basic personality.

However, it was clear that even as early as 2 years of age individuality features do appear in the Rorschach, and by 3 or 4 years these emerge with sufficient clarity to be clinically useful, provided that the maturity features are understood and allowance is made for them. Rorschach variations associated with individual personality become increasingly prominent throughout childhood, and we anticipated that at some later period, perhaps in adolescence or early maturity, they would substantially overshadow variations associated with age. We further suggested that at some still later age developmental factors might once again play a major role in determining the Rorschach response.

Having continued our investigation through another six years of life, we feel we can see this developmental process in better perspective, though our judgments of relative weighting of the factors are fairly impressionistic. Up to 5 or 6 years of age it appears clear that maturity factors outweigh individuality factors of other kinds. From a mixed group of Rorschach records it would probably be easier to sort out the records of the 2-, 3-, and 4-year-olds than to sort out individual children on some personality criterion. Somewhere around 6 or 7 years there appears to be a qualitative shift, and individuality features appear more strongly than before. Group averages and more qualitative patterning features do present a distinctive picture for each successive age, but individual records show considerable variation in their expression of this picture. This period lasts from 6 or 7 years until about 11, and within this period one does not get the impression of individuality being more and more distinctively revealed year after year. In many ways, in fact, 10 years of age appears to give a picture of particular child-to-child similarity. This is not to say that individual personality formulations cannot be drawn from a 10-year-old's Rorschach, but in a large collection of records a great many of the 10-year-olds seem to give variations on the same basic theme.

The next shift in level occurs around 12 years, and seems to represent not simply a waxing of individuality features and waning of developmental features, but an increasing definition of *both*. Through the adolescent years, we feel that there are rather clearly discriminate age changes, but that these are expressed by most individual subjects in definite yet *individual* fashion. That is, an individual subject can at the same time express his adherence to the common picture of the age and yet at the same time show himself clearly as an individual.

We can only speculate about the years following 16, though some normative data are available (e.g., McFate and Orr, 43). As mentioned before, we anticipate that developmental changes during adulthood must be conceived in larger intervals (we would certainly expect differences between the 20's, 30's, and 40's), and perhaps even then do not account for an important amount of the differences among individuals. By the 70's, however, we have found (2) that developmental factors are again of marked importance, not in terms of age-defined intervals but in functionally defined intervals. One can diagnose a senile subject but cannot describe his individual personality very fully.

The Introversive Phase of Adolescence

The literature on adolescence, both that describing Rorschach trends and the more general literature, abounds in reference to adolescent introversity. An "introversial crisis," appearing around 14 or 15 and marked in the Rorschach by high M, is proposed by some writers. Our own studies suggest that development in early adolescence cannot be so simply defined but includes several phases at variance with this introversivity.

Recent studies of adolescent behavior, as observed by parents, teachers, and adolescents themselves in a broad range of situations (11), indicate clearly enough that strong introversial trends appear during early adolescence. But the adolescent does not simply move into and then out of an introversive period. Rather, he moves through a sequence of phases in which introversive trends are succeeded by extratensive ones. Around 12 years behavior appears typically to reflect vigorous, enthusiastic, outgoing tendencies; around 13 an introversial swing appears, with withdrawing, often passive trends more in evidence. This is followed by a reaction, typically around 14, in the form of extraversion of behavior, lability, energetic expansiveness. The "introversive phase" is again in evidence around 15, this time often with greater apathy and more flattened affect than before (particularly in relation to home and family). Around 16 the sequence tends to stabilize, with greater balance between introversive and extratensive trends. (If one were plotting a dip into introversiveness between early and mid-adolescence for this particular group of subjects, the curve would not be V-shaped but W-shaped.)

Our Rorschach study appears to parallel these results (as it should, since the subjects of the two studies partly overlap). A fuller, more energetic response is typically found at 12, 14, and 16 years of age. Thirteen and 15 years, the more introversive ages, are not characterized by increased M, however, but rather by a general flattening and constriction of response. Developmentally, at least in this age range and for this sample, movement responses tend to accompany the ages showing relatively greater energy, zest, responsiveness. M as much as C is reduced at the "introversial ages." (This finding seems in keeping with the total picture of each age level as described here, but it was not an anticipated finding, and it serves as a warning against too glib assumptions concerning interpretation of Rorschach variables.)

A word might be added about the actuality of these proposed "phases" of development. Since the present study is a cross-sectional one, we can only point to the differences that appear from group to group and indicate that we believe that in part, at least, the group differences represent age changes and not sampling differences or other artifacts. Studies are now in progress to test just this point. The cases presented in Chapter 17 indicate that the changes we have described do take place in at least some individuals. And our longitudinal study is now sufficiently advanced that we can anticipate its findings as showing real phasic patterning in the development of many children's Rorschach responses.

Sex Differences

One of the most striking results of our analysis of Rorschach records for the age range 10 to 16 was the number of conspicuous sex differences that appeared. In the first 10 years, sex differences on the Rorschach were found to be relatively small and often inconsistent from age to age. In the preadolescent and early adolescent years, however, sex differences are large relative to age differences, and generally consistent throughout the period. The differences in response for the two sexes are for most determinants so large that we have considered it necessary to present figures separately for boys and for girls.

Specific differences found, for each variable and for the separate ages, are presented in detail in Chapter 18 and are summarized on pages 272–278. As indicated there, boys' responses tend to be more global, more restricted and thus less enlivened, less precise, less full, and less variable than the girls'. Girls' responses, conversely, tend to be more detailed, longer, more enlivened, and more precise.

"Danger Signals"

Certain types of response have pathognomic significance when appearing in the Rorschach record of an adult. Obvious examples are color naming, contamination, and perseveration. Less striking but still suspicious signs of disturbance are discussed at length in all the standard texts on the Rorschach. In some cases, such signs have been formalized as lists of "neurotic indicators," "psychotic indicators," etc., and the number of signs found per record is often used in attempts to discriminate normal and disturbed subjects. Whether or not an examiner uses these formal lists, he is certainly on the watch for the "classic symptoms" of various forms of disturbance in examining individual records.

The extent to which a particular sort of response is atypical is, however, partly a normative matter. Our earlier study pointed out that

. . . many types of response which are considered pathological or at least suggestive of disturbance in the adult occur quite normatively and characteristically at certain ages in the child. The implication of any given determinant is, of course, not reversed or invalidated simply because it occurs in a majority of subjects at any given age. A Clob response [dysphoric response to blackness], for example, is usually considered to express diffuse and deep emotions and to indicate an abnormal susceptibility to profound disturbance. We may assume that Clob responses have these meanings wherever they are found. However, both the clinical implications of such responses and the implications with regard to individuality may well be considered to vary with the extent to which such signs are found to occur in a presumably normal population. The pathological significance of a danger signal may presumably be diminished if this sign occurs in a majority or even in a large number of the population. (1, p. 280).

Such response qualities as contamination, confabulation, extensive anatomy response, use of oligophrenic details, use of pure C, and perseveration were found to be of common enough occurrence at certain age levels to assume relatively benign significance. Furthermore, the total configuration seen at certain ages, such as 5½ and 7 years, would appear to suggest marked psychic disturbance in many subjects. While we may question the peace of mind of the 5½ or 7-year-old who gives a characteristic record of this sort, we do not necessarily suspect him of being less well adjusted than the average child of his age.

In the present age period, 10 to 16, we again find both particular types of response and total response patterns that in the adult record could be considered indicative of disturbance. Yet some of these do occur with some regularity, and their significance must be evaluated in the light of this fact. Ives, Grant, and Ranzoni's study of the "neurotic" Rorschachs of normal adolescents (37) has already been discussed in Chapter 2. Our own findings generally parallel theirs in indicating that many of Miale and Harrower-Erickson's neurotic signs do occur with greater frequency than could be reasonably expected if the signs were valid indicators of neurosis. We would summarize and comment on these points as follows.

1. R<25. Our median R ranges from 16 to 20 for different total age groups; only 14-year-old groups reach a median of 25. Not quite 25 per cent of our subjects would pass this criterion. (It is important to note, however, that a majority of our subjects were tested longitudinally, and this may have had some effect in depressing R, though a facilitating effect is equally likely.)

2. R<12. This second, more stringent criterion for R falls at about the 25th percentile for all age groups. While only 25 per cent of our subjects would fail to pass this point, this still seems a large number to be receiving two points for neuroticism. We would consider 12R to be low, but not necessarily neurotic. Records having fewer than 10R could well be given critical consideration.

3. M<2. Two M is the median for every age group except 15 years. But 44 per cent of our subjects give either one or no M. The production of no M at all, which occurs in 18 per cent of our subjects, might be considered atypical.

4. No FM. Just 22 per cent of all subjects give no FM. Its complete absence in a record would seem noteworthy.

5. FM>M. This is true of mean responses at 10, 11, and 16 years. FM and M tend to be pretty evenly balanced throughout this age range.

6. FM>2M. FM equals or exceeds twice M in about 35 per cent of subjects for the total age period.

7. Color shock. While we have found some occurrence of color shock at every age, its occurrence as we have classified it ranges from 2 to 7 per cent. Our scoring was evidently much more strict than that of Ives, Grant, and Ranzoni, who found well over 50 per cent incidence for most of their ages.

8. Shading shock. Again, incidence is very low among our subjects as we have scored it, with not more than 7 per cent of subjects showing shading shock at any age. Ives, Grant, and Ranzoni find closer to 20 to 25 per cent incidence.

9. FC<2. Over 90 per cent of our subjects show this "neurotic" sign.

10. No FC. Median FC at all ages is 0. About 70 per cent of our subjects use no FC.

11. F%>50. Median F% for the total age range is 63. About 75 per cent of the total group have F% exceeding 50.

12. A%>50. Median A% is 46 for the total age range. Nearly half of all subjects have A% exceeding 50.

13. (A+Anat)%>65. Mean (A+Anat)% ranges between 50 and 55 per cent for the different ages. Percentiles have not been computed, but at least a good majority of subjects fail to show this sign.

14. Refusals. One or more refusals are given by 15 to 28 per cent of the different age groups, suggesting that refusal of a single card is not necessarily a malignant sign in itself. Refusal of more than a single card must certainly be considered unusual.

These signs have been discussed individually, not so much because many clinicians score and tabulate neurotic signs, diagnosing on the basis of some given number, but because most of them represent rules of thumb by which many clinicians judge records. "More than 50%F is constricted," and "FC should exceed CF and M should exceed FM," are statements apparently often made tacitly by the clinician in getting his first bearings on a record. For adolescent records, such statements are simply untrue.

The most useful sort of bench marks for judging adolescents' records, we would suggest, are percentile tables such as our Table 7. These have their limitations. Our subjects are not a representative sample; they are brighter-than-average adolescents, of mostly upper middle class status. All the more reason for not considering 50%F restricted when nearly 75 per cent of our subjects exceed that point. Tables such as these provide only a start for judging the significance of a given score, but they provide a real-istic start, in that they compare that score with a range of values given by one group of subjects of the same age.

We would finally point out that at each age we find a number of types of response that might be considered suspect in an adult protocol but appear for this brief age period with some frequency and with ap-parently softened significance. Discussed more fully in the age chapters, some of the more striking points are described below.

10 years: A seemingly excessive amount of indecision, qualification, changing of mind, denial. The giving of vague or alternative responses—"Skeleton or bell." Confusion of animal and human forms. Fanciful and violent responses, including many headless creatures. High WS.

11 years: "Stream of consciousness" type of response; introduction of much irrelevant comment and information. Much interpersonal banter and com-ment with examiner to the point of rudeness. Violent M, such as "Two witches on two sides tearing a girl apart and taking her head off." Denial and much qualification of own response. High number of refusals. Much fighting and much blood. Very high DW. More WS than at any other age.

12 years: Multiple responses to one area of the card. Belief that there are right and wrong answers to the blot. Much DW. Contamination or near-contam-ination: "Rabbit with wings," "Moose-ass," "Antenna coming out of the head of a turtle." Confabulations. Perseveration. People or animals seen as headless, as cut or split open, or with parts cut or chopped off. High P. High WS and S. Many m.

13 years: Extreme restriction—low R, many refusals, mean experience balance low (23 boys and 20 girls have 1M:1ΣC or less. Of these, 9 boys and 4 girls have 0M:0ΣC). Shading is increased and in some cases shading is the only nonform determinant. Shading occurs more than do all color responses together; mean F(C) exceeds ½M. A high point for unpleasant adjectives. High m.

14 Years: High (H). Suggestions for changes in the blots. Highest anatomy response of any age; many blood responses. Highly dysphoric, primitive response of dead or rotten leaf or tree given by girls on Card IV.

15 years: Extreme restriction of responses, fewest responses of any age in this range; very restricted experience balance (12 girls and 23 boys have 1M:1ΣC; of these one girl and seven boys give 0M:0ΣC). Lowest M of any age. Many refusals. Whole manner is one of rejecting the situation. Per-severation of comment. High number of mask, map, abstract responses.

16 years: Many shading responses, many anatomy responses, many abstract responses. A light, humorous sort of confabulation, which in some appears almost as free association to the blot. Many (H). High m. The largest amount of blood and of explosion of any age.

CHAPTER TWENTY

Summary

This study reports the analysis of 700 Rorschach records: those of 50 boys and 50 girls at each yearly age level from 10 through 16, in a relatively homogeneous group of subjects. These subjects, mostly living in New Haven, Connecticut, and in nearby towns and cities, are of predominantly above-average intelligence (mean I.Q.=116) and mostly from upper middle-class (professional and managerial) home backgrounds. Many children contributed records at more than one age, resulting in 33 to 50 per cent overlap of subjects between adjacent ages.

The main purpose of this study has been to determine developmental trends in Rorschach response in this pre- and early-adolescent age period, following up our earlier study of trends in the first 10 years of life. This has been approached in several steps. First, descriptive statistics were computed for boys and for girls at each age on the usual Rorschach scoring variables. Second, distributions were tabulated for a number of additional, "qualitative" variables, such as the semantics of identifying concepts, the types of adjectives used, the initial exclamations given. Finally, descriptive sketches were drawn up of the "typical" Rorschach response at each age level. These descriptions represent an attempt to integrate the Rorschach material, and they draw on the data quantified in Steps 1 and 2 and also on more qualitatively treated variables suggested by repeated readings of the records at each age.

An additional purpose of this study has been the description of sex differences in response. Sex differences appearing in the distributions of the major Rorschach variables, as well as in most of the other tabulations made, have been described and summarized.

Developmental Trends in Single Variables

The individual variables show trends of two types: first, the over-all direction of change for the whole period, and second, the changes from age to age in use of the variable. These latter, we believe, are not simply chance fluctuations from the over-all trend, occurring at random among the variables, but are the result of changes in the total organization of response at different levels.

The over-all trends of change are not generally very large. In our earlier study covering the first 10 years of life, it appeared that developmental changes, as reflected in the Rorschach, tended to occur more and more slowly. Changes for the major variables were proportionately less in the years from 5 to 10 than in the years preceding. This slowing down continues in the years from 10 to 16. The values for nearly all variables are closer to adult expectations at age 16 than they are at age 10, but the rate at which they approach adult values is more rapid in the period from 5 to 10 than in the period from 10 to 16. The degree to which 16-year-old values approximate the values commonly expected from normal adults differs considerably for the different variables.

R: The over-all trend is toward a slow increase in number of responses, with a median R of 16 at 10 years, 19 at 16 years. Twelve, 14, and 16 years are high points of responsiveness, while 13 and 15 years fall off in number of responses produced. Mean values are close to median values, and about three responses higher throughout. Though median R tends in the direction of that expected from normal adults, by 16 years it is still low by adult standards.

Area: W%, over all, tends to decrease; D% to increase; and Dd% to remain essentially level. The changes are small, however, and median W% remains close to 50 per cent throughout, with D% nearly as high, and Dd% remaining well under 10 per cent throughout. The low point for W% and the high points for D% and Dd% occur at age 14, which most nearly approximates adult expectancy, but by 16 years these variables have returned to close to their 10-year-old values.

Form: Median F% for the entire age range is 63 per cent, and the individual age samples approximate this fairly closely, though there is a slight over-all decrease in F%. The 16-year-old median of 59 per cent is the lowest value for F%, but this is still well over the limit of 50%F expected from normal adults.

F+%, on the other hand, is already well within adult limits by 10 years, with a median of 92 per cent, and remains essentially at this level throughout the age range. All but the lowest 10 per cent of subjects obtain an F+% well over 80 per cent at all ages.

Movement: Human movement responses are given by over 75 per cent of subjects at all ages, with the largest percentage of subjects giving M at 14 and 16 years. Median M is close to 2M throughout, but the mean reveals a slight upward trend. Dips in this over-all trend appear at 13 and especially at 15 years, when M is much reduced.

Animal movement responses are given by 78 per cent of subjects, the largest usage appearing at 12, 14, and 16 years. Median FM approximates 2, and the over-all trend is essentially flat except for dips at 13 and 15 years, the former sharper in girls, the latter in boys.

Inanimate movement is given by nearly half our subjects (46 per cent), with 12 years being the high point, 15 the low point. Mean occurrence suggests a slight over-all rise with age, the only drop in this trend appearing at 15 years.

Color: Close to two thirds of our subjects give at least one color response of some kind. Only at 13 and 15 years do fewer than 60 per cent of subjects use color, while close to 75 per cent use color at 16 years.

Only about 25 per cent of subjects give FC responses, over all. The percentage increases consistently from 10 to 16 years, except for a sharp dip at 15. Mean FC fails to show this curve, remaining flat at .3 until 16 years, when it increases to .5. This is obviously very far from its adult expectancy. FC is evidently the scoring variable in which growth comes slowest and latest—or for which our adult expectancies are furthest wrong.

CF responses are given by very close to half the total sample. From age 10 to 13 a gradual decrease appears in proportion of subjects using this variable; thereafter appears a gradual increase. In mean CF, the curve is essentially flat from 10 through 15 (between .7 and .9), followed by an increase at 16 years (to 1.2). The 16-year-old mean would be a reasonable value to find in an adult's record, but in its relationship to mean FC it deviates markedly from the classic ratio of 3FC:1CF.

C responses are given by only 12 per cent of all subjects. No particular age trends emerge, except that surprisingly many 14-year-old girls use C (24 per cent). Mean C is only .1 to .2 for the different age groups, and thus is close to adult expectancy (of no C) throughout.

Shading: F(C) responses are given by about 40 per cent of our 10- and 11-year-olds, by nearly 60 per cent of our 16-year-olds. Mean F(C) increases directly from .7 at 10 years to 1.6 by 16 years. This is the determinant that increases most strikingly during the adolescent period.

Response to the black or dark gray qualities of the blot, either as color (C′) or as diffuse shading (Clob), is rare. All Clob and C′ responses, form-controlled or not, together are given by just 7 to 12 per cent of subjects at any age. No over-all trends are evident.

Content: Nearly all subjects give both animal and human responses. Median A% varies around 56 per cent, median H% around 18 per cent, with neither showing an over-all upward or downward trend. Thus, by 10 years these variables are already close to adult expectancies.

The average subject uses 5 to 6 different content categories, with perhaps a very slight tendency for this value to increase with age. With exceptions at few ages, the six most commonly used content categories are, in order, animal, human, object, anatomy, nature, plant.

Popularity: All our subjects included at least one of the 16 responses we have scored as P; all but 10 per cent gave four or more P. The median is 6 to 7 P throughout the age range, with an over-all slight decrease evident.

Refusals: Between 12 and 28 per cent of our subjects refuse one or more of the Rorschach cards, with over 25 per cent refusing cards at 10, 11, and 15 years. The over-all trend is a downward one, however, except for the brief increase at 15 years. At 16 years, 16 per cent of subjects still refuse one or more cards (rarely more than one), which still seems like a high percentage by comparison with our expectations for the normal adult.

It appears then that in area, in F%, and in the color balance our 16-year-olds are furthest from adult expectancies. Closer to the adult expectation though still not reaching it are the total number of responses and the number of human movement and shading responses. The balance between M and FM is, on the average, nearly an even one, rather than one emphasizing M, as we would expect in adults. The 16-year-olds are closest to adult expectancies in F+%, in content scores, and in P. All these last scores relate importantly to orientation to reality, and it seems significant that near-adult values are already well established by 10 years.

"DANGER SIGNALS" In the first 10 years of life, the child commonly gives many responses that would be considered suspect in the adult protocol, but that appear relatively benignly at certain of the early ages. The present study reveals that many scoring values, cut-off points, and ratios listed by some authors as indicators of neurotic trends appear in substantial minorities, or even large majorities, of our essentially normal adolescent group. A number of these signs are discussed individually on pages 284–286. Such signs as appear to be statistically the rule, rather than the exception, we cannot consider to have particularly adverse connotation when they appear.

CARD DIFFERENCES The score distributions already described are, of course, built up from responses to the individual Rorschach cards. Different cards, however, tend to elicit different types of response. A knowledge of the area, determinants, and content typically produced by the individual cards is of value for clinical interpretation of records. The "card-pull" of the individual blots is described in Chapter 9.

Sex Differences

Sex differences in the Rorschach response in the years from 10 to 16 appear to be marked and relatively consistent. In fact, by contrast with the years preceding 10, the difference in typical performance of boys and of girls is one of the most striking characteristics of this age range. Differences for the major scoring variables may be summarized as follows.

R: Median R for boys is 16, for girls is 19. Girls' mean and median values exceed those of the boys at every age except 11 years, when they are about equal.

Area: Boys give the greater proportion of W responses, fewer D and Dd than girls at all ages except 16 years. Median approach for boys is 52%W, 44%D, 2%Dd; for girls, 41%W, 50%D, 6%Dd.

Form: Differences in F% are variable and nonsignificant. Differences in F+% are slight but consistent, with girls obtaining higher F+% than boys at nearly every age.

Movement: A sex difference appears in M, but none in FM or m. Slightly more girls than boys give M, and mean M for girls is slightly but consistently higher.

Color: Girls significantly exceed boys in FC, CF, and ΣC. This difference, especially in ΣC, tends to increase with age, particularly from 14 years on.

Shading: At every age except 11, many more girls than boys give shading responses. The difference in mean F(C), like that for color, tends to increase with age.

Content: No difference appears in A%, but girls exceed boys in median H% at every age except 10 years. Over-all median for boys is 15%H, for girls 19%H. Girls give more object, nature, fire, food, and architecture responses at nearly every age; more scenes and more reflections at most ages. Boys tend to exceed in anatomy, blood, explosion, and mask responses.

Timing: Though the extreme values for girls are considerably higher than those for boys, thus elevating the means, the median test shows no difference in timing for the sexes. Since R differs significantly for the sexes, the girls apparently do more talking in the same length of time.

The sex differences can be summarized by the statement that boys tend to be more global in approach, to be less productive of responses, to be slightly less precise in form, and to produce fewer of the enlivened determinants. Girls give a response that tends to be fuller, more detailed, and more precise, richer in the use of enlivened determinants—human movement, color, and shading—and more responsive to human forms.

Particular sex differences also emerge at the single age levels. These are summarized below.

10 years: The 10-year-old response appears to be rooted in clarity and banality, yet at the same time it shows confusion, uncertainty, and some unreality. Girls' responses tend to emphasize the banal side of the age; boys' the confused side. Girls give more detail responses than do boys, more M, more shading. They are more precise and give more popular responses.

11 years: Scores for the two sexes for most determinants are more alike here than at other ages. However, girls' responses tend to be longer and more detailed than those of boys, to express more interpersonal engagement with the examiner, and to contain more "stream of consciousness" material.

12 years: Sex differences, both qualitative and quantitative, are greater than at 11. Girls' records are more expansive than boys' and more detailed. Girls give more color, movement, shading, higher H%. Boys give more refusals, more DW and WS, more qualifying responses, more quarreling and fighting movement responses, all typical of the age.

13 years: The total Rorschach response is characteristically more restricted than at surrounding ages. Boys and girls both show changes in this direction, but for most variables this change is shown more strongly by boys than girls.

14 years: Fourteen is a more expansive age, and this appears more strongly in girls' records than in boys'. Girls give higher R, more M and F(C), higher ΣC, with pure C given by surprisingly many girls.

15 years: The change from the expansiveness of 14 to the flattening of 15 is stronger in boys than in girls. For boys the drop in M, FM, H%, P is greater from 14 to 15 than it is for girls, and now boys give more abstract and map responses. As usual, girls give higher mean R, M, F(C), ΣC, and fewer girls show the impoverished records given by many boys.

16 years: Both sexes appear to take large strides toward maturity at this period, but in different areas. Girls' increased use of color responses exceeds that of the boys, who also show increase since 15 years. Girls also increase more in use of FM. Boys, however, show greater increase in use of M and show marked reduction in median W%, moving in a more adult direction, while girls show increase in W%.

Total Age Configurations

The fluctuations in individual Rorschach variables at successive ages represent, we believe, more than simply chance variations of statistics approaching more and more closely to adult values. They reflect, instead, changes in the total patterning of the Rorschach response, as individuals move through successive levels of reorganization of their personalities. Since individuals move at different rates, and since chronological intervals accord only roughly with the timing of developmental events, the use of yearly ages can give only an approximate picture of the underlying stages. Nevertheless, it has been possible to describe a "typical" Rorschach response picture for each of the yearly ages, setting it apart from the ages preceding and following it.

These descriptions indicate that the Rorschach response does not simply become more and more like the adult response, though the over-all trend is in that direction. Superimposed on this over-all trend is a somewhat rhythmic pattern, in which some ages emphasize extraversion of behavior, some introversion; some ages appear full and expansive, others relatively restricted and flattened in responsiveness. The individual age pictures may be summarized as follows.

10 years: This is the first age at which the mean experience balance is introversive. The response is also more global and less "disturbed looking" than at 9 years. Subjects show much greater critical ability. However, compared with ages that follow, Ten's response appears somewhat restricted, with a low median R and many refusals.

In spite of the fact that many responses end up as popular, subjects experience much difficulty in defining and expressing what they see, much uncertainty and denial of response. Many give alternative or vague responses. Human forms are confused with animal. Thus Ten appears rooted in the utmost clarity, reality, and banality, and yet at the same time to be lost in confusion, uncertainty, and unreality.

Similar ambivalence is shown in the need to be basically conforming and yet to be nonconforming, oppositional, resentful, and even secretive. Opposition is suggested by high WS, secretiveness by the large number of "mask" and "map" responses, and also by the subjects' resentment of inquiry.

The somewhat unconforming nature of color responses, the many responses suggesting horror and violence, the large number of headless creatures, and the general tendency to restriction of responses suggest a personality less open and conforming, more guarded and violent, than our surface impression of Ten might lead us to suspect.

Though the experience balance is introversive, animal movement still exceeds human movement, showing Ten's spontaneity of impulse. And yet Ten's response shows him as trying to protect himself, trying to remain on the safe side. He protects himself negatively by restriction of output, refusals, giving few Dd, few F(C). He protects himself positively by high generalization, by sticking to reality, by conforming and identifying strongly with the group. When his protections break down, he gives vague "map" or protective "mask" responses, denies or changes his response, or resorts to ideas of magic and superstition.

11 years: Though many of the major Rorschach determinants occur to about the same extent as at 10, Eleven's responses reflect a breaking up of 10-year-old smoothness, which begins to be replaced with a belligerent expansiveness, an expression of conflict with the environment, a suddenly confiding exuberance. Eleven shows himself to be highly verbal, exuberant, critical, argumentative, ready to launch into greater activity with others.

Expansiveness is shown in the increased verbal output, in the "stream of consciousness" type of response, in the vigor and controversial nature of M and of FM, in the vigor of color responses, in the elaboration into DW of usual popular responses. Oppositional and critically antagonistic tendencies are seen in the large number of refusals, in the high WS, in the frequent use of critical and unpleasant adjectives. Eleven's confiding exuberance and strongly personal response to the examiner are shown in the large number of initial remarks, his warm interchanges with examiner, the relatively high H%.

However, Eleven is an age of paradox. The characteristic verbal exuberance and liveliness are in sharp contrast with the often flat and uninspired final scores. Eleven talks a lot but he may say little. He is argumentative and critical, and yet increasingly sensitive to criticism. Eleven tends to fantasy and embroidery of his concepts, yet increased practicality and a certain flatness are shown in increased D%, high A%, large number of object responses, lowest ΣC of any age but 15.

There is a paradox too in the fact that while qualitatively there is a marked difference between the responses of the two sexes, girls being inclined toward a warm interpersonal stream-of-consciousness response, on actual scoring the two sexes are more alike than at most ages.

Eleven seems willing to leave Ten's protective balance and to launch out into active engagement with others. Enlivened verbal exuberance characterizes the response, but paradox remains the key, producing many surprises. Eleven is expansive but querulous, active and vigorous but critical and argumentative.

12 years: At twelve there occurs a marked growth spurt—a long stride toward approaching maturity that throws the relative immaturity of Eleven into clear relief: mean R at 12 rises from 19.5 to 22; W% continues to decline; mean F+% rises from 90 to 92; mean M rises from 2.2 to 2.6 and now exceeds FM; mean F(C) increases from .6 to .9; and A% decreases.

Twelve's response seems to emphasize many of the good points of Eleven and to resolve many of the earlier difficulties. Twelve appears from his Rorschach response to be a realist, practical, precise, conforming, in good equilibrium.

Increased expansiveness is shown in increase in number of responses, in multiple responses to one card, in suggestions of multiple action, in decrease of refusals, and especially in the largest number of M in the first 16 years (especially an increase in two-figure movement responses on Cards I, II, and III). For the first time M exceeds FM; M are increasingly vigorous; and FM are even more vigorous. Twelve is also a high point for m, and the nature of m suggests greater restraint and stronger inhibition than earlier (decrease of explosion, increase of tension). Color is also increased.

Twelve's response suggests a strong drive toward conformity, with strong interest in rightness or wrongness of response and in responses of others. A characteristic combination of expansiveness and conformity appears in the many DW built upon popular responses. These DW may approach or reach confabulation or contamination.

Median D% now surpasses median W%. F+% is increasing, showing greater precision, which is also indicated by the use of many qualifying phrases. There appears less effort to evaluate self than at the ages that follow, but sense of self is strengthening and interest in others is high. Evidences of interest in magic and superstition appear in the increase in (H). Strong oppositional tendencies are shown in high mean S and WS. Concern about sex is suggested by the large number of figures that are headless or have parts chopped off or are split open.

13 years: The Rorschach response at this age reflects a withdrawal, inwardization, and restriction. The mean number of responses declines, number of refusals and number refusing increases. Both movement and color responses fall off, resulting in the most restricted record to date. Mean experience balance is only 2.1M:1.1ΣC.

The only major determinant that does not fall off at this age is shading, which increases to a mean of 1.1. In certain subjects the only enlivenment is shading. The largest number of shading responses describe fine differentiation within the blot, indicating an individual engaged in minute and anxious scrutiny, particularly vulnerable to inner doubts and misgivings. Thirteen is the high point for the giving of unpleasant, unhappy adjectives. Though there are fewer affect adjectives given than at any age except 15, at no age is as high a proportion of these dysphoric as at 13.

D% is increasing, and at this age for the first time mean D% nearly equals mean W%. But while this is a step toward maturity, the M:FM ratio is again more evenly balanced, indicating a less "mature" control of impulses. Reflection responses are increased, but vista and anatomy occur no more than at 12. A reduction in H% and in texture responses suggest some withdrawal from interpersonal contact, as does the increase in "mask" responses.

14 years: The Rorschach response at this age, in contrast to the restricted response of Thirteen, reflects the exuberance, the seemingly boundless energy, the tremendous appetite for experience of the typical 14-year-old. The response is fuller and more enlivened in many respects than at any other age in this range.

There are here more responses and fewer refusals than at any other age in this period; more different content categories per subject are used than at any age but 16. Both movement and color responses are higher than at surrounding ages (mean 2.4M:1.2ΣC). There are also more initial remarks than at other ages except 10 and 11.

The 14-year-old appears to be concerned about his own personality. Shading responses reach a high point, and of these vista responses are higher than previously, suggesting Fourteen's effort to see himself and his behavior in perspective and in relation to the behavior of others. Reflection responses too occur more than at any other age in this range, suggestive of the narcissism of Fourteen. Interest in the body is also confirmed by the highest anatomy response of any age. This is also a high point for flower responses.

Fourteen's marked interest in other persons as well as in himself is shown in a greater number of both H and Hd responses than at any other age. Some criticalness toward others is suggested in the relatively high (H). There is also some complaint about the inadequacy or inaccuracy of the blots.

In color response, Fourteen continues to appear relatively egocentric and unmodulated. Though FC has increased, this is a high point for C. Emotions appear to be deepening and to be expressing themselves positively. At 14 there occurs a larger percentage of emotion-toned adjectives than at any age to date, and also more pleasant adjectives than in surrounding ages.

Practical, detailed thinking, as indicated in D responses, reaches its high point at this age; global responses are fewest of any age to date except 9 years. The large number of object responses and the low number of abstract responses support this picture of objective, practical, detailed thinking.

15 years: A restriction of response again takes place at 15. This pulling in and giving of a minimal response is shown in the small number of responses (median of just 15), in the shortest records of any age and the shortest response time. There are fewer movement responses—M, FM, or m—than at any other age, and the mean ΣC of 1.0 is lower than at any age in this range except 11. Twelve girls and 23 boys have an experience balance of 1M:1ΣC or less; eight subjects have 0M:0ΣC.

The Rorschach response reflects Fifteen's tendency to withdraw and to shut himself off from the outside world. Mean number of refusals is higher than at any age since 11, and 32 per cent of boys refuse at least one card. There is also much manipulation of cards before responding, giving of sparse responses in monosyllables or in a whisper, giving of "mask" and "map" responses, and perseveration of comment, such as "folded piece of paper."

There is lack of detail and an increase in global responses (median W% increases from 39 per cent at 14 to 51 per cent at 15). At the same time that Fifteen is withdrawing, he seems to be pulling together his thoughts and perceptions. He seems to be thoughtful and reflective. More shading responses appear than at earlier ages and more abstract responses. More vista and more reflection responses also appear. The subject is trying to view himself and his actions in perspective.

The passivity, quietness, and lack of energy output often associated with the age is reflected in the prevalence of static movement responses. Among m, tension movements predominate and occur more than at other ages. Abstract responses are conspicuous and are for the most part of a distinctly troubled or unpleasant nature, particularly representing conflict between two sets of forces.

16 years: The Rorschach record at this age is in almost every respect fuller, more expansive, more enlivened than that of the 15-year-old. There are more responses and more different content categories per subject, records are longer and there is more elaboration of simple responses. Both movement and color responses have increased (mean of 2.3M:1.7ΣC), while F% of 55 per cent is by far the lowest of any age in this range.

Emotional expression is increasingly adaptive, mean FC being the highest of any age in this range and twice as high as at 15, though CF still predominates among color responses. The general manner of response to the cards is more open, easy, and pleasurable than a year ago. Overt refusals are fewer and there is less indirect refusal by muttering and card turning. The nature of content appears more positive, less concealing. Mask responses are sharply reduced, map responses slightly so. This is a high point for human responses and for flower responses. This is also the high point for pleasant, the low point for unpleasant adjectives.

Shading responses reach their high point, reflecting an increasing sensitivity and awareness. Outstanding are texture responses, especially soft and furry textures, and such responses as reflection, water, wax. Reflection and vista responses are both high. Concern about the subject's own body is suggested by the many anatomy, X-ray, and "biology picture" responses. Abstract responses, especially those symbolizing conflict, are conspicuous.

Girls especially express optimistic fantasy in elaborate though cheerful confabulation. Daydreaming and fantasy are emphasized in the large number of (H) responses—fairies, witches, mermaids. That inner tensions exist in spite of the seemingly general geniality and conformity is suggested by the many abstract responses, high m, especially tension m, and large number of blood, fire, and explosion responses among C.

These Rorschach pictures, with their implications for the subjects' behavior, appear to parallel closely our findings in a survey of developmental changes in a broad range of everyday behavior areas, as reported by 10- to 16-year-old subjects, their parents, and their teachers (11). They depict the changing patterns of organization of affect, intellectual approach, and energy as individuals progress from late childhood toward maturity.

Bibliography

1. AMES, L. B., LEARNED, J., MÉTRAUX, R., and WALKER, R. N. *Child Rorschach Responses*. New York: Hoeber-Harper, 1952.
2. AMES, L. B., LEARNED, J., MÉTRAUX, R., and WALKER, R. N. *Rorschach Responses in Old Age*. New York: Hoeber-Harper, 1954.
3. AMES, L. B., *et al. Longitudinal Rorschach Responses*. (In prep.)
4. BECK, S. J. *Rorschach's Test. Vol. I. Basic Processes*. New York: Grune & Stratton, 1944.
5. BECKHAM, A. S. Rorschach study of high school failures. *Am. Psychol.*, 1950, *5:* 346 (abstr.).
6. BOWLUS, D. E., and SHOTWELL, A. M. A Rorschach study of psychopathic delinquency. *Am. J. Ment. Deficiency,* 1947, *52:* 23–30.
7. BOYNTON, P. L., and WADSWORTH, B. M. Emotionality test scores of delinquent and nondelinquent girls. *J. Abnorm. & Social Psychol.,* 1943, *38:* 87–92.
8. COX, S. M. A factorial study of the Rorschach responses of normal and maladjusted boys. *J. Genet. Psychol.,* 1951, *79:* 95–113.
9. ENDACOTT, J. L. The results of 100 male juvenile delinquents on the Rorschach ink-blot test. *J. Crim. Psychopath.,* 1941, *3:* 41–50.
10. GESELL, A., and ILG, F. L. In collaboration with L. B. AMES and G. BULLIS. *The Child from Five to Ten*. New York: Harper, 1946.
11. GESELL, A., ILG, F. L., and AMES, L. B. *Youth: The Years from Ten to Sixteen*. New York: Harper, 1956.
12. GLUECK, S., and GLUECK, E. *Unravelling Juvenile Delinquency*. New York: Commonwealth Fund, 1950.
13. GOLDFARB, W. A definition and validation of obsessional trends in the Rorschach examination of adolescents. *Ror. Res. Exch.,* 1943, *7:* 81–108.
14. GOLDFARB, W. Effects of early institutional care on adolescent personality. Rorschach data. *Am. J. Orthopsychiat.,* 1944, *14:* 441–447.
15. GOLDFARB, W., and KLOPFER, B. Rorschach characteristics of "institution children." *Ror. Res. Exch.,* 1944, *8:* 92–100.
16. GOODENOUGH, E. W. Interest in persons as an aspect of sex differences in the early years. *Genet. Psychol. Monog.,* 1957, *55:* 287–323.
17. GORLOW, L., ZIMET, C., and FINE, H. The validity of anxiety and hostility Rorschach content scores among adolescents. *J. Consult. Psychol.,* 1952, *16:* 73–75.
18. GRANT, M. Q., IVES, V., and RANZONI, J. H. Reliability and validity of judges' ratings of adjustment on the Rorschach. *Psychol. Monog.,* 1952, *66:* 1–20.
19. GURVITZ, M. S. In General Newsletter. *J. Proj. Tech.,* 1950, *14:* 211.
20. HERSHENSON, J. R. Preference of adolescents for Rorschach figures. *Child Developm.,* 1949, *20:* 101–118.
21. HERTZ, H. A Rorschach comparison between best and least adjusted girls in a training school. *Ror. Res. Exch.,* 1939, *4:* 134–150.
22. HERTZ, M. R. Rorschach norms for an adolescent age group. *Child Develop.,* 1935, *6:* 69–76.
23. HERTZ, M. R. The normal details in the Rorschach Ink-Blot Test. *Ror. Res. Exch.,* 1936–37, *1:* 104–121.

24. HERTZ, M. R.   Scoring the Rorschach Test with specific reference to the "normal detail" category. *Am. J. Orthopsychiat.*, 1938, *8:* 100–121.
25. HERTZ, M. R.   Scoring the Rorschach Ink-Blot Test. *J. Genet. Psychol.*, 1938, *52:* 15–64.
26. HERTZ, M. R.   The "popular" response factor in the Rorschach scoring. *J. Psychol.*, 1938, *6:* 3–31.
27. HERTZ, M. R.   Some personality changes in adolescence as revealed by the Rorschach method. *Psychol. Bull.*, 1940, *37:* 515–516.
28. HERTZ, M. R.   Evaluation of the Rorschach method and its application to normal childhood and adolescence. *Char. and Personal.*, 1941, *10:* 151–162.
29. HERTZ, M. R.   The scoring of the Rorschach Ink-Blot method as developed by the Brush Foundation. *Ror. Res. Exch.*, 1942, *6:* 16–27.
30. HERTZ, M. R.   *Frequency Tables for Scoring Responses to the Rorschach Ink-Blot Test,* 3rd Ed. Cleveland: Western Reserve Univ. Press, 1951.
31. HERTZ, M. R., and BAKER, E.   Personality patterns in adolescence as portrayed by the Rorschach Ink-Blot method: I. The movement factors. *J. Gen. Psychol.*, 1942, *27:* 119–188.
32. HERTZ, M. R., and BAKER, E.   Personality patterns in adolescence as portrayed by the Rorschach Ink-Blot method: II. The color factors. *J. Gen. Psychol.*, 1943, *28:* 3–61.
33. HERTZ, M. R., and BAKER, E.   Personality patterns in adolescence as portrayed by the Rorschach Ink-Blot method: III. The "Erlebnistypus" (a normative study). *J. Gen. Psychol.*, 1943, *28:* 225–276.
34. HERTZ, M. R., and BAKER, E.   Personality patterns in adolescence as portrayed by the Rorschach method: IV. The "Erlebnistypus" (a typological study). *J. Gen. Psychol.*, 1943, *29:* 3–45.
35. HERTZMAN, M., and MARGULIES, H.   Developmental changes as reflected in Rorschach test responses. *J. Genet. Psychol.*, 1943, *62:* 189–215.
36. Institute of Child Welfare, University of Minnesota. *The Minnesota Scale for Paternal Occupations.* Minnesota. No date. (Pamphlet.)
37. IVES, V., GRANT, M. Q., and RANZONI, J. H.   The "neurotic" Rorschachs of normal adolescents. *J. Genet. Psychol.*, 1953, *83:* 31–61.
38. JACOBS, S. M., and GRAHAM, E. E.   A comparison of the Rorschach of juvenile auto thieves and juvenile burglars. *J. Colo.-Wyo. Acad. Sci.*, 1952, *4:* 4–76.
39. KLOPFER, B., and KELLEY, D.   *The Rorschach Technique.* Yonkers, N.Y.: World Book Co., 1946.
40. KLOPFER, B., AINSWORTH, M. D., KLOPFER, W. G., and HOLT, R. R.   *Developments in the Rorschach Technique. Vol. 1.* Yonkers, N.Y.: World Book Co., 1954.
41. KOGAN, W.   Shifts in Rorschach patterns during a critical period in the institutional experience of a group of delinquent boys. *Ror. Res. Exch.*, 1940, *4:* 131–133.
42. MARGULIES, H.   Rorschach responses of successful and unsuccessful students. *Arch. Psychol.*, New York: 1942, *38:* 271.
43. McFATE, M. Q., and ORR, F. G.   Through adolescence with the Rorschach. *Ror. Res. Exch.*, 1949, *13:* 302–319.
44. PAULSEN, A.   Personality development in the middle years of childhood: a ten-year longitudinal study of 30 public school children by means of Rorschach test and social histories. *Am. J. Orthopsychiat.*, 1943, *24:* 336–350.
45. PESCOR, J. J.   Age of delinquents in relationship to Rorschach test scores. *Pub. Health Rep.*, Washington, 1938, *53:* 852–864.
46. PHILLIPS, L., and SMITH, J. G.   *Rorschach Interpretation: Advanced Technique.* New York: Grune & Stratton, 1953.
47. PIOTROWSKI, Z. A.   *Perceptanalysis: A Fundamental Reworked, Expanded and Systematic Rorschach Method.* New York: Macmillan, 1957.
48. RABIN, A. I., and BECK, S. J.   Genetic aspects of some Rorschach factors. *Am. J. Orthopsychiat.*, 1950, *20:* 595–599.

49. RANZONI, J. H., GRANT, M. Q., and IVES, V. Rorschach "card-pull" in a normal adolescent population. *J. Proj. Tech.*, 1950, *14:* 107–133.
50. RICHARDS, T. W. Personal significance of Rorschach figures. *J. Proj. Tech.*, 1958, *22:* 97–101.
51. RORSCHACH, H. *Psychodiagnostics.* Berne: Verlag Hans Huber, 1942.
52. SCHACHTEL, E. G. Notes on Rorschach tests of 500 juvenile delinquents and a control group of 500 non-delinquent adolescents. *J. Proj. Tech.*, 1951, *15:* 144–172.
53. SCHMIDL, F. The Rorschach test in juvenile delinquency research. *Am. J. Orthopsychiat.*, 1947, *17:* 151–160.
54. STAINBROOK, E. J., and SIEGEL, P. S. A comparative Rorschach study of Southern Negro and white high school and college students. *J. Psychol.*, 1944, *17:* 107–116.
55. STEINER, J. The Rorschach Test. In FRANK, L. K. and OTHERS. Personality development in adolescent girls. *Monogr. Soc. Res. Child Develop.*, 1951, *16*, Ch. 5, 34–59.
56. SUARES, N. Personality development in adolescence. *Ror. Res. Exch.*, 1938, *2:* 2–12.
57. THETFORD, W. N., MOLISH, H. B., and BECK, S. J. Developmental aspects of personality structure in normal children. *J. Proj. Tech.*, 1951, *15:* 58–78.
58. WEBER, G. H. Some qualitative aspects of an exploratory personality study of 15 juvenile automobile thieves. *Trans. Kansas Acad. Sci.*, 1950, *53:* 548–556.

Index

A, 65, 66, 73
   tables:
      by ages, 64, 65
      of means, 25
A%:
   age trends in, 65, 66
   ratio A:Ad, 66, 67
      table, 67
   tables:
      means, 25
      percentiles, 28
   see also Content
(A) responses, 67, 68
   table, 68
Abstract responses, 64
   at 13 years, 174
   at 15 years, 226, 227
   at 16 years, 243, 244
Ad, 66–67
(Ad) responses, 67, 68
   table, 68
Adjectives used, 87, 88
   at different ages:
      10 years, 109, 112
      11 years, 129, 133
      12 years, 159, 161
      13 years, 175, 179
      14 years, 195, 202
      15 years, 227, 231
      16 years, 245, 247
   number of, 88
   pleasant, 87, 88
   sex differences in, 87, 88
   table of, 88
   unpleasant, 87, 88
Adjustment, measures of, 15
   signs, 9, 11
Administration of test, 17, 18
Adolescent scores:
   compared with adult, 280, 281
   compared with old age:
      table, 281
Adult expectations:
   for area, 32, 37, 39
   for color, 51

Adult expectations—*(Contd.)*
   for content, 73
   for form, 38
   for movement:
      animal, 50, 51
      human, 40, 50, 51
   for populars, 78
   for refusals, 79
   in scoring:
      approximation to, 5, 280, 281, 291
Age:
   changes in scores, 263–271
   trends in scoring variables, *see* F, M,
      C, R, F(C), etc.
   see also under different ages
Ambivalence at 10 years, 108, 113
AMES, L. B., 7, 299
Anatomy responses, 63–66, 68, 73, 177,
      200, 226, 243
Angel responses, *see* (H)
Animal:
   movement, *see* FM
   responses:
      age trends in, 65, 66, 73
      tables:
         by ages, 64, 65
         means, 25
      see also A, Ad, (A), (Ad)
Anxiety at 13 years, 173, 175
Apathy at 15 years, 224
Area, 32–37
   in adults, 32, 37
   age changes in, 32–37
      10 years, 105, 106, 111
      11 years, 124, 130, 132
      12 years, 152, 156, 157, 161
      13 years, 172, 176, 179
      14 years, 198, 201
      15 years, 224, 227, 230
      16 years, 241, 247
   developmental trends in, 289
   sex differences in, 36, 272, 291
   table, 24
   see also W, D, Dd

303